THE MARTINLINERS

THE MARTINLINERS
The Martin Twins, 202 to 404

by Gary L Killion

To my son, Scott D Killion

Printed in Singapore

Published 1998 by Airways International Inc, PO Box 1109, Sandpoint, Idaho 83864-0872, USA

Editor: John Wegg
Design: Marvin Reguindin

ISBN 0-9653993-2-X

ACKNOWLEDGEMENTS

The writer is greatly indebted to many persons too numerous to mention who have contributed information and photographs. Six persons are, however, worthy of special note.

A number of erroneous assumptions concerning the deficiencies encountered during the 202 type certification program have been published previously. Edward Gaydos, the CAA flight test analyst assigned to the 202 certification program, provided considerable insight into the true nature of those deficiencies and the corrective action taken.

Lawrence E Wilson of the National Air and Space Museum recognized and brought to the writer's attention the only photo of the Martin 303 known to exist at that time. Since the time the first photo of the Martin 303 was discovered, Stan Piet of the Glenn L Martin Aviation Museum found another photo which shows some details of the 303 not visible in the other photo. Mr Piet also supplied an invaluable list of 202/303 customer model numbers and assigned serial numbers.

The FAA maintains the official records for each US-registered civil aircraft. During the 1980s, the FAA microfilmed all of the official records of each airplane extant at that time (or at least those the FAA thought were still extant). Those records are readily available from the FAA. Unfortunately, the records for the other aircraft are in remote storage and not easily accessed. In order to fill in the resulting gaps, David M Nichols graciously shared the results of his earlier research of the 202/404 records. Through that research and the writer's review of the currently available records, a number of previously published errors have been corrected.

Former Martin test pilot Jack L King kindly contributed his recollections of test flying the Martinliners, and also provided a number of insights and illustrations.

Finally, the writer is especially indebted to John Wegg, editor of *Airways*, for collecting and organizing this comprehensive collection of Martin 202/404 photos.

Table of Contents

THE MARTIN HERITAGE

THE GLENN L MARTIN COMPANY DISCOVERED, as have other manufacturers, that success in the commercial airliner market can be elusive, regardless of the credentials of the builder or the quality of his product.

Martin established one of the first aircraft factories in 1909—little more than half a decade after the Wright Brothers's first flight. Between 1929, when he moved his company to Baltimore, Maryland, and the beginning of World War II, Martin produced such famous aircraft as the B-10 bombers and the Model 130 'Clipper' flying boats. The former earned for Martin the 1932 Collier trophy; the latter were used by Pan American Airways to inaugurate trans-Pacific airline service in 1935. During World War II, the company produced more than 5,200 B-26 Marauder medium bombers, nearly 1,400 PBM Mariner patrol bombers, and more than 1,500 A-30 Baltimore attack bombers. In addition to airplanes of its own design, the company also manufactured 536 B-29 Superfortress bombers under license from Boeing.

As the tide of the war began to change, Martin's engineering talents were directed towards the anticipated postwar boom in air travel. The giant JRM-1 Mars flying boat was about to go into production as a naval cargo transport, and Martin considered trying to regain its eminence in commercial flying boats by offering Pratt & Whitney Wasp Major-powered civil derivatives for the transoceanic market. One of the variants, the Model 170-24A, would have carried 105 passengers and 2,557cu ft (71.6m^3) of cargo at a cruising speed of about 170mph (150kt/270km/h). Although in late 1946, Martin was still advertising for engineers to develop the civil Mars flying boats, there was little or no airline interest. It was obvious that the new, much faster generation of Douglas and Lockheed land-based airliners would completely supplant commercial flying boats. The market for land-based, short- to medium-range airliners held a great deal more promise.

Martin was still president and manager of the company at that time; however, Harry T Rowland later assumed management duties as executive vice president. As vice president of engineering, William K (Ken) Ebel was responsible for the overall design of Martin products during that era.

Meanwhile, the Air Transport Association of America (ATA), which represented the major US airlines, recognized the tremendous improvements in performance, passenger comfort, and economy that could be realized with a new generation of transport airplanes. In order to focus industry attention on its anticipated needs, the ATA drafted four sets of requirements for postwar airliners in 1943. Specifications ATA-C1 and ATA-D1 described four-engine airplanes for use on transcontinental and intercontinental routes. Since the new Douglas and Lockheed airplanes were expected to fill those roles, Specifications ATA-C1 and D1 were not given a great deal of attention. Specification ATA-B1 described a large twin-engine design. It received little attention at the time; however, the ATA-A1 airplanes from Martin and Convair would eventually evolve to ATA-B1 standards. A fifth specification for all-cargo airplanes was planned, but apparently not completed.

*The Martin Heritage:
the B-10 bomber,
Model 130 'Clipper',
B-26 Marauder, and
PBM Mariner.*
(all via John Wegg)

Specification ATA-A1 covered a twin-engine cargo-passenger airplane for shorter route segments. With nothing in sight but the venerable Douglas DC-3s, this set of requirements received most of the industry attention with designs being offered by Boeing, Douglas, Curtiss-Wright, Martin, and Convair. (Douglas did not specifically promote its offering as an ATA-A1 airplane, but it was obviously intended for that market.)

The airplane envisioned in Specification ATA-A1 by the ATA Committee on Future Aircraft Requirements was to have seating for 25 to 30 passengers with 1,000 to 2,000lb (450-900kg) cargo capacity and a convertible cabin interior to provide at least 7,000lb (3,175kg) cargo capacity with fewer passenger seats installed. The normal crew was to consist of two pilots and one attendant. Maximum operating economy was a prime consideration with particular emphasis on low maintenance and service costs. In that respect, it was to have features to minimize ground turn-around time. A tricycle landing gear was specified, but it need not have

cabin pressurization. If it were a mid- or high-wing design, it had to provide the same degree of safety for passengers and crew as a low-wing design. There were also cabin requirements concerning such details as door size, overhead racks, lavatories, galleys, stowage compartments, etc.

Among the performance requirements of Specification ATA-A1 were that it was to have a cruising speed of at least 200mph (174kt/320km/h) and a range of 800mi (1,300km) with standard fuel capacity. There were also to be provisions for additional fuel to increase the range to 1,500mi (2,400km), and it was to be able to operate from 2,500ft (760m)-long runways under sea level, standard-day conditions. Subsequently, this latter requirement was eased to 3,000ft (910m).

Martin, like the other major US aircraft manufacturers, faced massive cutbacks in military production at the end of World War II. In order to keep its production capability intact for the coming postwar models, Martin converted 100 surplus military Douglas C-54 Skymasters into civil airlin-

Martin offered a commercial variant of the Model 170 Mars, which saw passenger service with the Naval Air Transport Command, but there was no airline interest postwar for flying boats. (via John Wegg)

Pioneers of the US aircraft and airline industries. Glenn L Martin (seated) and William A Patterson admire a model of the airplane that would have been the mainstay of United Air Lines's medium-range routes, the 303. (Martin via NASM)

ers. The program, which ran from shortly after V-J Day until April 1947, involved a thorough overhaul of the entire airframe and its systems, replacement of the large cargo door with a smaller passenger loading door, and the installation of an airline passenger interior. Pennsylvania Central Airlines (Capital) received the first conversion in January 1946, and

KLM the 100th airplane. Other customers included Braniff, Chicago & Southern, Eastern Air Lines, Northeast, Pan American, TWA, and Cruzeiro do Sul of Brazil. Martin—which had had little pre-war commercial experience—no doubt gained considerable insight into the needs and expectations of the airline industry through this program.

Martin converted more than 100 former USAAF Air Transport Command Douglas C-54 Skymasters to commercial standard for nine domestic and overseas airlines. The program began shortly after V-J Day and ended 18 months later, in April 1947, with the delivery of the final aircraft to KLM.

The first aircraft was delivered to PCA—The Capital Airline in January 1946. Fitted with 56 seats, PCA's DC-4s had the largest passenger capacity of any commercial transport at the time (TWA's Lockheed 49 Constellations accommodated 51 passengers). By spring 1946, PCA had introduced a 60-seat DC-4. (Howard M Svendsen)

THE MARTIN 202

THE DESIGN GOAL FOR THE MODEL 202 was a highly efficient airplane to meet the requirements defined in Specification ATA-A1. As a prelude to the design of this model, Martin engineers obtained the suggestions of various airlines. It was correctly envisioned that the vast technological advances of World War II could be combined with the operational experience of the airlines to produce an airplane far in advance of any existing transport type. American Airlines apparently had considerable influence in the early design of the Model 202.

Although Martin considered more than 25 designs for Specification ATA-A1, efforts eventually centered around three basic 30-passenger designs. The 202-11 and 202-12 were Wright R-2600 Cyclone-14-powered low-wing and high-wing designs, respectively. Either would have had a maximum operating weight of 32,500lb (14,740kg). Martin first favored the high-wing 202-12 because it was expected to cruise 4mph (6km/h) faster at comparable power settings and offer enhanced passenger visibility, easier loading, and better maintenance accessibility. The low-wing 202-11 design eventually found greater favor, however, because its empty weight was estimated to be 382lb (173kg) less than that of the 202-12. This was owing primarily to the additional longitudinal beams and heavy bulkheads that would have been required under each spar to support the wings of the 202-12 in a gear-up landing. The proposal ultimately chosen for development, the 202-15, was a low-wing design similar to the 202-11 except that it used more powerful Pratt & Whitney R-2800 Double Wasp engines. Although it undoubtedly made extensive use of the same technology, it bore little resemblance to either the Marauder or the Mariner.

The name Mercury was used in early references to the 202 design; however, this name had been dropped by September 1945 when it revealed the 22nd revision of its design to the press, and Martin referred to it simply as the Model 202. By the end of that year, '2-O-2' or 'Two-O-Two' was in vogue. Fortuitous as it may have been for later sales promotion, '202' had no particular significance. It was simply the next available number in Martin's model designation system following the Model 200, a proposed four-engine 100,000lb (45,400kg) short-haul passenger airplane, and a proposed twin-engine bomber, identified as the Model 201.

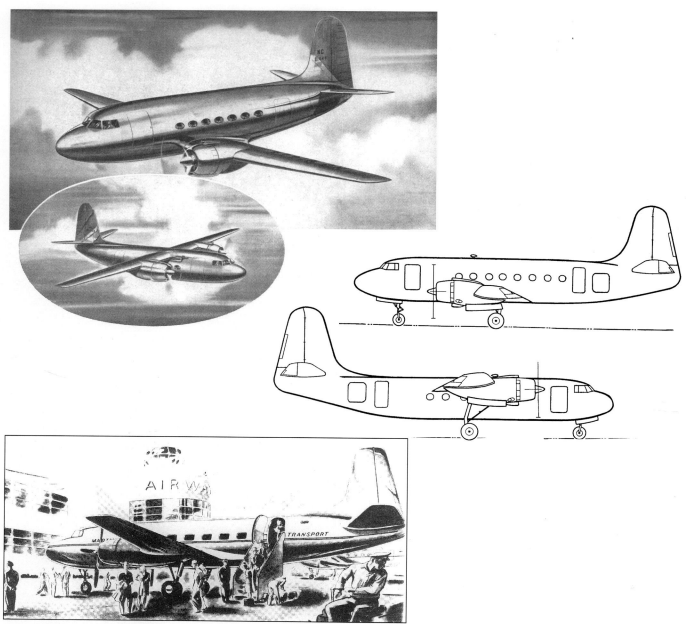

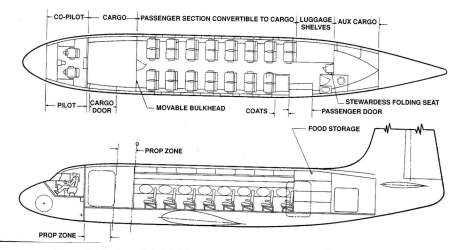

Sketches of the 202-11 (top) and high-wing 202-12 (middle) designs released in September 1944. These preliminary designs were submitted to the Aircraft Requirements Committee of the Air Transport Association to meet the ATA-A1 specification. Some sketches show the 202-11 with rectangular cabin windows (above).

Both proposals were similar in size and gross weight to the B-26 Marauder, and the 202-12 bore a strong resemblance to the medium bomber. Martin hoped that production facilities and equipment used for the B-26 could be rapidly converted to building the postwar transports. (The Martin Star/Author)

CO-PILOT — CARGO — PASSENGER SECTION CONVERTIBLE TO CARGO — LUGGAGE SHELVES — AUX CARGO

PILOT — CARGO DOOR — MOVABLE BULKHEAD — COATS — PASSENGER DOOR — STEWARDESS FOLDING SEAT

FOOD STORAGE

PROP ZONE

PROP ZONE

Plan and side views of the Model 202-11, published in September 1944. (The Martin Star)

202 Engineering

The key to the efficiency of the 202 was the wing which used Martin double-slotted flaps and a laminar-flow GLM-W-16 airfoil. The high lift characteristics afforded by this design enabled Martin to achieve satisfactory takeoff and landing performance with a wing of smaller area which, in turn, provided much greater cruise performance. Slow flight characteristics were further enhanced by the use of van Zelm ailerons. This feature, designed by Martin engineer W D van Zelm, incorporated vanes to direct airflow over the ailerons at extreme deflections. Martin claimed that conventional ailerons of 50 to 60% greater area would have been required to provide the same rate of roll. Although the ailerons did not directly improve takeoff and landing, they did so indirectly by enabling the use of longer-span flaps.

Extension of the large flaps resulted in a pronounced pitch-up moment because of the downwash over the stabilizer. In order to compensate for this moment, the stabilizer angle of incidence was increased by a flap-stabilizer interconnect system whenever the flaps were lowered. This system relieved the crew of making excessive trim changes whenever flap settings were changed and permitted a greater center-of-gravity range. A blow-back feature prevented the flaps from being extended beyond the setting appropriate for the airspeed involved.

The wing was of conventional all-metal, multi-spar construction. The major components were the center section, which extended to the outboard sides of the nacelles, and the two outboard sections; the wing tips were removable and interchangeable. Early studies were based on a wing area of 740sq ft (68.75m²); however, a larger wing of 864sq ft (80.26m²) was eventually adopted.

The total fuel capacity of 1,010USg (3,820l) was contained in four interconnected Mareng bladder-type cells located in each outboard wing section. Mareng cells were developed by *Martin engineering* during World War II and produced by the US Rubber Co under license. Locating the fuel outboard of the nacelles and using cells in lieu of conventional inte-

gral tanks afforded greater fire protection in a gear-up landing or a survivable accident. The airplane could be refueled by one person at a rate of 200USg (755l) per minute using underwing pressure refueling provisions.

The stabilizer and fin were of all-metal construction, as were the ailerons and interchangeable elevators. Curiously, the rudder was fabric-covered, a carry-over from the 1930s. The elevators and rudder featured servo-tabs to reduce control forces.

The fuselage was of all-metal monocoque construction with a constant circular cross section through the cabin. Although a passenger capacity of 30 and an aft cargo compartment were originally envisioned, as specified by the ATA, the aft cargo compartment was deleted later in favor of a standard cabin arrangement of ten rows of four comfortable MacArthur airline seats each. The increased capacity was a reflection of the fact that postwar traffic was greatly exceeding the wartime projections. As an option, Martin considered a convertible passenger-cargo interior. Although it would have enhanced the utility of a 202, it would have added 233lb (105kg) to the empty weight.

The Model 202 was one of the first transports offered with integral ventral stairs to facilitate passenger loading. (The contemporary Convair Model 110 also had this feature.) By eliminating the need for portable ramps at each terminal, these hydraulically operated stairs reduced the passenger loading and unloading times and freed ground personnel for other servicing. Martin also offered the Model

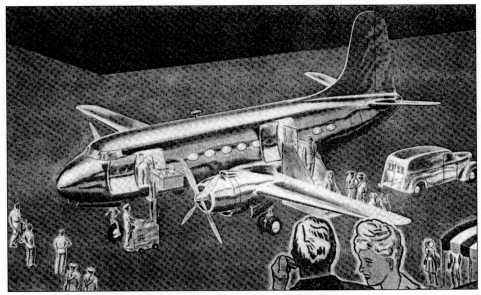

Another early impression of the Model 202 Mercury, which appeared in Air Transport *for January 1945, showing a 'convertible' design for passengers and cargo. It was envisaged that the Mercury could carry 1,560lb (700kg) of cargo with 30 passengers, or 7,560lb (3,430kg) of freight with 10 fixed seats empty (the other 20 seats would have been folded against the cabin wall).* (via John Wegg)

202 with integral stairs at the left forward end of the cabin, either in addition to, or instead of, the ventral stairs. Having both would have permitted simultaneous loading and unloading. It was also offered with a standard entrance door at the left rear end of the cabin.

As passengers ascended the rear ventral stairs, they first encountered shelves for carry-on luggage on their left. At the top of the stairs, the lavatory was on their right, and the galley and flight attendant's seat were on their left.

Advertisement from the December 1945 issue of Skyways *emphasizing the rapid passenger and cargo loading capabilities of the 202. By September that year, Martin had dropped the name Mercury in favor of Model 202, which was promoted as the 'Two-O-Two'. Within two weeks of V-J Day (August 15, 1945), Martin had produced a full-size mock-up of the new airliner. The 202 was first presented to the public (in mock-up form) at the National Aircraft Show in Cleveland in November 1946.*
(via Author)

A drawing of the Pratt & Whitney R-2800-powered 202-15 design that appeared in Air News, *January 1946. The chief designer for the 202 program was Maxwell Bassett. (via Author)*

A passenger entrance door was located at the left forward end of the cabin. Although seldom used for passenger entry, it provided access to the forward baggage compartment. An underfloor compartment was also provided aft of the wing for baggage and cargo.

The suggestions of airline flight crews were solicited in order to ensure that the cockpit was the ultimate in comfort and accessibility to controls and instruments. Protection of the two flight crew members from injuries caused by bird impacts was assured by tests conducted with a 202 windshield at the Civil Aeronautics Administration (CAA) Experimental Test Center at Indianapolis, Indiana. (The Experimental Test Center was the forerunner of the current William J Hughes Technical Center located at Atlantic City, New Jersey.) Two 'eyebrow' windows were added above the windshield after the CAA advised Martin that cockpit visibility was inadequate. The radio equipment, which varied according to customer requirements, could be located aft of the cockpit or in a compartment below the cabin floor. An optional Sperry A-12 autopilot could be installed.

Martin mistakenly believed that the airlines would not want their short-to-medium range transports to be pressurized because of the added weight and associated maintenance costs. Consequently, only cabin heating and air conditioning were provided for passenger comfort. Fortunately, the fuselage was designed for pressurization loads so that succeeding models could have that feature.

Conceivably, an airplane of the required size could have been designed around four Pratt & Whitney Twin Wasp or Wright Cyclone engines; however, a twin-engine configuration was chosen for a number of reasons. Although the four-engine design could have provided better performance with one engine inoperative, it would have had a greater empty weight, had more overall drag, and been more expensive to build, operate, and maintain. Operation on long over-water routes was, of course, not a design consideration. As the ATA had specified a twin-engine design, it would have been difficult to convince the airlines that they should buy a four-engine airplane in any event.

The engines chosen for the Model 202 were Pratt & Whitney Double Wasps. These were 18-cylinder, twin-row, air-cooled radial engines that had achieved excellent service records in such World War II military airplanes as the Republic P-47 Thunderbolt, Vought F4U Corsair, and Grumman F6F Hellcat fighters, and Curtiss-Wright C-46 Commando transports. They were chosen over the Wright R-2600 Cyclone-14 engines considered for the 202-11 and 202-12 because they afforded a much better operational ceiling with one engine inoperative. Martin's experience with Double Wasps in its own B-26 and PBM airplanes was undoubtedly a positive influence as well. In addition to the Model 202, they were also slated to power the postwar Convair 110 and Douglas DC-6 transports.

Three versions of the Double Wasp engines were eligible for use in the Model 202—the CA3, the CA15, and the CA18. All three were rated 2,100hp for takeoff and 1,800hp METO (Maximum Except TakeOff, or maximum continuous power in today's terminology). The CA15 and CA18 engines had an additional supercharger drive ratio (usually referred to as 'high blower') in order to produce more power at altitude. The CA3 engines incorporated only single-speed superchargers and were, therefore, intended for operators with routes over low elevations. The fuel consumption of each engine was about 150USg (570l) per hour in cruise.

The right and left hand engine installations were made interchangeable to reduce the number of powerplant spares that had to be stocked. New three-point engine mounts were developed to permit quick engine replacement. In order to alleviate cabin noise, a collector-ring discharged exhaust at the lower left side of each nacelle. The cowl, which was supported by the engine rather than the nacelle, incorporated five electrically actuated flaps—three on the left side and two on the right. The oil cooler was located on the lower right side of each nacelle opposite the bottom flap.

An anti-detonant injection (ADI) system was available to increase rated takeoff power from 2,100hp to 2,400hp with any of the three engine models. The 15USg (56l) of water-alcohol mixture used for this purpose were contained in a tank located in the left wing-fillet at the trailing edge.

Four-bladed Hamilton Standard or Aeroproducts propellers were specified early in the design program; however, three-bladed Hamilton Standard 23260/2H17 series propellers were eventually chosen. These were hydraulically

New Martin Transports Being Built for the Airlines

Combining luxurious comfort, high speed and low operating costs, new Martin transports will soon be entering service on the world's airways. With hundreds of these airliners on order, and with other important developments in the making, Martin sets the pace in commercial aviation! THE GLENN L. MARTIN CO., BALTIMORE 3, MD.

Martin's 1947 advertising promoted the primary advantages of its new model—comfort, speed, and low operating costs.
(Aircraft Year Book via John Wegg)

controlled, constant-speed, reversing propellers with three hollow-steel blades. (Like most propeller manufacturers, Hamilton Standard uses a model designation system in which the hub model precedes the slash and the blade model follows.) Many 202s were later retrofitted with Hamilton Standard 43E60/6895A propellers which had solid dural blades. Non-reversing Hamilton Standard 33E60/6899A propellers were also eligible; however, it is doubtful if any airplanes in service were so equipped. (California Central Airlines did operate 202s without reversing, but it apparently did so by simply deactivating the reversing features of the original 23260 propellers.)

The Model 202 was the first airplane in which an auto-feather system was used to improve performance during takeoff and climb with an inoperative engine. This system was designed to sense an engine failure and automatically feather the propeller, thereby eliminating the time interval otherwise required for the pilot to recognize the failure and manually feather the propeller. As an added benefit, it also eliminated the possibility of inadvertently feathering the wrong propeller. In order to preclude unwanted feathering because of a transient power interruption, a 0.2 second time delay was designed into the system. Martin made approximately 75 demonstrations of complete power loss on takeoff to demonstrate the reliability of the auto-feather system for CAA certification. Although airline pilots were reluctant to accept them at first, auto-feather systems became standard equipment on nearly all subsequent propeller-driven transports.

The Model 202 incorporated a 24-volt dc electrical system. Two 300 ampere engine-driven generators and a 34 ampere-hour battery provided electrical power for use in flight, while external power was normally used for ground loads, such as heating and ventilation.

Enticing potential passengers by emphasizing how much time they could save flying in a Martin product. (via John Wegg)

The tricycle landing gear incorporated dual wheels on the main landing gear; however, a single wheel sufficed for the steerable nose gear. The hydraulically operated landing gear could be fully retracted in less than 4½ seconds. This rapid retraction enhanced the climb profile by eliminating the drag of the landing gear almost immediately. The landing gear could extended for emergency descent at airspeeds up to 190mph (165kt/305km/h).

For operation in icing conditions, four nacelle-mounted combustion heaters were used to heat the wing, stabilizer and fin leading edges. The propellers were electrically de-iced.

Ease of maintenance was a primary consideration in the design of the Model 202. Hydraulic systems, other accessories and, if desired, radio equipment were located under the cabin floor to enable maintenance personnel to service them without entering the cabin or cockpit. Numerous ground-accessible service doors were provided, including a special door in the nose-wheel well for access to the instrument panel. Engine maintenance was facilitated by designing lower nacelle sections to open downward and form stands for performing engine maintenance. A removable panel was also provided in the firewall so that engine accessories could be reached from the wheel well. A small flood-light installed in the nacelle eliminated the need for an external light with a long power cord.

In order to relieve ground personnel from the tasks of installing and removing control surface gust locks, a built-in cockpit-controlled lock system was provided. If the pilot were to attempt a takeoff with the gust locks engaged, they could be unlocked by exerting an aft pressure of about 40lb (18kg) on the control column.

The 202 was also offered in an all-cargo version called the Merchantman (or in some instances, the Marketer) with 2,240cu ft (62.72m³) of cargo space, approximately that of a Curtiss-Wright C-46, and a large 72in x 96in (1.83m x 2.44m) cargo door in the aft left fuselage. The cabin floor would have been reinforced with one of the earliest applications of honeycomb construction.

In order to reduce the cabin temperature while the airplane was parked, Martin engineers developed a simple, but unique, water evaporation system for the Merchantman. Basically, it consisted of a perforated aluminum tube running along the top of the fuselage from the fin to the nose. When there was a cabin load of perishable cargo, ground personnel could simply connect a garden hose to the tube. The spray of water on the exterior surfaces of the fuselage was expected to

*A retouched photo of NX93002 represent-
ing the all-cargo version of the 202.
Martin usually referred to the cargo model
as the 'Merchantman'; however, 'Marketer'
appears on the nose in this illustration.*
(Martin P20905 via Smithsonian Institution)

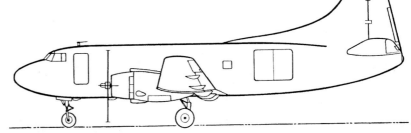

The Merchantman all-cargo 202. (Author)

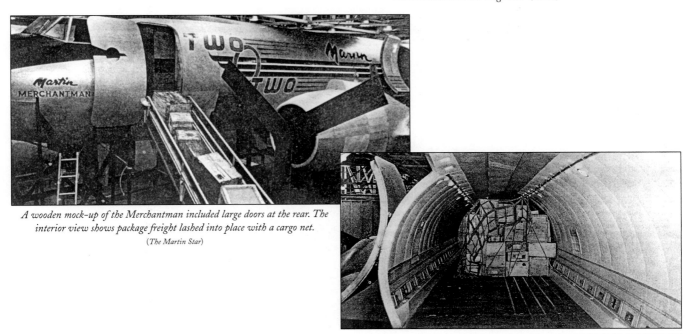

*A wooden mock-up of the Merchantman included large doors at the rear. The
interior view shows package freight lashed into place with a cargo net.*
(*The Martin Star*)

lower the cabin temperature as much as 10° to 15°F (5° to 8°C).

The maximum weights of the Model 202 were 39,900lb (18,100kg) and 38,000lb (17,240kg) for takeoff and landing, respectively. Weight reductions were required when certain tires were installed, the auto-feather system was inoperative, or ADI was not used. The empty weight varied considerably depending on the type of interior and equipment installed; however, it was typically about 25,000lb (11,340kg) with an airline interior. The empty weight of NC93041, manufacturer's serial number (msn) 9162, was, for example, 24,745lb (11,224kg) when originally delivered with the 40-passenger interior and 25,236lb (11,447kg) after conversion to the 36-passenger configuration.

FLIGHT TESTING

In light of its successful World War II production experience, Martin planned to build the Model 202 with no prototype. By placing it in production immediately and using the first production airplanes for development and certification, Martin anticipated placing the Model 202 in service long before any competitive type would be available. Two parallel production lines were set up in Martin's D Building to provide an initial production rate of five 202s per month. It was expected that the two lines could produce as many as 25 airplanes per month; however, sales failed to support a rate that great. All of the 202s could have been built in a couple of months if the lines were operating at their full potential! Following the demise of the 303 program, a third production line established for that model was apparently used for modification of completed 202s. Each 202 consisted of 27,000 parts, 200 sub-assemblies, and 35 major assemblies.

Martin's chief test pilot Orville Edwin (Pat) Tibbs made the first flight of the Model 202 on November 22, 1946. A former Army pilot, Tibbs joined Martin on December 16, 1941.
(The Martin Star)

The first 202 (NX93001) with the original wing and fin configuration. Martin was proud that it had completed and flown the first 202 just 368 days after the first drawings were submitted to its production department, and that it had introduced the idea of going straight into production without a prototype in order to save "every possible minute."

The 202 first flew on November 22, 1946, and by spring the following year, two more aircraft had been flown and 14 'planes were on the production line, with minor assemblies completed for 25 additional airplanes.

Considering the stability problems experienced by the original 202, W K Ebel's (Martin's vice president of engineering) statements in a December 1947 press release that "I can't imagine any 'plane having any more stability than our 202 has—directionally, longitudinally and laterally" are rather startling! (A U Schmidt via Peter M Bowers/A R Krieger)

Development testing began on November 22, 1946, at Baltimore, Maryland, with the first flight of NX93001 (msn 9122). Veteran test pilot O E (Pat) Tibbs was at the controls for this milestone that occurred just one year and three days after the first 202 drawings were submitted for engineering review. The second airplane (NX93002, msn 9123), was added to the flight test program during the following January. Both flew with an attractive company livery consisting of blue trim and red lettering on the natural aluminum finish. The fourth airplane (NC93003, msn 9128) was later used as a company demonstrator with this same livery. The third (msn 9124) was a non-flying airframe used for structural tests conducted at Martin's Strawberry Point Navy seaplane delivery hangar.

Although later mitigated somewhat by the cancellations and resulting excess production, using production airplanes for testing proved to be a gamble that Martin lost. Despite early enthusiastic statements about the flight characteristics, it was soon found that extensive redesign was required before the Model 202 could be certificated. Engine oil cooling was deficient; however, that was a relatively minor problem compared to the stability and controllability problems that plagued the 202.

The deficiencies of the 202 should have been apparent even before the first flight; however, Martin personnel seemed almost entranced by the prevailing exuberance. G T Willey, Martin's vice president of manufacturing, was led to write, "In the Martin 2-0-2, we of the Glenn L Martin Company feel we have designed and are building *the* commercial air transport of the postwar age. We don't consider the Martin 2-0-2 a 'forerunner' or a prototype or the 'start' of a trend. It is, in itself, the answer to the need of the world's airlines…." This example of gross overconfidence appeared in an article written for the June 1947 issue of *Air Trails*.

Some writers claim that the 202 was intentionally designed with poor lateral stability at the request of American Airlines because the airline wanted an airplane that could be steered down an ILS (Instrument Landing System) with rudder movement alone. This is undoubtedly in error because American would have been well aware that an airplane with poor lateral stability is difficult to control during instrument flight. It appears, instead, that Martin greatly over-estimated the stability and controllability of the 202 during preliminary design. At one point during the development of the 202, Martin conducted a series of tests with a 0.0875-scale powered model in the Wright Brothers wind tunnel at the Massachusetts Institute of Technology. The 202's inadequate lateral stability should have been recognized then. Perhaps Martin failed to appreciate the degree of stability needed for a civil design as its recent experience had all been with military airplanes. In any event, the Model 202, as originally designed, incorporated a constant dihedral of 3° from the fuselage to the wing tips.

After seeing the early sketches of the 202, CAA flight test personnel advised Martin that they seriously doubted the airplane would have sufficient lateral stability for civil certification.

Second 202 (NX93002) after the change to 10° dihedral in the outboard wing panels and a long sweeping dorsal fin. The long test boom protruding from the nose was used to calibrate the airplane's airspeed indication system.

Former aerodynamics engineer George Trimble recalls that Glenn Martin himself had wanted a 2° wing dihedral. Jack King, a Martin test pilot, remembers that the original tail was chosen to save weight, and that Glenn Martin randomly chose the largest dorsal fin out of two or three proposals which was subsequently known as the 'Presidential Tail'.

(Martin P30436 via A R Krieger/Martin via Author)

Certification test team in an obviously posed photo. From left to right: CAA flight analyst M Edward Gaydos, Martin chief flight test engineer Don K Covington, CAA flight test pilot H C 'Hank' Faller, and Martin test pilot E R 'Dutch' Gelvin. The pressure rake protruding from the nacelle was used to test the novel auto-feather system. (Martin via A R Krieger) *The certification team boarding NX93002 through the ventral stairs. From a legal standpoint, the manufacturer's pilot is always the pilot-in-command during CAA/FAA flight tests.* (Martin P30478/P30477 via Ed Gaydos)

So strong were the CAA doubts that the National Advisory Committee for Aeronautics (NACA) was requested to analyze the handling qualities of the 202. Based on data from the earlier Martin wind tunnel tests, NACA confirmed the suspicions of the CAA. In its Research Memorandum L7A31, NACA warned, "Considerable negative effective dihedral is probable in the landing and approach conditions which could make the airplane difficult if not dangerous to fly." Martin rationalized that in-flight wing deflection would increase the effective dihedral. Perhaps the manufacturer failed to take the warnings seriously because it remembered that the Marauder was eventually vindicated of similar criticism. The flight test program confirmed the suspicions of the CAA, and Martin had to increase the dihedral of the outboard wing sections to correct the deficiency in lateral stability. The first prototype (msn 9122) was tested with 8° dihedral in the outboard wing sections. It was found necessary, however, to adopt 10° as tested with the second airplane (msn 9123). In addition, the test program revealed a serious deficiency in lateral controllability that required considerable tailoring of the van Zelm ailerons.

The increased dihedral left the 202 with a tendency to Dutch roll. (Dutch roll is a flight condition in which the airplane oscillates in both yaw and roll. The term 'Dutch roll' comes from the fact that the roll slightly precedes the yaw in a motion similar to the weave of a skater's body.) That prompted the addition of a large, sweeping dorsal-fin that extended as far forward as the wing trailing edge. The 202 was also subject to rudder-lock (a condition in which the rudder stalls at high deflection angles and, with a reversal of pedal forces, floats to the rudder-stop). In order to solve that problem, so-called 'bumper springs' were added to supplement the aerodynamic rudder forces at the extremes of rudder travel.

Ten airplanes were nearing final assembly, and subassemblies for a further 20 had also been completed by the time all the needed changes were developed. Each had to be modified to the new configuration before it could be delivered. In addition to the revenue that was lost because of the delivery delays, it was reported that nearly $1.3 million worth of obsolete parts and assemblies had to be scrapped. Convair, in contrast, obtained much valuable flight experience with its Model 110 before it placed the definitive Model 240 in production.

The 202 was the first airplane required by the CAA to endure an extensive functioning and reliability (F & R) test

Busy production lines in Martin's D Building at Middle River on April 30, 1947. Outboard wing panels have already been installed without the required dihedral on at least five of the 16 airplanes, including LAN's CC-CLU (msn 9126) in the foreground. The nose of the next airframe is marked 'FOR 1' and 'M 15' (msn 9130), and was almost certainly intended for Air France. The third airframe behind CC-CLU, PCA's No 2 (msn 9132), was also destined to be reallocated.

Initially, the D Building was the final assembly location for the B–26 Marauder before Plant 2 was built, then used for assembly of the PBM Mariner and Mars before the 202 and 303 program. (Martin P30120 via A R Krieger)

Before—and after. Similar pre-delivery publicity photos of msn 9158 (NX93037) before and after the addition of outboard wing dihedral and the 'Presidential Tail'. This ill-fated airplane, shown here in Northwest's early post-World War II black trim, crashed October 13, 1950, at Almelund, Minnesota. (via Jim Borden/Logan Coombs via Walt Redmond)

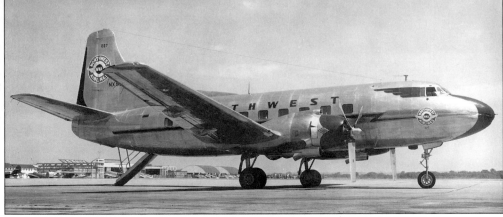

As a precursor to Northwest's unhappy experience with the 202, and its own fate, NX93037 (msn 9158) suffered a left main gear failure at Middle River during pre-certification tests. (via Jack L King)

Pat Tibbs demonstrating the use of automatic feathering for a single-engine takeoff. With the airplane loaded to maximum gross weight, fuel was cut to the left engine at V_1. The Model 202 was required to meet stringent postwar engine-out climb performance standards. Even with one propeller feathered, its cruise speed of 185mph (298km/h) was faster than that of contemporary DC-3s. (Martin P31308 via William T Larkins)

program. The purpose of such testing is to show that an airplane can withstand the rigors of actual airline service. Unfortunately, the 17,000mi (27,400km) F & R program conducted with the 202 failed to predict the difficulties that awaited the first 202 operators.

During that period, all type certificates were issued by the CAA headquarters in Washington, DC. The regional office (in this case, Region One located in New York) would administer the type certification program and, upon its completion, give tentative approval and issue tentative standard category airworthiness certificates for the eligible individual airplanes. At the same time, the regional office would advise headquarters of its completion. Assuming there were no unforeseen difficulties, the type certificate was then issued sometime later. It was, therefore, not uncommon for an operator to place a new model in service before the actual issuance of the type certificate and cause considerable confusion for future historians!

The completion of the 202 type certification program on August 13, 1947, was marked with a ceremony in which

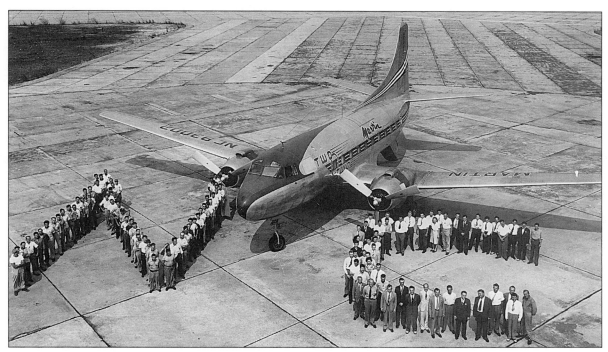

Following completion of the CAA type certification program on August 13, 1947, Martin employees formed 'NC' to symbolize the fact that msn 9123 was no longer an experimental airplane.

Apart from the extensive redesign necessary, 202s also experienced two in-flight incidents during the test program. During a high-speed test flight, the forward door came off and damaged the fuselage and propeller; however, an uneventful single-engine landing was made. A serious engine fire also occurred on a separate occasion. (Martin P31094 via W T Larkins)

the registration numbers of msn 9123 were repainted 'NC' in lieu of 'NX'. Serial number 9122 would have been eligible as well if the changes needed for type certification were incorporated. Martin chose, instead, to leave it with 8° dihedral in the outboard wing sections and just use it as an experimental test bed.

The redesign notwithstanding, the time that elapsed between the first flight and September 3, 1947, when Type Certificate No 795 was issued, was relatively short. The maximum takeoff weight of the 202 was limited to 38,000lb (17,240kg) at the time the type certificate was issued; however, that was increased to the definitive 39,900lb (18,100kg) two months later on completion of additional testing.

Although Martin frequently referred to the new model as the '2-0-2' (which, apparently, was the style stamped on the airplane data plates) or 'Two-O-Two', the official model designation is '202' as shown on the type certificate. Apart from the official model designation, Martin also used the following unofficial designations to facilitate

Advertising late in 1947 heralded the long-awaited completion of the CAA type certification program. (via Author)

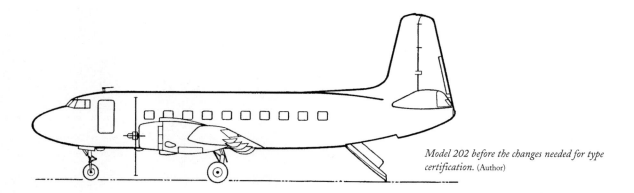

Model 202 before the changes needed for type certification. (Author)

negotiations with various potential customers and account for the differences in the airplanes offered:

202A	American Airlines
202AP	Aeroposta Argentina
202B	Braniff Airways
202C	Colonial Airlines
202CR	Servicios Aéreos Cruzeiro do Sul
202CS	Chicago & Southern Airlines
202D	Delta Air Lines
202DO	Compañía Argentina de Aéronavegación Dodera
202E	Eastern Air Lines
202EXEC	typical executive version
202F	unidentified French customer (undoubtedly Air France)
202FA	Flota Aérea Mercante Argentina (FAMA)
202FL	Línea Aérea Nacional de Chile (LAN)
202LAN	LAN follow-on order
202LAV	Línea Aéropostal Venezolana (LAV)
202M	prototype msn 2123 when converted for Martin executive use
202N	Northwest Airlines
202NW	Northwest Airlines (alternative to 202N)
202P	Pennsylvania Central Airlines (PCA)
202PAT	Pacific Airways Transportation Corp
202S	Empresa Guatemalteca de Aviación (AVIATECA)
202U	United Air Lines

These unofficial model designations probably never appeared outside Martin's own records. The designation 202A used during the unsuccessful negotiations with American Airlines should not be confused with the official model designation 202A assigned later to the airplanes delivered to TWA.

One of the 202 prototypes on final approach to Martin Airport.
(Martin P30422R via Jack L King)

THE REAL WORLD

Early optimism notwithstanding, the marketplace was to prove even more unkind to the Model 202 than certification had been. The first harbinger of the troubles awaiting 202 sales occurred in early September 1945, when American Airlines announced its order for 100 Convair 240s. That was a major blow to Martin as it had worked closely with American in the development of the 202. Sales were finally launched a month and a half later with the announcement of an order from Pennsylvania Central Airlines (PCA). By late 1946, Martin had orders and options for about 270 202s—more than Convair had garnered for the 240. Martin's advertising proudly announced sales to PCA (50), Eastern Air Lines (50), Colonial Airlines (20), Braniff Airways (18), Chicago & Southern Airlines (17), Delta Air Lines (20), and several other operators, including Línea Aérea Nacional (LAN) of Chile. (Delta had not actually signed a contract, but it had tentatively agreed to take ten with an option for ten more. Some of the other numbers quoted also included options.) Ten additional 202s were to be leased to Northwest Airlines pending delivery of a fleet of 303s. Five airlines, including Flying Tiger (or National Skyways Freight, as the airline was known at the time), had ordered the Merchantman all-cargo version. Martin claimed the 202 would be serving more than 200 cities in 41 of the United States!

Contracts for the purchase of new airline airplanes typically have penalty clauses that reduce the purchase price of any airplane that is not delivered by the date specified in the contract. Instead of simply having such penalty clauses, the 202 contracts reportedly gave customers the option of canceling their orders altogether and receiving full refund of their down payments when delays occurred. The option would prove to be the 202's nemesis.

Westinghouse Electric Corporation also planned to acquire about 60 pressurized variants of the Model 202 to serve as airborne television relay stations in a scheme known as 'Stratovision', devised by the corporation's C E Nobles in 1945. For this program, which was jointly sponsored by Martin and Westinghouse, a network of 14

Sky of dreams. Impressions of the 202 in the colors of Eastern Air Lines, United Air Lines, Pennsylvania Central Airlines, Braniff Airways, Chicago & Southern, and Colonial Airlines. Not one would fly 202s, although Eastern did take delivery of the 404. (The Martin Star)

Artist's impression of the 202 in service as a Stratovision broadcasting station. In this configuration, the 202 would have had a maximum gross weight of 39,900lb (18,098kg) and carried 7,000lb (3,175kg) of radio and support equipment, including a four-man crew. With 1,250USg (4,730l) of fuel, endurance was estimated at 3hr on station at 180mph (290km/h), plus reserves, climb (32min), and descent. The 202 would have been used for experimental operations with oxygen equipment; the commercial application would have used the pressurized Model 303. (Martin)

Stratovision stations would have been needed to span the United States completely. At each station, an airplane was to orbit continuously at 25,000 to 30,000ft (7,600 to 9,100m) and broadcast television signals downward to serve an area 422 miles (680km) in diameter. Each airplane would have been on station for three hours before being relieved. In order to promote the concept, Martin flew a group of radio and aviation writers to Zanesville, Ohio, on June 23, 1948, to witness a Stratovision broadcast of the Republican National Convention. Appropriately, the group was flown there in a 202, scheduled for delivery to LAN. Although this and a number of other tests were successfully conducted with a Boeing B-29, the idea was eventually abandoned. Television transmission by coaxial cable or microwave relay proved to be more practical.

Early 1945 advertising showing the 36-passenger Curtiss CW-20E in the markings of Eastern Air Lines. The new model would have had a 'dolphin' nose to improve the pilot's angle of vision.
(via John Wegg)

REAL—AND IMAGINED—COMPETITION

Although Martin did not seem to take it seriously, there was competition—both real and imagined. Curtiss-Wright had hoped to market its Model CW-20E, a 36-passenger civil version of the military C-46E Commando with two 2,100hp Wright Cyclone 18BA (R-3350 series) engines. The original CW-20 first flew in 1940 and promised to replace the already obsolescent Douglas DC-3. The intervention of World War II, however, precluded it from entering airline service then. Shortly after the wartime curtailment of US airline operations, Curtiss-Wright offered an early version of the CW-20E as a Pratt & Whitney Double Wasp-powered replacement for the few DC-3s that remained in high-priority civil service. In addition to the standard 36-passenger version, high density versions with 44 or 55 seats were offered for short stage lengths. Although CW-20Es would have been more efficient than the DC-3s, military C-46 production was deemed more important; and the CW-20E had to wait until the end of the war. Eastern Air Lines and National Airlines placed orders in 1944 for ten and 16, respectively; however, the CW-20E never really had a chance as a new-production postwar airliner. By the end of the war, it was obsolete compared to the planned postwar designs. Furthermore, the CW-20E had little to offer over the many surplus military C-46s that would be available shortly at bar-gain-basement prices. No additional orders were received, and those placed by Eastern and National were canceled.

Even the military-surplus C-46s found little favor for passenger service among the scheduled airlines, despite their cheaper purchase costs. A few were used for non-scheduled passenger service in the US during the early postwar period, and Northeast operated one briefly in scheduled passenger service between Boston and Montréal in 1957. Some were also used for passenger operations in Latin American countries. Non-commercial use of the C-46 was even more limited. Curtiss-Wright retained a C-46E until 1960 for its own use as an executive airplane, and another C-46E was used for personal transport by a Los Angeles area dentist. With those minor exceptions, the C-46 was destined to serve only as a workhorse in cargo service.

Curtiss-Wright's proposed Model CW-28, a contemporary of the early 202 designs, did not fare any better. It would have been a modern 32-passenger development of the CW-20 series with a new wing of higher aspect-ratio, a slimmer fuselage, redesigned tail surfaces, and a dual-wheel, tricycle landing gear. Considering that the CW-20 was originally designed for cabin pressurization, the CW-28 would probably have incorporated that feature. In order to keep as much of the airplane in the corporate family as possible, it was designed around two 2,500hp Cyclone 18BD engines rather than Pratt & Whitney Double Wasps. With the greater power afforded by the Wright engines, the CW-28 was expected to cruise at 288mph (250kt/463km/h), faster than the competing Double Wasp-powered models. Like Martin

Proposed Curtiss-Wright successor to the CW-20/C-46 series, the Model CW-28. (Curtiss-Wright)

and Convair, Curtiss-Wright targeted American Airlines as a launch customer for the Model CW-28. The September 1945 announcement of American's order for 100 Convair 240s apparently sounded the death knell of the CW-28 (and quite possibly Curtiss-Wright as an aircraft manufacturer) as it was never mentioned in subsequent airline trade publications. On top of that blow, Curtiss-Wright's enthusiasm for building airliners reportedly was dampened by other manufacturer's threats to boycott Wright engines.

In what would be described charitably as wishful thinking, Fairchild released sketches of its Model F-78, a proposed civil passenger variant of the military C-82 Packet. The C-82 proved to be less than satisfactory as a military cargo transport; and it would have required considerable change before it could have been considered for civil use, even in an all-cargo role. The F-78 would have been hampered also by its slow cruising speed of about 220mph (190kt/355km/h). Nevertheless, in 1945, Fairchild proposed a 45-passenger version with four-abreast seating. Lavatories would have been installed at the rear of the cabin, and the nose would have been lengthened slightly to accommodate a seven-seat lounge with a bar and buffet. As the cockpit would have been located above the cabin, the lounge could have provided passengers with an unobstructed forward view. In another sketch, Fairchild proposed a lounge at the aft end of the fuselage to provide passengers a panoramic view of whatever they had just passed over. The cabin floor would have been raised to provide space for baggage below the

cabin. Not surprisingly, there was no airline interest in the passenger variant of the Packet. Nevertheless, one airplane, no doubt a C-82 loaned by the US Army Air Force, was flown briefly in 1947 with United Air Lines markings and the civil registration NC8855 in an experimental program to determine the feasibility of in-flight mail sorting.

Boeing offered a 30-passenger high-wing design known as the Model 431-16. Like the 202, it would have been powered by two Double Wasp engines; however, its cruising speed was only expected to be 252mph (219kt/405km/h). Consequently, it received little consideration; and a companion design with four 1,200hp engines, the Model 431-17, received even less. After concluding these models had little potential, Boeing sold the design studies to Fokker. The F.27 Friendship is reputed to have evolved from them; however, it is doubtful whether it owed more than just the basic high-wing configuration to the Boeing models.

In today's world, the Douglas DC-8 is an airliner with four turbojet or turbofan engines. The model designation DC-8 was originally assigned, however, to a passenger derivative of the novel XB-42 Mixmaster. That DC-8 would have been powered by two liquid-cooled, 1,650hp Allison V-1710 engines buried in the lower forward fuselage and two contrarotating propellers at the aft end of the fuselage. Although it had about two-thirds as much power, the performance of the DC-8 was expected to equal that of conventional 40- to 50-passenger airplanes because of the absence of drag from wing-mounted engines and propellers. Despite its promised

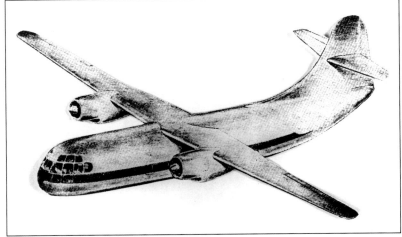

Proposed Boeing Model 431-16. Note the family resemblance of the cockpit and fin to those of the Boeing Stratocruiser. This design study was later sold to Fokker. (Boeing)

Artist's sketch of the first DC-8. (Douglas via Harry Gann)

The big one that got away! Although later reduced to 75 airplanes, American Airlines's 100-plane Convair 240 order was a fatal blow to the Curtiss-Wright CW-28 program and a big disappointment to Martin.
(American Airlines)

performance, the airlines were reluctant to order the DC-8 because of the safety and maintenance problems that might arise with the buried liquid-cooled engines and the long propeller drive-shafts. Consequently, the first DC-8 was never seen except in attractive artists's illustrations.

The only real competitor, insofar as new airplanes were concerned, was the Convair 240. Similar in design objectives and even in appearance, the two models were in direct competition for the meager market that existed immediately after the war. Performance figures were comparable, and both had accommodations for 40 passengers.

The comparison of passenger capacities was misleading, however. The total length of the 202 cabin, including the service areas and forward compartments for cargo or baggage, was about 2ft (0.61m) shorter than that of the 240. Furthermore, the 240 utilized about 5.5ft (1.6m) more of the fuselage aft of the cabin for an externally accessed cargo or baggage compartment. The effective length of the 240 cabin was, therefore, considerably greater than that of the 202.

Because of the deficiency in space for service and cargo or baggage, the 202 proved to be a 36-passenger airliner insofar as trunk airline use was concerned. The 202 cabin was 3.5in (9cm) wider than that of the 240.

Initially, Martin had a delivery time advantage over Convair; however, all but about seven months disappeared with the redesign and rework required for certification of the 202. Martin was also at a disadvantage because the 202 did not incorporate cabin pressurization. As noted earlier, American ordered 100 Convair 240s in September 1945. The order was later reduced to 75, but that was still large enough to give Convair a solid competitive base.

A Dream Unrealized

Although competition from the 240 did exist, it was really the prevailing economic conditions that devastated 202 sales. It was originally conceived during a period of great enthusiasm on the part of almost everyone involved in aviation—operator and manufacturer alike. Unfortunately for the 202, the reality of the late 1940s differed considerably. Most of the trunk airlines found financing the purchase of new airplanes quite difficult, and priorities had to be given to the new longer-range Douglas DC-6s and Lockheed Constellations. Because of short-sighted Civil Aeronautics Board (CAB) restrictions, the Local Service operators found such financing completely impossible. Although much less than optimum equipment, Douglas DC-3s were relatively cheap to acquire and operate because of a temporary abundance of military surplus airframes and spares. As a result, many operators continued using them for several years until better financing was available. In fairness, it must be noted that the economic conditions also affected Convair 240 sales.

Martin's 1947 advertising campaign for the 202 won

The Martin 202 appeared on a 10-cent (black) US air mail stamp issued on August 30, 1947, during the annual convention of the American Air Mail Society held in Washington, DC. The building on the stamp is the Pan American Union Building in that city.
(via Jack L King)

an award from the American Newspaper Publishers Association. Despite that achievement, Martin not only failed to attract any new customers, but lost all but three of its original customers by the time the 202 was certificated. Some orders were lost simply because the customers could not obtain financing; others were undoubtedly lost because Martin's contracts conveniently allowed them to cancel without penalties when the delays occurred. The large 50-airplane order placed by Pennsylvania Central Airlines (PCA—later renamed Capital Airlines) had been reduced to 20. Within another month, it was lost altogether, leaving only Northwest and LAN. Martin did pick up an order for two from Línea Aéropostal Venezolana (LAV) around the same time. Northwest converted its order for ten leased 202s to a purchase contract and, on December 23, purchased three airplanes (msn 9133 and Martin's demonstrators, msns 9128 and 9132). Northwest also purchased 12 of the airplanes under construction for other customers on February 10, 1948; however, Martin could find little consolation in those sales as Northwest would no longer be receiving 50 Model 303 airplanes. Because there were no other prospective customers, the 202s were undoubtedly sold to Northwest at a tremendous loss.

There was a press report in September 1948, that AVIATECA (Empresa Guatemalteca de Aviación) would buy two of the remaining 202s; however, none were delivered. An order for three placed about the same time by Líneas Aéreas Nacionales SA (LANSA) of Colombia was also canceled.

Altogether, 31 Martin 202s were delivered—four to LAN, 25 to Northwest and two to LAV. A dozen more were left uncompleted when the orders ran out. In addition,

One of a series of advertisements which promoted the speed and efficiency of the 202. (The Martin Star)

Martin placed an unsold 202 Merchantman (purported to have been msn 9171) in storage partially completed.

MILITARY AND SPECIAL VERSIONS

Martin unsuccessfully offered the Model 202 for several military uses. The staff-transport, medical-evacuation or troop-carrier versions would have been, in essence, the standard airline 202 with interior changes appropriate to the mission. The changes for the cargo, pilot-trainer, navigation-trainer and bombardier-trainer versions would have been considerably more extensive.

The cargo version would have been similar to the Merchantman with strengthened cabin flooring, cargo tie-down provisions and a large cargo loading door in the aft fuselage. Like that of the later 202A, the maximum takeoff weight would have been increased to 43,000lb (19,500kg). The company demonstrator (NC93003, msn 9128), was used to show the potential of that version to the US Air Force at Wright Field in December 1947, and later the same month to the US Navy and Marine Corps at Washington, DC. It did not have the large cargo door installed; however, the passenger interior was stripped to represent a cargo airplane.

The pilot-trainer version, which would have had two duplicate instrument panels for the use of trainees while they were not at the controls, would have had a reduced maximum takeoff weight of 36,000lb (16,330kg).

For the navigation trainer, Martin would have made modifications similar to those made by Convair to transform the airline 240 into the T-29; ie, the cabin would have contained provisions for 17 navigational students including duplicate instrument panels, LORAN (LOng-RAnge Navigation) scopes, drift meters and working tables. It too would have had a maximum takeoff weight of 43,000lb (19,500kg).

The bombardier trainer would have been the most recognizable with a large radome on the underside of the fuselage just forward of the wing, and a bomb bay designed to carry 23 100lb (45kg) practice bombs aft of the wing.

There would have been five student stations with visual bombsights and one station for radar bombing. Unlike the other versions, which would have retained their 202 model designation, the bombardier trainer was re-identified by Martin as the Model 268.

The military services faced an even greater shortage of funds than the airlines and could not immediately procure airplanes for such purposes. When orders were eventually placed, they went to Convair for versions of the Model 240. Despite earlier press reports that Martin's offerings were favored, Convair's 240-17 and 240-18 were selected as the T-29A and T-32, respectively, for the navigational and

An impression of the Model 268 bombardier trainer proposal for the USAF.
(courtesy Stan Piet, Glenn L Martin Museum)

Proposed convertible cargo/troop carrier/medical-evacuation version of the 202.
Despite reports that Martin's proposal was favored, Convair's 240-53 won the contract and became the
US Air Force's C-131A. (Martin P21070 via William T Larkins)

bombardier training roles. The 240-53 was also chosen later to become the C-131A for medical evacuation duties. Convair's T-32 contract was canceled before any were built; however, a number of T-29Ds were later produced for bombardier training.

Martin's failure to obtain a military contract may have been the result of a purported feud between Martin executives and military officials going back to the days of World War II production. Regardless of the reason, it was most unfortunate for Martin, considering that the military market eventually garnered Convair orders for a total of 380 T-29s and C-131As.

In addition to the nearly $1.3 million Martin lost because of 202 parts and assemblies that had to be scrapped, it lost almost as much on what was described as a 'special 202 model'. Special 202 probably referred to the proposed military variants of the 202.

Martin offered a luxurious executive version of the Model 202, but none were sold. In a late 1948 sales effort, the company also promoted an advanced civil cargo version with the maximum takeoff weight increased to 43,000lb (19,500kg) and additional fuel cells installed to provide a total fuel capacity of 1,550USg (5,860l). In addition to the 72in x 96in (1.83m x 2.44m) rear cargo door planned earlier for the Merchantman, the advanced cargo version would have had a 66in x 57in (1.68m x 1.45m) door in the front end of the cabin. Although this cargo version was equally unsuccessful, the increased weight and fuel capacity did show up in the Model 202A.

INTO SERVICE WITH NORTHWEST

LAN is sometimes credited erroneously with the honor; however, Northwest was the first customer to place the 202 in service. The exact date is uncertain as the airline used 202s as extra sections to supplement other models before the time dedicated 202 flights were initiated. Although dates as late as December 1947 are quoted, the 202s were in service by October of that year. *American Aviation Daily* reported on October 27 that the Northwest 202s had gone into service 'recently', and Northwest's fourth aircraft (NC93040, msn 9161) is reported to have entered service on October 12. LAN, of course, did not even receive its first airplane until November 5. In any event, the 202 was carrying passengers at least seven months before American placed the Convair 240 in service.

Small symbols were generally used then in airline schedules to indicate the airplane model used for a particular flight. In some cases, there was a special significance in the chosen symbol. For example, a star denoted a Lockheed Constellation flight, and the colon used for a Boeing Stratocruiser flight represented the double-lobe fuselage of that model. A small square was adopted by most of the airlines to represent a Martin 202 flight. Unfortunately, several stormy years would pass before the 202s would live up to the honesty and dependability that were implied by that symbol.

Northwest Airlines received two 202s (NC93037 & NC93038) in August 1947 which were used for crew training and route familiarization. The airline placed the 202 in service by October 1947, the first customer to do so. (via John Wegg)

After the 202s went into service, the rear galley installation was found to be inadequate. As predicted by Northwest's flight attendants, this arrangement did not provide sufficient working space. This, of course, was long before meals were prepared in advance and simply heated before serving. The lack of space forced the attendant to stack service items in the aisle which, in turn, precluded access to the lavatory during food preparation. Having to restock the galley through the ventral stairs was also inconvenient. In addition, there was a definite need to provide more storage for passengers's coats and other carry-on items. After further consideration, Northwest elected to provide more passenger service space by removing the front row of passenger seats. A larger galley was located at the front end of the cabin, along with a large coat room; and carry-on luggage racks were provided in the left rear of the cabin opposite the lavatory. The carry-on racks were quite popular with passengers as they eliminated the need for checking and later reclaiming baggage. A prototype conversion was made at the Martin factory, and the other nine airplanes already built were modified to the new configuration by the Texas

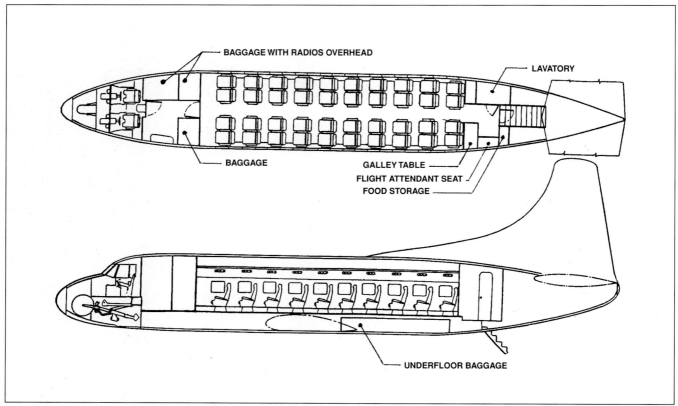

Northwest Airlines 202 configuration with the original 40-passenger interior. (Author)

Engineering and Manufacturing Company (TEMCO) in Dallas, Texas. All of Northwest's subsequent 202s were completed with the new interior arrangement before delivery. Apparently LAN made similar modifications to its 202s as later photos show them with only nine passenger windows on each side.

As a precursor of Northwest's future experience with the 202, one of its 202s suffered substantial damage on December 10, 1947, when forced to land in an open field near the Great Northern Railroad's main line following a takeoff from Fargo's Hector Field with the engines inadvertently set in the high blower position. With the use of airbags, the airplane was raised and set on its landing gear by a maintenance crew dispatched from Minneapolis-St Paul. After its engines and propellers had been replaced, a strip was bulldozed out of the snow and frozen earth and the 202 flown to St Paul for final repairs.

Another 202 suffered substantial damage on April 2 of the following year when the front service door failed and struck the left propeller just after takeoff on a ferry flight.

So far, no one had been injured in a 202. That changed, however, on August 29, 1948, when NC93044 (msn 9165) crashed at Winona, Minnesota, following a structural failure of the left wing. All 37 persons aboard were killed. In service for just five months, it had logged only 1,321 hours of

Passengers deplaning through the ventral exit in Northwest Airlines' Fleet No 552 (NC93052). After passing from Northwest to California Central Airlines, then Allegheny Airlines, this airplane was damaged beyond repair by an engine fire during a November 14, 1955, training flight at New Castle, Delaware. (Martin P37092 via Donald Falenczykowski)

Routine servicing of a Northwest 202 (NC93042). This airplane, which is shown in Northwest's definitive 202 era livery, gave many years of satisfactory service with California Central, Allegheny (as N170A), and RAPSA (as HP–431) before being scrapped at Panama City around 1972. (Martin P37073 via Donald Falenczykowski)

Northwest Airlines's NC93044 in an experimental livery. In contrast to the drab colors typically used by Northwest, the painted nose area of this airplane was bright yellow. It crashed on August 29, 1948, at Winona, Minnesota, following a fatigue failure of an outer wing attachment fitting. With only 1,321 hours total time when the crash occurred, it can be surmised that the fatal cracks had already begun when this photo was taken. (Martin P31971 via Smithsonian Institution)

This plan view of N93039, obviously on public display, shows off the 202's eyebrow cockpit windows and the positioning of the airline titles and registration on the upper surfaces of the wings, which were reversed on the underside. (Bob Redden collection)

In-flight view of Northwest's N93051 (the gap between N and the numbers shows where 'C' has been removed following new regulations effective January 1, 1949). This airplane was damaged in a forced landing on September 4, 1950, at Billings, Montana. However, it survived to enjoy a long career with Pioneer Air Lines, Allegheny Airlines (as N173A), and RAPSA (as HP-427) before being scrapped at Panama City. (Northwest Airlines)

flight time. Although there was considerable turbulence in the area because of thunderstorms, the failure was found to have resulted from fatigue cracks in the front outer wing panel attachment fitting. That was one of the four fittings that had been redesigned during the flight test program to increase the dihedral in the outer wing sections. Similar cracks were found in five other Northwest 202s, including NC93042. (Three of the five had cracks in both wings.)

The CAA quickly responded by issuing an Airworthiness Directive (AD) that required an immediate inspection of the fittings of the remaining 202s. The initial action was followed by a definitive AD (49-15-02) that required interim rework of the fittings, periodic inspections within 900-hour intervals, and reductions in airspeed limits pending a complete rework of the wings at the Martin factory. During the following year, each remaining airplane of Northwest and those of LAN and LAV were returned to Martin for wing spar modifications. This program required about six to eight weeks per airplane and was undoubtedly very costly to the manufacturer.

Unfortunately, Northwest's troubles with its 202s were just beginning. Four more non-injury accidents were experienced through January 1950: a forward service door blew off at Spokane, Washington, on the same day as the Winona accident; an airplane was substantially damaged on December 28, 1948, at Yakima, Washington, because of inadequate snow removal from runways; a 202's left main gear failed to extend on September 30, 1949, at Milwaukee, Wisconsin; and the non-reversal of a propeller on landing caused an aircraft to skid off an icy runway at Kalispell,

Montana, on January 17, 1950.

Tragedy struck again on March 7 of that year when N93050 (msn 9134) crashed into a residence during a missed approach to the Minneapolis-St Paul Municipal Airport. (The registration number prefix displayed on Northwest's 202 fleet had been changed from 'NC' to 'N' a month or so earlier.) The left wing had failed but, unlike the Winona accident, the failure was not caused by structural deficiency. During the approach, the airplane had struck the 70ft (21m)-high steel flagpole of the National Soldiers Cemetery at nearby Fort Snelling. All 13 persons on board plus two occupants of the residence were killed.

Later that year, on October 13, all six aboard N93037 (msn 9158) were killed when it crashed at Almelund, Minnesota. That accident was attributed to the unwanted reversal of the right propeller during flight. Following hard on its heels was the destruction of N93040 (msn 9161) on November 7, when it was flown into a mountain during an approach to Butte, Montana.

By then, the Northwest flight crews were reluctant to fly the 202s, and passengers were fervently avoiding them. The 21 remaining airplanes were grounded for a short time, but were returned to service after they were determined to have no structural defects.

The year 1951 was not to prove more favorable for the 202. On January 16, N93054 (msn 9144) experienced a sudden loss of control while in cruise near Reardan, Washington, and crashed, killing all ten persons aboard. The reason for the loss of control could not be determined.

Illustrating Northwest's misfortunes with the 202, all six aboard N93037 were killed on October 13, 1950, at Almelund, Minnesota, when it crashed following a reversal of the right-hand propeller during a training flight. A trail of wreckage (above) leads to msn 9161's final destination, alarmingly close to several houses.

Northwest voluntarily grounded its 202 fleet three times. After the August 29, 1948, accident at Winona, it had to return some of its fleet of 13 Douglas DC-3s to service to supplement DC-4s (NWA had planned to retire all its DC-3s from passenger service effective September 1). The 202 returned to service on September 30, 1948. The 202 was grounded a second time between November 12 and 19 following the accident of msn 9161; and for the third and final time on March 17, 1951. (Leo J Kohn)

MORE TROUBLES

Apart from the accidents, the 202s suffered many maintenance difficulties. Because of these and the accidents, the CAA formed a special review team of aeronautical experts. The purposes of this team, appropriately known as the 'Martin 202 Modification Board', were to discover anything that might have caused the series of accidents and recommend modifications and operating procedures to make the airplanes safer. Similar teams had been formed earlier when the Douglas DC-6 and Lockheed Constellation were having their problems. The Board found no basic design faults that could have contributed to the accidents; however, it did recommend a number of changes. As a result of the team's recommendations, several ADs were issued to require numerous improvements in the electrical, hydraulic, windshield heating, landing gear position indication, and fuel systems, and to the combustion heater and autopilot installations. The ADs were applicable to TWA's 202As as well as to the 202s. Many of the improvements undoubtedly involved adapting design features that had been developed for the Model 404. Airworthiness Directives requiring structural inspection and modifications of 202s were also issued in 1951.

None of the recommended modifications warranted immediate grounding of the 202 fleet. Although the modifications could have been performed over a period of time without removing the airplanes from service, Northwest elected to ground the remaining 202s voluntarily on March 17, 1951. 'Expediting the program' and 'efficient utilization of resources' were the reasons given, but the real reason was that its pilots had given Northwest an ultimatum—they would not fly the 202s after that date.

While the 202s were undergoing the modifications, Northwest tentatively decided to retire the fleet prematurely—a move reminiscent of the disposal of its Lockheed 14 Super Electra fleet several years earlier. Rumors that the entire fleet was being sold to National Airlines were quickly denied by that operator. Eight were sold; however, Northwest did retain ownership of the remaining 12 airplanes as it had not ruled out returning them to service in its own fleet. Most were transferred to Transocean Air Lines.

OVER TO TRANSOCEAN

Transocean flew the leased airplanes in the basic Northwest color scheme on domestic military airlift operations. (Photos showing those airplanes with 'Airlift' titles have led to the erroneous assumption that they were operated by an airline with that name.) Three airplanes purchased outright by Transocean were used initially for non-scheduled passenger service between San Francisco, Los Angeles, and New York

Look alikes! Three-quarter rear views of a Northwest Airlines 202 on lease to Transocean and a Western Air Lines Convair 240-2 show how similar the competitive designs were in appearance. The only differences obvious at first glance from this angle are the stabilizer and outer wing dihedral of the 202, and the augmenter exhaust system of the 240. Lowering the ventral stairs of both airplanes would have made the similarity even more striking. (William T Larkins)

via Salt Lake City, Denver, and Chicago. When those flights proved to be unprofitable, Transocean transferred its three owned 202s and two of those leased to Japan.

At the close of World War II, the Allied occupational forces disbanded the Japanese commercial airline, Dai Nihon Koku, and prohibited all aviation by Japanese nationals. The subsequent recovery of the Japanese economy was accompanied by a developing need for domestic airline service; therefore, a new airline, Japan Air Lines (JAL), was formed on August 1, 1951, held by private financial interests. As the Japanese were still prohibited from flying their own airplanes, JAL contracted with Northwest to provide airplanes and crews for a period of one year. Under subcontract to Northwest, Transocean inaugurated postwar airline service on behalf of JAL on October 25, 1951.

Unfortunately, the propensity of the 202s for accidents continued with Transocean. On November 5, 1951, N93039 (msn 9160) crashed with one fatality on approach to Tucumcari, New Mexico. The next year, on April 9, N93043 (msn 9164) crashed into Mount Mihara in Japan. (It was one of the three owned by Transocean.) All 37 persons aboard were lost in that accident. In little more than four years since their introduction in airline service, only 24 of the 31 delivered 202s were extant.

By the end of Northwest's contract period, a peace treaty had been signed, enabling a reformed Japanese government-owned JAL to begin its own service on October 1, 1952. With

the completion of the Japanese contract and a diminishing need for military airlift, Transocean returned the leased airplanes to Northwest and sold the four owned airplanes to Southwest Airways. (Transocean had purchased two of the leased airplanes in the meantime; however, that was apparently just a transaction to facilitate their sale to Southwest.)

Although retaining the basic Northwest livery, N93043 has been purchased by Transocean Air Lines for non-scheduled coast-to-coast passenger service. It would later crash into Mount Mihara on April 9, 1952, while flown by Transocean on Japanese domestic service.
(William T Larkins via Clinton H Groves)

Photographed at Oakland, California, N93055 is leased to Transocean Air Lines for domestic military airlift operations. (William T Larkins)

CALIFORNIA CENTRAL

Before the Airline Deregulation Act of 1978, the Civil Aeronautics Board (CAB) exercised almost complete domination of the US airline industry. There was, however, one situation in which the CAB had no authority. Provided there was no carriage of mail, it had no jurisdiction in any airline operations conducted entirely within one state. Generally, that was academic then. With one exception, there were no states with large population centers separated by enough distance to support airline service without mail subsidy. The one exception was California.

California Central Airlines was formed in 1948 by Colonel Charles C Sherman to operate between the metropolitan areas of San Francisco and Los Angeles, a sector that probably had the greatest traffic potential of any airline route in the world. Sherman had previously operated on this route as a so-called Large Irregular carrier under the name of Airline Transport Carriers; however, all service by such airlines was curtailed by the CAB to eight flights per month in December of 1948—hardly enough to be profitable or provide any semblance of service to the public. In order to escape the constraints of the CAB, he quickly split off the California intrastate portion and reformed it as California Central Airlines. The remaining portion continued to operate separately as a Large Irregular carrier under the name California Hawaiian Airlines.

There were, of course, a number of trunk airlines that also served the route; however, California Central was able to

California Central Airlines 202 City of San Diego *seen at Lockheed Air Terminal, Burbank, California, and* City of San Francisco *(N93052) on approach to the same airport.*

In an unusual transaction, CCA exchanged three DC-3s and two DC-4s with Northwest Airlines for five 202s. The 202s were modified to carry 44 passengers and were fitted with an air/ground radio telephone for use by passengers. A Lockheed Constellation flown by Colonel Sherman's affiliate, California Hawaiian Airlines, also used this attractive red, white, and blue livery. (via Jukka Kauppinen/Robert Hufford)

offer much lower fares because its tariff was under the cognizance of the California Public Utilities Commission (PUC). Unlike the CAB, the PUC strongly supported low cost fares. At one point, California Central's fares were about half the CAB-dictated fares of the trunk airlines and were even competitive with train tariffs. Operations were conducted with Douglas DC-3s from 1949 to 1951 when they and some DC-4s were traded to Northwest for five 202s. The Martins were an immediate success, and record numbers of passengers were carried after their introduction. Unfortunately, California Central was undercapitalized, and

Interior of a CCA 202 looking through a plastic bulkhead which separated an eight-seat 'business class'. (The Martin Star)

the low fares did not provide sufficient income for it to ever become profitable. Although it eventually went into bankruptcy in 1954, California Central's trouble-free operation had finally overcome the reputation of the 202s for being accident-prone airplanes.

BACK TO NORTHWEST (ALMOST)

Meanwhile, Northwest had made a detailed study of each accident and identified a number of operations and maintenance deficiencies. Those were corrected with some sweeping changes in its organization. Except for the wing failure at Winona, Northwest concluded that there was no correlation between any of the accidents and the 202 design. Its conclusion was also supported by Trans World Airlines's successful operation of 202As. As a result, Northwest decided to return the airplanes it still owned to service. This, of course, was dependent on convincing its pilots that the 202s were safe airplanes.

Whether the pilots changed their position is not clear at this late date. In any event, the 202s never did go back into service with Northwest. It appears that Northwest ultimately decided to dispose of them because of one very real fact of life. As it had been the sole US operator of 202s, Northwest alone bore all of the bad publicity from the accidents. Should there have been another accident, regardless of the cause, the additional bad publicity would probably have spelled the end for Northwest. The routes the 202s formerly served were flown with a less efficient combination of Douglas DC-3s and DC-4s. A fleet of new Convair 440s was considered in 1957, but it was not until the merger with Republic Airlines three decades later that Northwest actually flew any other post-World War II twin.

Mexico made this a moot point, anyhow. As traffic grew, the airline was given CAB permission to replace its initial fleet of Lockheed 10-A Electras with DC-3s. The CAB did not directly control the types of airplanes the airlines operated; however, it did so indirectly by allowing or disallowing additional subsidy to cover the costs of introducing new types in service.

By early in the 1950s, traffic had increased to the point where the DC-3s were inadequate to serve the routes effectively. As none of the Local Service airlines were given permanent operating certificates, financing anything newer than DC-3s was very difficult. Nevertheless, Pioneer—as Essair had become—convinced the lending institutions that its routes would support the use of modern airplanes with larger capacities. As a result, financing for better equipment was made available.

Douglas Super DC-3s, SAAB Scandias, and new Convair 340s or Martin 404s were considered in addition to the almost new 202As leased temporarily to TWA. The Super DC-3s were deemed too costly for the little improvement they would offer over standard DC-3s. Although Boeing was considering license production of Scandias, the Swedish transport was quickly ruled out because it could not be supplied on a timely basis from either Boeing or SAAB. Boeing production of Scandias, of course, never did come about; and three years would pass before license-built Scandias were available from Fokker. Convair 340s and Martin 404s were expensive, and they too were not readily available. Following a very thorough review of the Northwest difficulties and corrective action taken, Pioneer contracted with Martin to buy nine of the 202As for $450,000 each upon return from the TWA lease. When TWA decided to exercise a purchase option and keep the 202As, Pioneer had to settle for the nine 202s returned to Northwest from the

A PIONEERING LOCAL SERVICE

Texas-based Pioneer Air Lines began operations in 1945 under the name Essair, an acronym for *E*fficiency, *S*afety and *S*peed by *Air*. Unlike California, Texas could not then generate sufficient passenger volume for an airline to operate without mail subsidy. Essair, therefore, operated as a Local Service airline under the jurisdiction of the CAB. Later, Essair's extension of service into New

Pacemaster Kit Carson *was one of nine 202s acquired in 1952 by Local Service carrier Pioneer Air Lines to upgrade its DC-3 fleet, the first such airline to do so. When this photo was taken at Oakland, California, in 1954, Pioneer had been forced by the CAB to retire its 202s.* (A R Krieger)

Pioneer Air Lines referred and named its 202s 'Pacemasters'. This schedule covers the second month of Pacemaster operation which started on June 2, 1952.

(via John Wegg)

Transocean lease. TEMCO, which had performed 202 modifications earlier for Northwest, was selected to carry out an extensive overhaul, refurbishment, and modification program. Although this raised the total cost of introducing the 202 fleet in Pioneer service to more than $4 million, it was still $1 million less expensive than the anticipated cost of the 202A fleet. After completion of this program, Pioneer placed its 202s in service on June 2, 1952.

An order was also placed for the delivery of five new 340s in 1954; however, that deal fell through when Pioneer was unable to get the necessary government approval to purchase them. (Because of Korean War production priorities, airlines had to obtain government certification for their orders by showing that they had a need for new airplanes.)

In light of its experience in stepping up from Electras to DC-3s, Pioneer and its lenders were confident that the CAB would quickly approve the additional mail subsidy needed temporarily to cover the costs of introducing the first modern, postwar airplanes in Local Service operation. Unfortunately, Pioneer had not anticipated the ensuing short-sighted, biased action of the CAB. In the early post World War II period, the CAB policy concerning Local Service airlines was based on two premises. First, those carriers were not permanent entities; their very existence was at the pleasure of the CAB. Second, they were not to be allowed under any circumstances to expand or improve their lot in any way that might result in competition with the Trunk airlines. The CAB certainly did not want a Local Service airline to offer any kind of service that might draw traffic away from the Trunks! After holding Pioneer in suspense for almost a year, it finally denied the additional sub-sidy. The CAB was able to rationalize its action because the DC-3s were relatively inexpensive to operate—owing, of course, to the temporary abundance of war-surplus airplanes and spares. As if to emphasize its contempt for the progressive thinking of Pioneer management, the CAB offered less subsidy than Pioneer was receiving a year earlier when it was still using DC-3s.

The CAB denial of additional subsidy placed Pioneer in an untenable position. The airline had spent a large sum of money in placing the airplanes in service and operating them for almost a year while the CAB decision was pending. Although it could not afford to continue operating its fleet of 202s without additional subsidy, it could not readily obtain a replacement fleet of DC-3s. An interim fleet of DC-3s was leased from Eastern, and these were followed by a long-term lease of ten DC-3s from M M Landy. In the meantime, the 202s were transferred to a newly formed subsidiary, Pioneer Aeronautical Services, for disposal.

Ironically, Pioneer was able to lease some of the 202s back from Pioneer Aeronautical Services and reintroduce 202 service on September 1, 1953, on a route from Houston to Midland-Odessa via Austin and San Angelo. It was, of course, impossible to remain profitable using an entire fleet of leased airplanes. The only solution was a forced merger with Continental Air Lines on April 1, 1955. The patrons of the former Pioneer routes were then forced back to flying in DC-3s altogether. Pioneer Aeronautical Services leased one of the 202s to Martin for use as an electronics test bed; however, the others remained in storage until their eventual sale to Allegheny and Southwest.

The capricious action of the CAB obviously sent a chilling message to the surviving Local Service airlines and their potential lenders.

Although too late to help Pioneer, the CAB policy concerning Local Service operators was reversed in two steps by Congressional action. First, a bill was passed in May 1955, to force the CAB to grant permanent operating certificates to the 13 surviving Local Service airlines and make them more attractive to potential lenders. In order to ensure the availability of financing, a second bill passed on September 7, 1957, enabled the federal government to guarantee loans made to Local Service airlines for new equipment. The two measures just about eliminated any risk to the lenders. CAB resistance to Local Service airlines did not die easily, however. CAB officials were extremely critical a few years later when Local Service airlines placed their first orders for jet-powered airplanes.

Back to California

Meanwhile, California-based Southwest Airways had obtained four 202s from Transocean. Like that of Pioneer, its request for additional subsidy was denied by the CAB; however, Southwest was able to survive without it because its 202s were used to supplement DC-3s, rather than replace them entirely. As traffic grew and routes could absorb them, four more 202s were obtained from California Central and Pioneer.

One 202 (N93061, msn 9150) was damaged beyond repair in a hangar fire at San Francisco on December 30, 1955; however, none of Southwest's 202s were lost in accidents, and there were no injuries during their operation. Southwest changed its name to Pacific Air Lines on March 6, 1958, for better identification with the area it served. Eventually, the remaining 202s were sold to TWA in trade for a fleet of 404s.

The partially completed 202 Merchantman remained in storage until 1955 when it was used at sea off Norfolk, Virginia, in the CAA's *Operation Ditch*. For the test program, the outer wing panels were replaced with large drums for buoyancy, a partial airline interior was installed, and the rear half of the cargo door was removed to simulate an open passenger door. The airplane was then taken out to sea to represent a ditched airliner. With 40 CAA volunteers aboard, including 13 women, tests were conducted to study the best procedures for getting passengers off the airplane into the 20-man life rafts. In these tests, the volunteers were able to leave the airplane in as little as 3min 37sec after the evacuation began. The same airplane was used for another series of simulated ditchings in San Francisco Bay a year later.

The airplane used in San Francisco Bay is sometimes claimed to have been the Southwest Airways 202 (msn 9150) damaged in the hangar fire. It could not have been that airplane, however. First, serial number 9150 did not have the Merchantman cargo door. Furthermore, it is clear from photos that it was the same plane as that used in the earlier Norfolk tests. Photos of those tests appeared in *Aviation Week* several months before the fire occurred.

Southwest Airways was the second Local Service 202 operator, starting service in April 1953. Here, N93049 shows the Martinliner's characteristic nose-down attitude during final landing approach. This airplane, originally assigned to Air France, was first used by Martin as a demonstrator (as NC93004), then it enjoyed a long, successful career with Northwest Airlines, Transocean Air Lines, Japan Air Lines, Southwest (later Pacific Air Lines), and a number other operators before ending its days in San Juan, Puerto Rico, in the 1970s. (Robert Hufford)

After touting itself as 'The Pacific Air Line' since 1956, Southwest Airways changed its name to Pacific Air Lines in March 1958 as displayed by ex-Northwest/Transocean/Pioneer 202 N93059 at Los Angeles in February 1963. It has been fitted with a Chamberlain nose radome—weather radar was required by the FAA on all 202s and 404s used in air carrier service from January 1, 1962. (Clay Jansson via Walt Redmond)

The uncompleted 202 Merchantman, believed to have been msn 9171, being used in October 1956 for ditching evacuation practice by a Transocean crew in San Francisco Bay. This airframe had been used by the CAA a year earlier for Operation Ditch, *a series of ditching evacuation tests off Norfolk, VA.*
(Ralph Lewis via Arue Szura)

ALLEGHENY AIRLINES

Allegheny Airlines, or All American Aviation (as it was originally known), began mail-carrying operations before World War II using Stinson Reliants and a unique in-flight mail pick-up system. After World War II, the airline evolved into a Local Service carrier. Although it did not rush to replace its DC-3s, as did Pioneer and Southwest, Allegheny found by 1955 that some of its routes could support the operation of more modern equipment without additional subsidy. The Fokker F.27 and Handley Page Herald were considered promising DC-3 replacements; however, neither was expected to be available for at least two years. (Although Handley Page had not then formally decided to proceed with the Rolls-Royce Dart-powered model, Allegheny was probably considering that variant rather than the original reciprocating-powered Herald.) In order to accommodate increased traffic while definitive DC-3 replacements were being developed, a transitional fleet that eventually included eight 202s was acquired from California Central and Pioneer. Once the 202s were in service, Allegheny found that their seat-mile operating costs were less than those estimated for either F.27s or Heralds.

One 202 (N172A, msn 9142), was damaged beyond economical repair by an engine fire during a 1955 training flight. Another (N174A, msn 9159), was lost along with all 25 persons aboard on December 1, 1959, when it crashed into a mountain near Williamsport, Pennsylvania. That was, of course, not the fault of the 202 design in any way. Following about a decade of satisfactory service, Allegheny withdrew its remaining 202s from passenger service in March 1966. Three all-cargo 202s remained in service for another year, then they too were sold to Fairchild Hiller in trade for F-27s.

Two Allegheny 202s, N176A The Detroiter *(foreground) and* N173A The Pennsylvanian, *seen at Pittsburgh in June 1958. Allegheny introduced the 'Martin Executive' on June 1, 1955.*

In 1956, in a promotional scheme, 15 English-speaking hostesses from Air France served on the 202s (Allegheny did not hire female flight attendants until the following year, perhaps as a result of the experimental program!). (Ken Sumney via Peter M Bowers)

Allegheny Cargoliner N175A photographed in July 1964, wearing the airline's Convair 440-era color scheme. All 15 of Allegheny's surviving 202 and 202A fleet were traded-in to Fairchild Hiller for F-27Js; 13 of these plus spares were sold by the manufacturer to Associated Products of America. (Roger F Besecker via Eric W Wagner)

A TARNISHED REPUTATION

The reputation of the 202s never did recover completely; however, the years of successful operation with Pacific and Allegheny did much to remove the stigma that resulted from the early crashes and their association with the financial difficulties of California Central and Pioneer.

Although none resulted in any injuries, at least five 202s were involved in accidents involving the landing gear—either failures of the gear or inadvertent retraction by the crew.

The gear-up landing of a LAV airplane (YV-C-AMC, msn 9131) on August 26, 1952, notwithstanding, its airplanes and those of LAN apparently enjoyed relatively trouble-free service for several years before their eventual retirement.

As Martin had dropped the name Mercury early in the design stage, the operators coined various promotional names for their 202s. Northwest referred to its 202s as 'Martin Luxury Liners' in the *Official Airline Guide* and other advertising. California Central, and later Southwest, used the term 'Martinliner' in an apparent attempt to benefit from public familiarity with the name

Three rare airplanes. Línea Aéropostale Venezolana's YV-C-AMB Rafael Urdaneta at La Guaira (the airport and seaport that serve Caracas), Venezuela, in 1951 in company with a British West Indian Airways Vickers Viking and a Chicago & Southern Douglas C-54, N53102 City of New Orleans. This C-54, one of six converted for C&S by the Glenn L Martin Co to civilian DC-4 standard, was one of the few, possibly the only one, converted (by C&S) to use Wright R-1820 series engines in lieu of the original Pratt & Whitney R-2000 series engines. (The Aeroplane/Flight via Tony Merton Jones/Propliner)

Following the demise of Pioneer Air Lines 202 service, N93058 was transferred to Pioneer Aeronautical Services and leased back to Martin in January 1955 for use as an electronics test bed (indicated by the covered rear windows and the bulge forward of the ventral air stairs). Except for replacing Pioneer's buffalo with Martin's logo on the fin, it is still painted in basic Pioneer colors. Underneath the cockpit is a cartoon figure of a pilot riding a rocket. (A R Krieger)

'Convair-Liner'. Pioneer called its 202s 'Pacemasters'; and Allegheny, recognizing the predominant nature of its patronage, referred to its fleet as 'Martin Executives'. Allegheny also referred to its airplanes erroneously as 202Bs.

The availability of used Convair-Liners and Martin 404s at affordable prices in the 1960s spelled the end for 202s in scheduled service with major airlines. One ex-Pacific 202 was used by California Time Airlines for California intrastate service in 1963; and, farther south, another was used in 1966 and 1967 by Servicio Aéreo Baja (Baja Air Lines) for local service in México's Baja California. The latter airplane operated with the attention-getting registration XA-SEX. Three others—the last 202s to see scheduled passenger service—were used from 1965 to 1970 by Rutas Aéreas Panamenas SA (RAPSA) for flights between Panama City and David. A few others lingered for awhile in miscellaneous non-scheduled activities; however, most remained in storage until they were finally scrapped. The remains of one (msn 9142) were reported on a farm in Delaware late in the 1970s. In Colombia, Aeroproveedora 'Proa' used a single 202 as a freighter. Although withdrawn from use in 1977, the hulk was still languishing at Bogotá-Eldorado as late as 1995. One 202 (N93041, msn 9162), still remained on the US register by 1995, but is not believed extant. Thus, for all practical purposes, the 202 may be considered extinct.

Another California-based second-hand operator of the 202 was California Time Airlines, which used N93059 in the early 1960s for short-lived intrastate service. (Clay Jansson via Walt Redmond)

Msn 9143 following a two-year lease to Baja Air Lines, which used the 202 on scheduled flights between Tijuana and Puerto Vallarta with en route stops at some very short landing strips. It still retains the Baja livery and titles; however, the former eye-catching Mexican registration XA-SEX has been converted to the more modest N22AA. (Harry Sievers via Peter R Keating)

RAPSA used its 202s primarily in scheduled domestic service between Panama City and David. HP-427 was formerly N93051 of Northwest, Transocean, and Pioneer, and N173A of Allegheny. (Dan Hagedorn via Gary Kuhn)

In later years, RAPSA painted its 202s in a striking orange color scheme. All three of RAPSA's 202s—the last of the type to see scheduled passenger service—are believed to have been scrapped at Panama City around 1972. (via Elliot H Greenman)

End of the line. Possibly the last operational 202 anywhere, Aero Proveedora's HK-1484, photographed at Bogotá, Colombia, in November 1992, after more than a decade of inactivity, has definitely made its last flight. (Michael Magnusson)

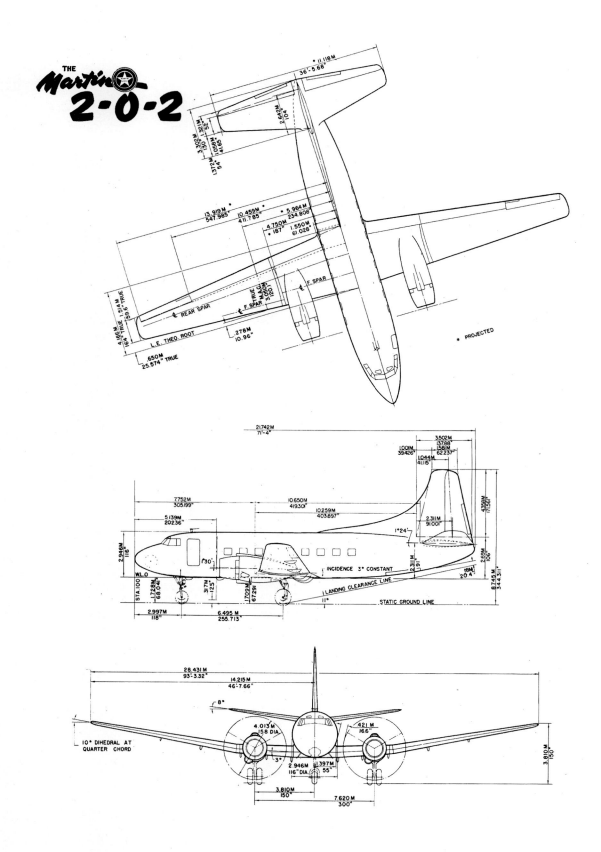

THE MARTIN 228

The Model 228 was offered late in 1945 as a 'junior' version of the Model 202 for use on relatively short, low-density routes. It differed from the Model 202 primarily in that two nine-cylinder, single-row Wright Cyclone engines would have been used. Those engines were developed from the World War II military R-1820 series engines used in such airplanes as the Boeing B-17 Flying Fortress bombers and Grumman FM-2 Wildcat fighters. The C9HD, the version selected for the Model 228, was rated at 1,425hp for takeoff and 1,275hp METO (maximum except takeoff: the term 'maximum continuous power' had not yet come into use).

In order to provide satisfactory performance with the less powerful engines, it would have been necessary to decrease the takeoff weight drastically to 28,500lb (12,930kg)—only slightly more than that of a DC-3. This would have been accomplished primarily by reducing the fuel capacity to 650USg (2,460l). The reduction in fuel capacity was compatible with design requirements because the airplanes were intended for use on short routes and the fuel consumption of the Cyclones was much less than that of the Double Wasp engines. Also consistent with the intended use, the cabin capacity would have been reduced to 26 passengers; and the aft cargo compartment deleted. The lighter weight of the Cyclone engines would have made another substantial contribution to weight savings.

Structurally, the 228 design was purported to be the same as that of the 202 except that the fuselage was shortened by 39in (1m) to accommodate one less row of passenger seats. Because the structure was designed for the weights of the Model 202, it would have been stronger and heavier than necessary for the lighter weights of the Model 228 in most areas. Therefore, it appears that the Model 228 would not have had a very attractive useful load without extensive structural redesign.

There is a big difference between increasing the weight of an airplane and efficiently reducing it. When maximum weights are increased, the structure has only to be strengthened in the areas that are deficient. Because much of the structure does not require strengthening, the increased structural weight is minimal. Insofar as empty weight is concerned, this results in an airplane that is more efficient than its forebear. On the other hand, it is very difficult to identify and remove unnecessary strength from the structure when maximum weights are reduced. The resulting airplane is, therefore, over-strength in many areas and the structure is heavier than necessary accordingly. This is why there is almost no example of successfully reducing the power and weight of an existing design. Nevertheless, Martin claimed a useful load of 8,371lb (3,797kg) for the Model 228.

Although less than that of a 202, the estimated cruising speed of 244mph (212kt/393km/h) was considered adequate for the short stages on which the Model 228 would have been operated.

The comparisons with the Model 202 were based, of course, on that model as it was envisioned in late 1945. The

Model 202 had undergone considerable evolution by the time it went into service two years later.

Owing to the dismal market conditions that prevailed in 1946, Martin did not proceed with construction of the Model 228. In fact, the manufacturer had its hands full making the Model 202 viable. Financing was difficult to obtain for any airline airplane at that time, and those intended for short routes were given the lowest priority of all. There was no point in wasting precious financing on airplanes for routes that could be served effectively with Douglas DC-3s.

This sketch of the Model 228 by Air Trails *staff artist S Calhoun Smith appeared in the July 1946 issue.*

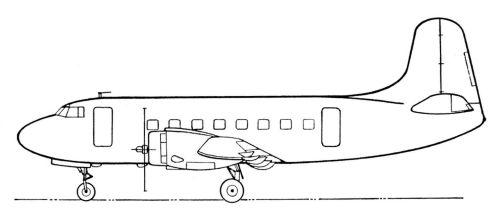

Side-view of the proposed Model 228. (Author)

THE MARTIN 303

CONTRARY TO MARTIN'S INITIAL BELIEF, the airlines showed a strong preference for short-to-medium range airplanes with cabin pressurization. Although the Model 202 was unpressurized, the fuselage was designed structurally with pressurization in mind. It was, therefore, possible to add pressurization system components and offer a pressurized companion known as the Model 303. United Air Lines was the primary sponsor of the model, eventually investing one million dollars of its own money in the development of the 303.

The 303 was expected to cruise at about "five miles a minute," or 14mph (12kt/22km/h) faster than the 202. Whether Martin could have gained that much additional cruise performance is questionable; however, the wing span was shortened about 4ft (1.2m) in an attempt to gain speed at the expense of takeoff and climb performance. It is somewhat surprising that United wanted Martin to sacrifice these for additional speed, considering that it encouraged Convair to do just the opposite in the later evolution of the 240 into the 340. There would also have been a small increase in empty weight because of the cabin pressurization.

To facilitate production and reduce the empty weight by 125lb (56kg), Martin elected to redesign the wing with a single-piece, tip-to-tip construction. The Model 303, at least the version for United, would have had nine rows of four seats each plus a semi-circular lounge seating four more passengers in the aft end of the fuselage. In lieu of ventral stairs, that configuration would have had a passenger entry door and integral stairs in the aft left side of the fuselage.

Northwest specified more cockpit headroom; therefore, the windshields of its airplanes would have been extended upward 3in (8cm) more than United's 303s and the 202s. The 'eyebrow' windows of the 202 were unnecessary in either case because the pilots were seated closer to the windshield.

Instead of interspersing 303s in the two lines set up for 202 production, Martin established a third production line for the 303s. There was, however, a common stockroom located between the 303 line and the two 202 lines. The first 303 was completed on July 1, 1947, making a first flight two days later, again with Pat Tibbs at the controls, accompanied by co-pilot W R Turner. The 57-minute flight was pronounced highly successful; however, that assessment is dubious considering the stability and controllability deficiencies the 303 shared with the early 202s.

Martin had a very impressive list of orders for the Model 303 at one time. United was, of course, the first customer with an order for 35 airplanes placed in January 1946, scheduled for delivery from July 1947. That order was later increased to 50, and Northwest contributed an order for 50 (35 firm plus 15 options). Braniff ordered 12 in addition to the 202s it had on order, and Pan American-Grace (PANA-

GRA) had seven on order at one time also.

As in the case of the 202s, Martin used unofficial customer designations to account for the differences in the 303s ordered by various airlines. The United, Northwest, Braniff, and PANAGRA configurations were designated 303U, 303N, 303B, and 303PG, respectively. Also, 303T was used during unsuccessful negotiations with Transcontinental & Western Air (TWA).

Like most of the 202 orders, the Model 303 sales quickly disappeared. Northwest dropped its 15 options early in May 1947. Within another week, Braniff was no longer a 303 customer. Then United canceled its order in October because of nine-month delivery delays and a desire to re-examine its equipment needs in light of 'changes in the general economic conditions'. That loss would prove to be doubly tragic for Martin. It not only represented the loss of a $16 million order from one of the major US airlines, but it also set in motion the sequence of events that led to the development of a formidable competitor—the Convair 340. United's down payment, which had reached $1,480,000, was returned upon cancellation of the order.

Martin had experienced some problems in developing a satisfactory pressurization system; and, because of the single-piece wing construction, it would have been extremely difficult to redesign the 303 to correct the stability deficiencies identified in the 202 test program. In view of those obstacles and the prevailing market conditions, Martin announced on December 16, 1947, that it had discontinued the Model 303. Because of somewhat overzealous Internal Revenue Service requirements for a tax write-off of Martin's reported $15 million loss, the prototype airplane and a second nearing completion fell victim to acetylene torches; and most, if not all, records of the Model 303 became fuel for a giant bonfire.

Model designations 305 and 306 were assigned to unpressurized and jet-powered versions, respectively, but those died with the 303 itself.

The first 303 was painted in United's newly adopted color scheme—ironically the same livery in which its large Convair 340 fleet later flew.

Two rare D Building production-line views of the first 303 (msn 9222, NX93162) taken on May 26, 1947, with United Air Lines paint applied (masking material and tape is still on the airframe). The second 303 can be seen in jigs. Although the first 303 accumulated 87 flight hours, no in-flight photos appear to have survived the wholesale destruction of 303 materiel and records in order for Martin to be eligible for tax carry-back credits after the cancellation of United's order for 50 aircraft. (Martin P30303 & P30306 via Stan Piet/Glenn L Martin Museum)

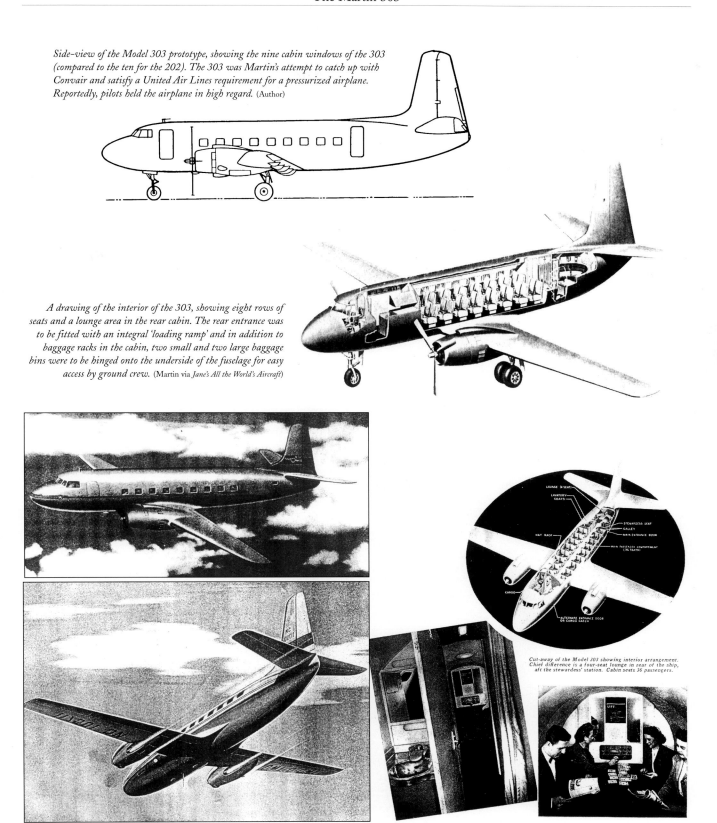

Side-view of the Model 303 prototype, showing the nine cabin windows of the 303 (compared to the ten for the 202). The 303 was Martin's attempt to catch up with Convair and satisfy a United Air Lines requirement for a pressurized airplane. Reportedly, pilots held the airplane in high regard. (Author)

A drawing of the interior of the 303, showing eight rows of seats and a lounge area in the rear cabin. The rear entrance was to be fitted with an integral 'loading ramp' and in addition to baggage racks in the cabin, two small and two large baggage bins were to be hinged onto the underside of the fuselage for easy access by ground crew. (Martin via Jane's All the World's Aircraft)

Cut-away of the Model 303 showing interior arrangement. Chief difference is a four-seat lounge in rear of the ship, aft the stewardess' station. Cabin seats 36 passengers.

Impressions of the 'Three-O-Three'. The side view shows a small window in the rear fuselage for a lounge area. The cutaway drawing shows a 36-seat (at a 39in/0.99m pitch) main cabin, with a four-seat lounge aft of the stewardess station. On the 303, the lavatory was moved to the right side of the fuselage. The doorway leads to a lounge.

The in-flight view accents the 'jet thrust augmentation' engine exhaust system proposed for the 303 which was to "add considerably to speed of the planes," according to the contemporary caption. (The Martin Star)

THE MARTIN 304

D<small>URING THE INITIAL DESIGN PHASE OF THE</small> M<small>ODEL</small> 202, turbine engines promised major breakthroughs

in performance and passenger comfort. Martin, being mindful of those possibilities, designed the basic air-

frame so that it could be adapted to this radical new form of power.

Two General Electric TG-100 turbopropeller engines were chosen for the Model 304, as the turbine-powered version was known. These were the first US turboprop engines and among the first in the world. They were axial-flow engines expected to produce approximately the same power as the Pratt & Whitney Double Wasp engines. Like the 303, the 304 would have had cabin pressurization. It was expected to have a maximum takeoff weight of 39,000lb (17,690kg) and the rather optimistic cruising speed of 365mph (317kt/587km/h). Maximum speed was estimated at 385mph (334kt/619km/h). The 304 was designed to weigh 4,000lb (1,810kg) more than the 303, and carry a maximum cargo payload of 11,500lb (5,215kg); landing weight was 34,000lb (14,420kg).

An all-cargo example was to have been delivered to United Air Lines in 1947 for service testing; however, it was never built. After a total of 66 flights and approximately 50 flight hours in the Convair XP-81 and Ryan XF2R-1 Fireball fighters, development of the TG-100 for military use was discontinued. Without military funding, it was unfeasible to continue developing the engine for civilian use. Even if the engine program had continued, Martin would probably have been too preoccupied with the 202 and 303 to have pursued the Model 304 actively at the same time. Fortunately, Martin's investment had only reached about $10,000 by the time the 304 was canceled.

An artist's impression of the turbine-powered 304, which was identical to the 303 except for new engine nacelles to accommodate the TG-100 engines. At around the same time that United placed its initial order for the 303, the airline agreed to test the 304 in cargo-carrying operations, starting in 1947. In the event, the TG-100 would not have developed enough power to operate the 304 at high-altitude stations on United's network, such as Cheyenne and Denver, and in high temperatures. (Martin via *Skyways*)

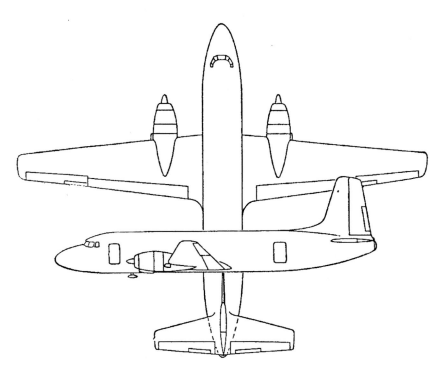

A three-view sketch of the turbine-powered 304.

THE MARTIN 202A

Martin completed and delivered the last of 31 Model 202s in June 1948. Because of the prevailing market conditions, no buyers could be found for the 12 additional partially completed airplanes and they were placed in storage.

After a year, economic conditions began to improve, and Martin found that there was a market for a pressurized airplane of slightly greater passenger capacity. Accordingly, development of what became the Model 404 was started. Transcontinental & Western Air (TWA—later Trans World Airlines) was interested in the Model 404; however, it needed very early deliveries so its aging four-engine Boeing 307 Stratoliners could be retired. Howard Hughes started the selection process on behalf of TWA by holding a fly-off competition late in 1949 between Martin and Convair at his Culver City, California, airport.

Convair had an apparent advantage in that it had 15 completed 240s on hand and could offer almost instant delivery. Martin successfully countered by offering to complete the 12 unsold 202s immediately and lease them to TWA pending delivery of a fleet of 404s. Some improvements were incorporated, and they were designated as Model 202As to distinguish them from the airplanes completed earlier. The second 202 (msn 9123) was partially converted to the 202A configuration and used for the brief 202A type certification program.

The Model 202A was identical to the Model 202 in appearance; however, there were a number of internal differences. The structure of the wings and fuselage was strengthened to permit maximum weights of 43,000lb (19,500kg) and 41,000lb (18,600kg) for takeoff and landing, respectively. (The increased maximum weights were,

however, partially offset by an increase in empty weight to about 27,000lb (12,245kg).) These changes, which were developed in 1948 for the advanced cargo version of the 202, facilitated an increase in fuel capacity to 1,350USg (5,100l). Pratt & Whitney Double Wasp CB16 engines, which were to be used later on TWA's 404s, provided better altitude performance than the CA15 or CA18 engines used in the 202s. Although Hamilton Standard 23260/2H17 series propellers were also eligible for use on 202As, 43E60/6895A propellers were used exclusively.

Type Certificate No 795 was amended on July 10, 1950, to include the 202A; and TWA introduced the new model in service on September 1, replacing Boeing 307s on one route and DC-3s on two others. Martin service was initiated with little fanfare because TWA did not want the public to associate them with the Northwest 202 accidents. The big public relations effort would come later when the definitive 404s were ready.

Like its later 404s, TWA flew the 202As with the promotional name 'Martin Skyliners'. As originally delivered, the 202As had TWA's red trim on natural aluminum finish. Shortly afterward, they received the brilliant white fuselage background that became a feature of the TWA fleet.

As noted earlier, nine of the 202As were to have been sold to Pioneer Air Lines upon return from lease; however, TWA chose to exercise a purchase option in 1952 and retain all 12 in its fleet along with its 404s. One airplane (N93211) was lost in a mid-air collision with a DC-3 on January 12, 1955, at Covington, Kentucky. All 13 persons aboard the 202A were killed; however, the accident was in no way the fault of the design. There were other minor, non-injury accidents, including two gear-up landings; but TWA's overall satisfactory service experience with 202As was in marked contrast to that of Northwest with 202s.

After about eight or nine years with TWA, a few of the 202As were leased briefly to Pacific Air Lines in 1958 pending delivery of 404s. Three were also used by Lone Star Airlines in 1960 for a Dallas–Houston shuttle that proved to be even more brief. The majority of the 202As complet-ed their scheduled passenger service by joining the 202s in the fleet of Allegheny Airlines. Most of the 202As were scrapped after Allegheny retired them in 1966; however, a few were used occasionally by other operators. Southeast was the last airline to use the 202A in the US (early in the 1970s). Elsewhere, Comercialisadora Aérea Mixta Bolivia Ltda (CAMBA) operated one (msn 14075, registered CP-1441) in Bolivia until about 1984. Propeller spinners, befitting an executive airplane, belied its use in hauling meat.

Of the dozen 202As, only the former Allegheny airplane displayed at the Aviation Hall of Fame and Museum at Teterboro, New Jersey (N93204, msn 14074), is known to exist today.

The first 202A, as originally delivered on July 14, 1950, with the TWA red trim on natural aluminum. TWA had an option to buy—later exercised—the leased aircraft. The price of a new 202A was quoted as $408,000, compared to the 202's price of $204,000 (in 1946) and $247,000 in 1947.
(TWA)

TWA's promotion of its 'Martin Skyliner' fleet was rather modest because the 202As were intended only for interim use pending delivery of its 404s. (via John Wegg)

Skyliner Albuquerque (N93208) at Chicago-Midway in August 1953, after receiving the white fuselage background introduced with TWA's 404s. Baggage and mail are being loaded into the forward fuselage compartment and the cargo doors under the aft fuselage are open. (Howard M Svendsen)

A few TWA 202As, including N93205, were leased to Pacific Air Lines in 1958 pending delivery of 404s. Pacific simply replaced 'Trans World Airlines' with its own name in blue letters on this and its other leased 202As. (Author)

Lone Star Airlines leased three 202As (N93204 illustrated) from California Airmotive Corp for a short-lived shuttle service between Dallas and Houston. (Eric W Wagner collection)

'Martin Executive' N93201 of Allegheny Airlines. Allegheny planned to re-register its 202As N178A through N181A, but chose instead to retain the original registration numbers and simply use 178 through 181 as fleet numbers. (Robert O'Dell via Peter M Bowers)

Allegheny's N93205 at Baltimore in August 1965, with the addition of weather radar and the Convair 440-era paint.
(Dave Lucabaugh via Walt Redmond)

Another view of N93205, this time in service with Southeast Airlines at Miami in May 1970. (John P Stewart)

Still showing portions of its previous Allegheny Airlines livery, N93205 was used by rock musicians for concert tours after its days of scheduled service. With joint 'Herman's Hermits' and 'The Animals' titles, Fleet Number 184 also carries crew names ('Capt L W Skelly and 1st Off D R Creato') by the cockpit. (MAP)

N93204 at Wildwood, New Jersey, where it would eventually be scrapped. (via John Wegg)

CAMBA's CP-1441 was never operated by Piedmont; nevertheless it is seen at La Paz, Bolivia, on January 10, 1981, with a Piedmont-like red paint design and propeller spinners, probably from a Douglas DC-6.
(Rolf Larsson)

Cover of the first sales brochure issued by the Glenn L Martin Co for the Martin 202 in 1947. (courtesy Jack L King)

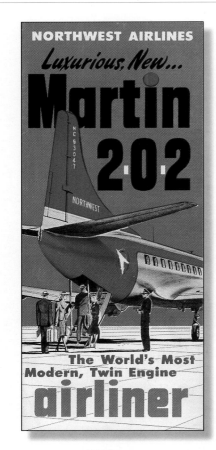

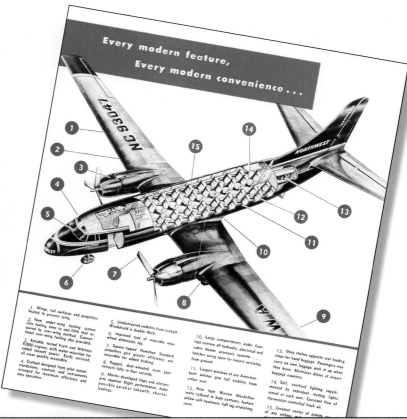

Cover and contents of a promotional brochure for the Martin 202, issued by the General Traffic Department of Northwest Orient Airlines.
(John Wegg collection)

Rare color views of Northwest Airlines N93051 and NC93037, in the livery adopted for the airline's post–World War II fleet. (courtesy Jim Borden)

The crew members standing in front of NC93039 (Fleet Number 539) are Casimer Falenczykowski (left) and Bill McGinn. (via Donald Falenczykowski)

Some of Northwest's 202s were first painted in a black, red, and silver scheme which was standard for the NWA fleet in the immediate postwar years, and NC93042 can be identified in this view of the ramp at Minneapolis–St Paul Airport (now the St Paul Airport). (courtesy Jim Borden)

Before adopting its trademark red fin, Northwest tried several experimental color schemes on the 202, including this yellow trim on the lower forward fuselage of NC93044 (msn 9165), also illustrated in black & white on page 27. Casimer Falenczykowski (left) and Tom North flank Julie North in front of Fleet Number 544. (via Donald Falenczykowski)

In marked contrast to the numerous crashes that Northwest Airlines suffered with its 202s, those of LAN-Chile— including Fleet No 263 (CC-CLMC/msn 9127) seen here at Santiago—gave many years of trouble-free service.
(Peter R Keating via MAP)

Pacemaster William B. Travis (N93053/msn 9143) at Cannon AFB, Clovis, New Mexico, in 1952, during Pioneer's bold attempt to take Local Service airlines out of the DC-3 era. (David Lusk via Brian Lusk)

Southwest Airways, later renamed Pacific Air Lines, was the first Local Service operator to successfully supplement, then replace, aging Douglas DC-3s with modern postwar airliners. A Southwest 202 (N93060/msn 9149), is seen parked proudly in company with TWA Constellations and a United DC-7 at Los Angeles. (Mel Lawrence)

City of Oakland (N93042/msn 9163), at a crisp and clear Burbank, California, on December 4, 1953, in the attractive paint scheme of California Central Airlines. (Clay Jansson via Walt Redmond)

N93059 (msn 9148) at Burbank, California, March 1965—probably following the demise of planned intrastate service by California Time Airlines to Palm Springs and San Jose.
(Clay Jansson via Walt Redmond)

Rutas Aéreas Panamenas SA (RAPSA) was probably the last operator to use 202s in scheduled passenger service. HP-398 (msn 9133) sports a colorful scheme at Panama City in April 1972. (Jean-François Belet via Jean-Marie Magendie)

Central American Airways Flying Service specialized in charters to sports teams and rock bands. Judging by the 'Chicago' logo seen on the aft fuselage of N71R (msn 9167) in June 1970 at Columbus, Ohio, it was probably chartered then to the band of that name. (Harry Sievers)

A number of Martins were used to fly prospective purchasers to view land developments. In a variation on that theme, International Crystal Manufacturing Co of Oklahoma City used N93059 (msn 9148) as a showcase to fly its products to prospective purchasers. (Clay Jansson via Walt Redmond)

Seen at Denver on July 10, 1965, N93053 (msn 9143) was used for charter flights by Salt Lake City-based Edde Airlines. (Ronald C Hill)

The timeless elegance of fleecy clouds and a highly polished airliner! This brand-new 202A will soon become the first of 52 Martin airliners flying the routes of TWA, replacing DC-3s.

As with most of the TWA Martin fleet, Fleet No 210 was delivered to TWA at the airline's maintenance base at New Castle, Delaware. After the paperwork had been signed, the airplane made a brief stop at Martin Airport, Baltimore, before heading west to Kansas City.

(TWA via Jon Proctor)

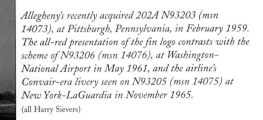

Allegheny's recently acquired 202A N93203 (msn 14073), at Pittsburgh, Pennsylvania, in February 1959. The all-red presentation of the fin logo contrasts with the scheme of N93206 (msn 14076), at Washington-National Airport in May 1961, and the airline's Convair-era livery seen on N93205 (msn 14075) at New York-LaGuardia in November 1965.

(all Harry Sievers)

Lone Star Airlines leased three 44-seat 202As (N93207/msn 14077 illustrated), which it referred to as 'Customliners', from California Airmotive in 1960 for Texas intrastate service. All flights were 'manned by Captain, First Officer, and Texas-Belle Stewardess in attendance'. (Elliot H Greenman)

Two of the five 202As acquired by Modern Air Transport for charter service, at Miami, Florida, in May 1968. One distinguishing feature of 202s, as seen on N93212 (msn 14082) in the foreground, is the lack of aerodynamic rudder balance. A 404 would have a cutout at the top of the fin to accommodate the aerodynamically balanced rudder.

N93205, msn 14075, in Modern Air Transport's later livery, also at Miami, Florida, in May 1968. (both Bo-Göran Lundkvist via Ted Gibson)

Florida intrastate operator Southeast Airlines acquired four 202As from Modern Air Transport, including N93205 (msn 14075) seen at Miami International Airport on December 12, 1971. (Harry Sievers)

THE MARTIN 404

MARTIN, TO ITS DISMAY, SAW THE VERY IMPRESSIVE LIST OF 202 AND 303 CUSTOMERS dwindle to three

airlines buying a total of 31 Model 202s. As this was primarily because of economic conditions rather than

dissatisfaction, most remained potential customers. None had rushed to San Diego to fill the remaining

voids in their fleets with Convair 240s. United Air Lines, in particular, evaluated the 240s and concluded

that they would be uneconomical when operated in the Rocky Mountain area. Although well-suited for

operations from low elevation airports, the 240s lacked sufficient wing area to operate from higher elevation

airports without severe restrictions in payload.

TWA attempted earlier to purchase a fleet of 303s; however, that deal was never completed because of financial and management problems. Like United, TWA had concluded that the 240 lacked sufficient wing area for operation on its western US route system. Although the TWA routes passed further south where the terrain was not as high, they did include airports that suffered from very hot ambient temperatures as well as moderately high elevations. Later, TWA and Eastern Air Lines negotiated jointly with Convair for an improved variant of the 240 with more wing area; however, those talks ended abruptly when Convair adopted a 'take it' (the standard 240) or 'leave it' attitude. Convair believed that Martin had been eliminated from the market by the 202 problems and there would be no point in spending money to develop a new model when, with no viable alternatives, the airlines would have to settle for 240s in their existing form.

By mid-1949, it appeared that improving economic conditions would revive the market for airplanes of this class. Contrary to Convair's expectations, Martin responded by offering the Model 404, a development of the 202 with a stretched, pressurized fuselage. The 'Four-O-Four', as Martin referred to the new model, also incorporated a number of subtle, but nevertheless important, detail improvements. Its efforts were rewarded with orders for 65 airplanes from TWA and Eastern Air Lines. United, Braniff, Chicago & Southern; Colonial, National, and Delta were also considered likely prospects.

The cabin pressurization of the Model 303 was not fully developed when that model was discontinued late in 1947. With the advent of the Model 404, efforts to develop a satisfactory system were renewed. The resulting system incorporated an AiResearch cabin compressor driven by the right-hand engine. A variable-ratio drive was used to compensate for varying engine speeds and to account for the changing demands of pressurization. This system enabled the Model 404 to operate above much of the turbulence and provide greater passenger comfort. At an actual altitude of 16,000ft (4,900m), for example, the equivalent cabin-altitude was less than 8,000ft (2,450m). In addition to cabin pressurization, the system was also designed to provide cabin air conditioning and de-humidification during ground operation.

The fuselage was designed for a maximum pressure differential of 3.25psi (0.23kg/cm^2). In order to provide a better fatigue life, the fuselage skin gauge was increased somewhat over that of the 202. The windows of the 202 also had to be replaced with windows designed to withstand pressur-

The second 202 (msn 9123) was modified for brief use as the 202A prototype, then further modified to serve as the aerodynamic prototype of the Model 404 and repainted with a gold vertical stabilizer and rudder and a wide gold band along the fuselage. The new registration N40400 and a 39in (0.99m) stretched fuselage notwithstanding, it retained its original Model 202 identity in official records. (Martin via Author)

ization loads. The structural integrity of the 404 under such loads was demonstrated by testing a fuselage completely submerged in the Middle River near the Martin plant.

Space for an additional row of seats was gained by adding 13in (0.33m) and 26in (0.66m) sections in the fuselage fore and aft of the wing, respectively. The standard cabin arrangement consisted of ten rows of four seats; however, additional seating could be provided in a high-density configuration. Like that of the 36-passenger 202, the standard arrangement included a lavatory in the aft right side of the cabin and carry-on luggage racks on the opposite side. The galley was located forward of the cabin on the left side in the TWA airplanes and on the right side in the Eastern airplanes. As originally envisioned in the ATA Specification ATA-A1, the TWA airplanes were designed to be flown in a combination cargo-passenger configuration with the first three rows of seats removed. Up to 2,600lb (1,180kg) of additional cargo could be carried in this 'combi' mode.

The integral ventral passenger-loading stairs of the Model 202 had proven quite popular, and they were retained on the Model 404. Because of their success in the 202s, it was recognized that the door in the left forward end of the cabin would not be needed for passenger entry. Because it would be used only as a service door, it was reduced in height in the 404. It was also simplified by replacing the troublesome translating opening-mechanism with hinges.

Cockpit visibility was substantially improved by extending the windshield and side windows 3in (8cm) in height. The enlarged windshield eliminated the need for the small triangular 'eyebrow' windows used in the Model 202. This was probably the same as the windshield configuration developed earlier for Northwest's 303s.

Higher capacity combustion heaters and redesigned wing heating ducts were incorporated to improve the thermal anti-ice system.

Some consideration was given to the use of Wright Cyclone-18 engines. This was probably in deference to pilot resistance to auto-feather systems, although commonality with the engines used in the Lockheed Constellation fleets of both TWA and Eastern would have provided some advantages as well. The higher-powered Cyclone-18 engines would have enabled the same takeoff weights without auto-feather; however, they were considerably heavier and would have reduced the useful load of the 404s. Pratt & Whitney engines were, therefore, retained. Double Wasp CB3 and CB16 engines were used in the 404s delivered to Eastern and TWA, respectively. Like the earlier CA series engines used on the Model 202, the CB engines were rated at 2,400hp with anti-detonant injection (ADI) for takeoff and 1,800hp for maximum continuous operation. The CB series did, however, provide better altitude performance. Like the CA3 engines, the CB3 engines had only single-speed superchargers and were, therefore, intended for use on routes over low elevations. The maximum certificated altitude was 25,000ft (7,600m), however, operations were effectively limited by practical considerations to about 14,000ft (4,300m) when CB3 engines were installed, or 19,000ft (5,800m) with CB16s.

The CB3 and CB16 engines used 100/130 grade aviation gasoline. By simply using 108/135 grade fuel (or 115/145 after 108/135 was phased out), they became CB4 and CB17 engines, respectively, and were eligible for increased ratings of 2,500hp for takeoff with ADI and 1,900hp for maximum continuous operation. Both the Douglas DC-6s and the competitive Convair 340s were approved for alternate operation at the higher CB4 or CB17 power. Although Martin once proposed a high-density 48-52 passenger variant with CB17 engines, neither the manufacturer nor any of the operators ever conducted the necessary flight tests for operation of 404s at the higher powers.

Hamilton Standard 43E60/6895A propellers were used exclusively on the Model 404.

To provide aerodynamic balance, the rudder was modified slightly at the upper end. This change was purportedly made to accommodate the possible installation of higher-powered turbine engines, but it also reduced the minimum control speed to about 100mph (87kt/160km/h) with one engine inoperative. The rudder pedal force was considerably less than the maximum allowed by the Civil Aeronautics Administration (CAA) under those conditions. The elevator was also modified slightly to reduce control forces.

The mechanical flap-stabilizer interconnect system of the 202 sometimes failed when there was a sudden change in the direction of flap travel—during a missed approach, for example. As that could leave the flight crew with choosing to land with either an incorrect flap setting or an airplane that was severely out of trim, the mechanical system was replaced with an electrically actuated system in the 404.

Maximum weights of the Model 404 were considerably greater than those of the 202s. Drop tests, of course, had to be conducted to show that the landing gear was satisfactory for operation at the new weights. The takeoff weight was initially limited to 43,650lb (19,800kg) by the performance requirements for en route climb with one engine inoperative. Shortly after initial certification of the 404, the CAA adopted more realistic standards for en route climb performance, enabling Martin to obtain CAA approval for a maximum takeoff weight of 44,900lb (20,370kg). It is understood, however, that TWA pilots refused to fly the 404s at takeoff weights greater than the original 43,650lb (19,800kg). As with the Model 202, weight reductions were required if ADI were not used.

Initially, the landing weight was limited to 42,000lb (19,050kg) or 43,000lb (19,500kg), depending on which of two types of Menasco main landing gear shock-strut assem-

blies was used. Reportedly, those limited to the lower weight for landing were the TWA 404s. Both types of shock-strut assemblies were high-efficiency units designed in answer to complaints that the landing gear of the 202 was too stiff. Within a few months after the first 404s went into service, the maximum landing weight was set at 43,000lb (19,500kg) for all 404s regardless of which shock-strut assembly was installed.

TWA airplanes typically weighed about 29,100lb (13,200kg) empty. Those for Eastern generally weighed about 700lb (320kg) more despite the use of lighter CB3 engines.

The second 202 (msn 9123) had been converted previously for use as the Model 202A prototype. The fuselage was then stretched so that it could serve as the aerodynamic prototype of the Model 404. The first flight in that configuration took place on October 21, 1950, at Baltimore, in the hands of Pat Tibbs and co-pilot Jack King. Because it did not incorporate cabin pressurization, some of the development and certification testing had to be held in abeyance until the first flight of a true 404 on July 27 the following year. The final testing was completed, and Type Certificate No 1A7 was issued for the Model 404 on October 5, 1951. (By that time, the authority to issue type certificates had been delegated to the regional offices.)

Despite the similarity of the two models in appearance, Martin claimed that 80% of the tooling used to produce 404s differed from that used for 202s.

Martin sometimes referred to the new model as the 'Four-O-Four' or, as stamped on at least some of the airplane data plates, '4-0-4'; however, the model designation generally shown in official records is '404'. Although occasionally identified as the '4-0-4P', serial number 9123 retained its Model 202 identity in official records and was approved in its stretched form under Type Certificate No 795 rather than 1A7.

A COMPETITOR EMERGES

The future of the 404 looked very bright at first as it offered some advantages over its closest rival, the Convair 240. As noted earlier, Convair had rebuffed TWA and Eastern in their earlier attempts to acquire an improved variant of the Model 240. Shocked into reality by the market entry of the 404, Convair responded by offering an improved version tentatively designated the Model 240A. The sequence of the changes that led from the 240 to the 240A is not cer-

The basic Convair–Liner, the Model 240, was developed into the 340, with a stretched fuselage and greater wing area, to compete with the Martin 404. A United Air Lines 'Mainliner' Convair 340-31 (N73201), carries the same livery as that on the first Martin 303. (United Air Lines 4390-1)

The second step in the evolution was to increase the wing area. This improved takeoff and climb performance considerably, enabling operations from high-elevation airports without severe reductions in payload. Eventually, the new variant became known as the Model 340. Ironically, it was very similar to the improved 240 that Convair refused to develop earlier for TWA and Eastern. Comparable to the 404 in performance and superior in passenger capacity, it proved to be a worthy adversary.

Although both TWA and Eastern placed follow-on orders, Martin's sole additional customer was the US Coast Guard. Of the prospects noted earlier, only Colonial failed to order Convair 340s. (Chicago & Southern was acquired by Delta before delivery of its 340s, so that order was integrated with Delta's.)

Linee Aeree Italiane (LAI), 40% of which was then owned by TWA, requested the Italian government to finance a fleet of Martin 404s in 1950. The financial assis-

tain as Convair was offering several different configurations; however, the changes eventually focused on a longer fuselage and greater wing area. The fuselage of the 240 was stretched 54in (1.37m) to provide space for an additional row of seats and regain the advantage in passenger capacity that the 240 enjoyed over the 202.

(As in the case of the 202 versus the 240, a comparison of the cabin lengths generally quoted for the two new models was misleading. The length of 36ft 7in (11.15m) quoted for the new Convair model included only the passenger seating area, while 37ft 11in (11.56m) included both the cabin seating area and the aft service area of the 404. The Convair model also included an externally accessed cargo or baggage compartment aft of the cabin, making the effective length of the cabin about 9ft (2.75m) greater than that of the 404.)

A comparison in Convair-Liner (American Airlines 240 N94258) and Martinliner (Eastern 404 N474A) final approach attitudes. (Mel Lawrence via Clinton H Groves/Airliners America/ATP)

tance was not granted, and reports a year later that TWA would assist in financing the 404s proved to be untrue. Eventually, LAI had to settle for some used Convair 240s. The managing director of Air-India International also expressed an interest early in 1952 in acquiring a fleet of Martin 404s, Convair 340s, or Vickers Viscounts. Martin and the other manufacturers mentioned were equally unsuccessful in that respect.

The first 404 for Eastern (N440A) being towed out by a 'mule' in August 1951 from the still-camouflaged Martin final assembly building. The in-flight view shows an unusual shadow-style application of the word 'Eastern' and the registration on the upper wing surfaces, and the positioning of the registration on the fuselage underneath the horizontal stabilizer. In service, Eastern 404s carried their registrations on the fin.
(Martin via David Ostrowski & via John Wegg)

The Airlift 404

Martin attempted to sell a version described as the 'Military Airlift 404' for use as a combination trainer, staff transport, and utility cargo airplane. It would have differed from the civilian 404s primarily in that the integral ventral stairs would have been replaced by large outward-opening clamshell doors and a built-in loading ramp. Structural changes would have permitted an increase in takeoff weight to 50,000lb (22,680kg). Wingtip fuel tanks would have been provided, and optional Allison T-38 turbopropeller engines were offered. Martin promoted the fact that a 404 could carry almost as much cargo or personnel as a Douglas C-54 at much less cost. Nevertheless, no orders resulted.

Martin may have been hampered in its competition with Convair by the financial crisis it experienced late in 1951. Despite having a backlog of orders totaling almost $400 million, Martin had an acute shortage of ready working capital.

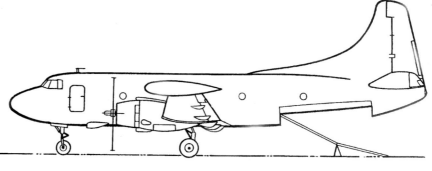

Sketch and side-view of the proposed military 'Airlift' 404, offered to the US Air Force and Navy in 1950 with either Pratt & Whitney R-2800-CB14 engines or Allison T-38 turboprops. Most vehicles would have experienced difficulty moving from the steep ramp onto the cabin floor. (Author)

THE 404 ENTERS SERVICE

Dedicated 404 flights were inaugurated by both TWA and Eastern on January 15, 1952. TWA, however, operated the first commercial 404 service on November 10, 1951, and had nine airplanes in service by the official inauguration date. Similarly, Eastern used its 404s from December 20, 1951, as extra sections to back up Constellation flights.

TWA made no distinction between the 404s and 202As in published schedules, referring to both models as 'Martin Skyliners'. Its airplanes were quite striking in appearance with their bright red trim on a brilliant white fuselage background. In contrast to the white fuselages of TWA's 404s, Eastern's airplanes were placed in service with gleaming natural aluminum finish and the class name 'Silver Falcon'.

Production of the Model 404 was concluded early in 1953 with a program loss of $17.5 million and a total of 103 airplanes— 41 for TWA, 60 for Eastern and two for the US Coast Guard. In addition, one non-flying airframe was used for structural tests. Actually one airplane of the TWA order (N40437, msn 14172) went directly to the Hughes Tool Company. (Howard Hughes, of course, owned TWA as well as Hughes Tool Co.) Its intended use by Hughes was characterized as 'special experimental work'; however, it was placed in storage for about two-and-a-half years pending resale to The National Supply Co as a luxurious executive airplane.

The unit price of $647,140 for each of the US Coast Guard airplanes was greater than that of the TWA and Eastern airplanes, a reflection of Martin's sharply increasing production costs. As Martin's backlog and employment were both at a low level at the outbreak of the Korean War, the rapid expansion that followed adversely affected the 404 program. Much of its already small force of experienced production workers had to be transferred to defense production, forcing Martin to build the 404s with less experienced help. The loss of productivity contributed significantly to the $17.5 million program loss.

Fortunately, the 404s were relatively free from design-related fatal accidents. But like the 202s and 202As, they were prone to minor accidents involving the landing gear. The first accident involving a 404 occurred a little more than a year after the type was placed in service. A TWA captain

Skyliner Harrisburg *being run-up for the photographer's benefit at St Louis in 1957. Martin demonstrated a 202, and later the prototype 404, to Howard Hughes at Culver City over a period of about six weeks in competition with Convair. Hughes became Martin's best commercial customer, buying a dozen 202As and 41 Model 404s (although only 52 airplanes entered service with TWA).* (Peter M Bowers)

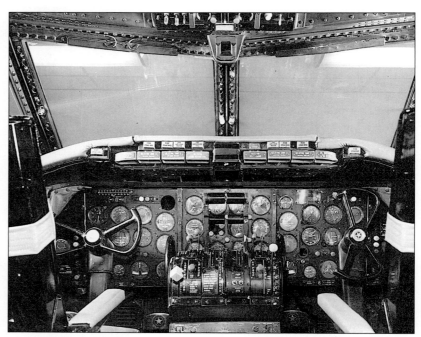

The Martin Star logo in the center of the control wheels and the lack of 'eyebrow' windows confirms that this is the cockpit of a 404—TWA's N40414. TWA pilots appreciated the 404's quiet, comfortable cockpit, and cited the 404's heating system as superior to that of the Convair 340/440. (courtesy Edward G Betts)

inadvertently raised the landing gear of N40439 during roll-out at Pittsburgh, Pennsylvania, on November 10, 1952. There were no injuries other than that suffered by the captain's pride. Eastern experienced the next non-injury accident on April 17, 1953, when the left landing gear of one of its 404s retracted following a landing at Greensboro, North

Aft-facing and forward-facing views in TWA's N40414. Compare its comfortable spacious seats with those in the typical 40-passenger commuter airliners of today! The first three seat-rows were occasionally removed from TWA airplanes for night flights in a 'combi' passenger–cargo mode. TWA flew its Martinliners with one hostess and it was common practice for the co-pilot to assist in the cabin on short legs with a full load of passengers. (courtesy Edward G Betts)

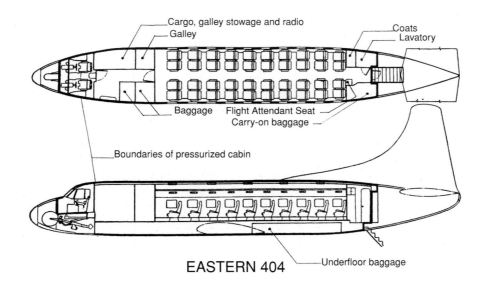

EASTERN 404

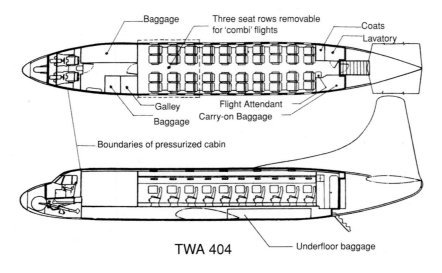

TWA 404

The 40-passenger Eastern and TWA cabin interiors. (Author)

After serving as the aerodynamic prototype of the Model 404, the stretched 202 (msn 9123/N40400) was retained by Martin for company travel. Known as the 'Two-by-Four' within the company, it carried the body of Glenn L Martin from Baltimore to Orange County in December 1955. It was displayed in a livery resembling that of TWA, but with black trim, at Las Vegas on April 14, 1959. The airplane in the background is a true 404, which was soon to be delivered to Houston Lumber Co as N333G. (Larry Smalley via Walt Redmond)

Carolina. TWA and Eastern experienced at least ten more accidents involving the landing gear. Some were caused by hard landings or a gear malfunction; many others were simply brought about by the inadvertent retraction of the gear during the landing roll. None resulted in any injuries—owing in large measure, no doubt, to the fact that all fuel was carried in the outer-wing panel fuel-cells.

Naturally, there were other incidents, such as in October 1960, when a TWA 404 collided with a flock of wild geese some 50 miles (80km) north of Pittsburgh. The collision "dug a two-foot hole in the nose and ripped the port wing and fuselage," according to Capt Samuel H Mariani, who turned the airplane back for a landing at Pittsburgh.

The first fatal accident involving a 404 was caused by a deviation from the intended flight path. TWA's N40416 was destroyed and all 16 aboard were killed when it was flown into Sandia Mountain, near Albuquerque, New Mexico, on February 19, 1955, on a flight from Albuquerque to Santa Fe. The reasons for the deviation could not be determined.

Eastern's N445A crashed on February 17, 1956, after stalling out of a turn on an approach for landing at Owensboro, Kentucky. Miraculously, only one person was seriously injured in that crash even though the fuselage came to rest in an inverted position. Then on April 1, TWA lost N40403 at Pittsburgh, Pennsylvania, following an engine failure just after takeoff. The result was 22 fatalities and seven persons with serious injuries. No injuries occurred, but

TWA's N40404 was damaged beyond repair on November 15, 1956, following an attempted single-engine go-around at Las Vegas, Nevada. Eastern's N453A crashed on March 10, 1957, at Louisville, Kentucky, in a landing that was so hard that the left wing failed inboard of the nacelle. Again, there was only one injury even though the fuselage of that airplane, like that of N445A, came to rest in an inverted position. Eastern's N496A was also damaged beyond repair after striking a pile of gravel on approach to Melbourne, Florida, on March 17, 1958, fortunately without casualties. None of these accidents could be attributed to any fault of the 404 design.

COAST GUARD 404S

The two US Coast Guard airplanes were ostensibly ordered for logistics and general transport under the military designation RM-1G; however, they were actually delivered in 1952 as RM-1Z airplanes with accommodation for 22 passengers in the main cabin and six in a forward lounge area. In 1962, when Secretary of Defense McNamara ordered the services to adopt a common model designation system, they were redesignated VC-3As. Both were transferred to Naval Air Reserve Training Unit VR-52 in 1969 (as C-3As), then to the Military Aircraft Storage and Disposition Center (MASDC) at Davis-Monthan Air Force Base, Arizona, about a year later.

One of two VC-3As (1283) at Baltimore on April 27, 1969, in the attractive white and red-orange livery adopted by the US Coast Guard for all of its airplanes, helicopters, and ships. (Dave Lucabaugh via John P Stewart)

Following service with the US Coast Guard, in 1969 the two VC-3As were transferred to Naval Air Reserve Training Unit VR-52 and assigned new Navy military serial numbers. USCG 1282 became USN 158202, as shown here at NAF Andrews, Maryland, on March 28, 1970.
(Steve Miller via David Ostrowski)

THE SECOND-HAND MARKET

Following their eventual retirement by TWA and Eastern, the 404s were eagerly sought by Local Service airlines as DC-3 replacements. Like the Convair 240s, they had less resale value than Convair 340s and 440s because there were no apparent prospects for later turbopropeller conversion. (Convair had not yet embarked on its installation of Rolls-Royce Darts in 240s.) Their lower cost made the Martin 404s quite desirable for airlines that were short of financing, or were only looking for interim equipment. The resale value of TWA's 404s was slightly greater than that of Eastern's airplanes because the former had CB16 engines with two-speed superchargers. Also, the Eastern airplanes typically had about half again as many hours of time in service. California Airmotive Corporation served as the sales agent for many, if not all, of TWA's 404s; and Charlotte Aircraft Corporation served in a similar capacity for those of Eastern. Both companies also purchased some of the 404s for later resale.

One of the most significant contributions to airline safety and passenger comfort was the development of airborne weather-mapping radar in the mid-1950s. The installation of such equipment enabled flight crews to avoid hail and severe thunderstorm activity. Some of the airlines, notably United, pioneered the installation of radar in their entire fleets on a voluntary basis. Others, such as TWA and Eastern, chose to install it voluntarily only on their long-range airplanes. After its merits were thoroughly proven, the

FAA adopted Special Civil Air Regulation SR-436 that, with certain exceptions, required the installation of radar on all airplanes used in US air-carrier operations. (The exceptions were for operations with Curtiss-Wright C-46s or any non-transport category airplanes, such as Douglas DC-3s, and for airline operations in Alaska or Hawaii with any kind of airplanes.) In order to lessen the impact, a phase-in schedule was adopted. Compliance was required for all turbine-powered airplanes by July 1, 1960. Operators had to have radar installed in their Douglas DC-6s and DC-7s, and Lockheed 1049s and 1649s, within the next six months and in all others, including the Martin 404s, by January 1, 1962. TWA had retired all of its 404s by then; however, Eastern and the second-generation users were required to install radar. The 202s and 202As that were still in air-carrier service were, of course, required to comply as well. Most Martin operators installed the Chamberlain Aviation (Cair) radome that lengthened the nose slightly and gave it an upturned-snout

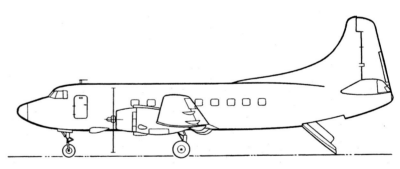

Side-view of Model 404 with the later addition of weather radar. (Author)

appearance. A few other 404s had radomes that retained the original nose shape.

Southwest, Allegheny, and Mohawk were the first Local Service operators to supplement their DC-3s successfully with modern postwar equipment. As noted earlier, Southwest (which was later renamed Pacific) and Allegheny did so by acquiring a few used 202s.

Following several years of successful operation with a mixed fleet of DC-3s and 202s, Pacific needed additional airplanes in order to expand its operations and to replace the DC-3s. As there were no more 202s available, the airline turned first to Fairchild and ordered a handful of turbine-powered F-27s. It was impractical, however, for Pacific to build its entire fleet around F-27s because of their high cost.

Eventually, a fleet of 404s was acquired to replace both the DC-3s and 202s. The 404s were a natural addition. Pacific was already experienced in operating Martin products, and many spares were common to the two models. Most came from TWA; however, two ex-Eastern 404s were also flown. Pacific received Supplemental Type Certificate (STC) SA4-1042 to install 44-passenger interiors in its 404s.

After its time as a first-line passenger airplane had passed, Pacific received another STC (SA1428WE) on June 9, 1967, for the conversion of N40438 (msn 14173) to an all-cargo configuration. A similar conversion of N40441 (msn 14176) had been planned, but the modification of that airplane was apparently not completed.

Pacific merged with Bonanza Air Lines and West Coast Airlines in 1968 to form Air West. The 404s had been retired by then, and the once familiar sight of a Martin airplane was almost gone from West Coast skies.

Allegheny chose Napier Eland-powered Convair 540s as its next-generation airplanes. Although the Eland-powered version did not work out, Allegheny was committed to a Convair fleet and was not interested in acquiring any 404s.

Like Southwest and Allegheny, Mohawk Airlines was an early Local Service operator of modern, postwar airplanes. Its first were three of the Central Air Transport Corp Convair 240s that had been rescued from the Chinese communist regime by General Chennault. Eventually, a large fleet of 240s, 340s, and even brand-new 440s was acquired. In 1961, Mohawk was given an opportunity to take over a number of routes in the northeastern part of the US from Eastern Air Lines.

This Pacific Air Lines 404 (N40408), photographed at Las Vegas on June 24, 1961, features a Chamberlain radome to comply with the FAA's soon-to-be mandatory weather radar requirement. The large 'Four O Four' title was a hallmark of the Local Service carrier. (Robert E Hufford)
The same aircraft at San Francisco on March 30, 1965, in the airline's newly adopted livery.
(Author)

Pacific Air Lines converted N40438 to an all-cargo configuration as evidenced by the large 'Air Freight by Pacific' titles and netting visible through the cabin windows. (MAP)

This, together with other growth, required its fleet to be almost doubled. Undoubtedly, Mohawk would have preferred to continue operating an all-Convair fleet; however, locating that many additional Convairs on short notice would have been difficult, if not impossible. As an expediency, 15 404s were acquired from Eastern in the deal. Instead of making the last of these operational, Mohawk leased another ex-Eastern

404 from Charlotte Aircraft Corp. As with its 240s, Mohawk's Martins were operated with the class name 'Cosmopolitan'. Identical paint schemes emphasized the similarities and differences in appearance between the Convair and Martin airplanes.

Mohawk's leased airplane (N449A) crashed following loss of control in a severe thunderstorm shortly after takeoff

Mohawk's newly acquired Air Chief Potawatomi *(N466M) far from home at Decatur, Illinois, on September 16, 1962.* (Leo J Kohn)

from Rochester, New York, on July 2, 1963, with seven fatalities and 30 persons seriously injured. Another Mohawk 404 (N472M), contributed to the list of embarrassed captains who had inadvertently retracted the landing gear during the landing roll-out.

Eventually, Mohawk traded its 14 operational 404s to Ozark Air Lines in late 1964 and 1965 for about a third as many Convair 240s. It was a mutually beneficial trade. Because it was taking delivery of a new fleet of BAC One-Elevens, Mohawk did not need as many propeller-driven airplanes then and could benefit from having a standardized Convair-Liner fleet. Ozark, on the other hand, had a temporary need for additional airplanes pending delivery of new Fairchild Hiller FH-227s about two years later. Mohawk was also considering conversion of its Convair fleet to Rolls-Royce Dart engines, and it was unlikely that such a conversion would be available for the 404s.

Compañia Panamena de Aviación (COPA) became the first non-US airline to operate a 404 when its HP-302 (msn 14170) replaced a Curtiss C-46 on the 200mi (320km) Panama City–David route in fall 1961. The 404 was flown in the color scheme of Pan American with which it was affiliated at the time. After a few years of Panamanian service, it was replaced with a Hawker Siddeley 748 in 1965 and added to the Piedmont Airlines fleet.

Of the second-generation users, Piedmont had the largest fleet of 404s. At least 36, predominantly ex-TWA, are known

to have been operated by Piedmont; and possibly others were used on short-term leases. Piedmont originally purchased a few F-27s as its first DC-3 replacements; however, like Pacific, it found the F-27s to be too costly to be viable replacements for an entire fleet. After the F-27s had been in operation about three years, TWA started to dispose of its 404s; and, Piedmont signed a contract on July 31, 1961, to supplement the F-27s with an initial fleet of 16 404s. The Piedmont F-27s were later replaced with FH-227s; however, even those were outlasted by the 404s. Piedmont also performed maintenance for other 404 operators, including COPA and Ray Charles.

Three 404s were lost in accidents while in service with Piedmont. The first production 404 (N40401) was damaged beyond repair on August 22, 1962, following an unselected

Local Service airlines developed quick turnarounds at intermedistops to a fine art. Piedmont's Shenandoah Valley Pacemaker *is seen at Greenville-Spartanburg, South Carolina, on June 11, 1967, on a typical five-minute turnaround with only the No 1 (left) engine shut down. That practice made it somewhat breezy for the ground crewman trying to load the aft belly cargo compartment.* (Robert E Hufford)

Piedmont's Tidewater Pacemaker, *the first 404, just made its last landing. The accident occurred on August 22, 1962, at Wilmington, North Carolina, when the left-hand propeller went into reverse prematurely. A released blade grazed the head of Piedmont's chief pilot, John 'Pappy' Wilkes sitting in the jump seat. Pilot Bob Carter and FAA Flight Inspector Sills in the right seat were unscathed. After the dust had settled, Sills gave Carter his type rating.* (Paul J McDaniel)

reversal of the left propeller during a landing at Wilmington, North Carolina. There were no injuries in that accident; however, all three occupants of the former COPA 404 (N40406) were killed on November 20, 1966, when it crashed at New Bern, North Carolina. The third airplane (N40446) was damaged beyond repair when the landing gear collapsed at Roanoke, Virginia. There were no injuries in that accident, nor in two other landing accidents involving Piedmont 404s.

Eventually, the remaining Piedmont 404s were retired late in the 1960s in favor of a fleet of NAMC YS-11A airplanes.

Southern Airways was one of the last operators of an all DC-3 fleet. As it apparently lacked the financing needed for new F-27s, it was content to acquire a fleet of 22 404s beginning in 1961.

Although Martin 404s were never approved for ditching *per se*, Southern was granted an exemption on April 28, 1965, to fly its 404s in extended overwater service. The exemption was based on the general similarity of the Model 404 to the Convair Model 440. The National Advisory Committe for Aeronautics (NACA) had previously tested a $1/15$-scale model of the 440 and concluded that it would have excellent ditching characteristics.

There were no fatalities in 404s operated by Southern; however, one (N251S) was damaged beyond economical repair in a hard landing at Oxford, Mississippi, on New Year's Day 1968. By then the market-value of 404s had dropped to the point where they were not worth the cost of repairing damage that would have been considered minor when they were newer.

At one time, there were rumors that General Motors would purchase Convair 440s from Eastern Air Lines for conversion to 580s and subsequent delivery to Southern. That did not happen, and Southern continued to operate 404s into the 1970s—long after the other Local Service airlines had gone on to more modern equipment. Southern's last scheduled 404 service was a roundtrip flight on April 30, 1978, from Atlanta to Gadsden, Georgia. That service, using N144S, marked the last scheduled flight with a reciprocating-powered airplane by a 'major' US airline.

Non-scheduled operators also found used 404s to be worthwhile additions to their fleets. The two most prominent non-scheduled operators of 404s were ASA International Airlines and East Coast Flying Service.

Aerovías Sud Americana, or ASA International Airlines as it was generally known, began non-scheduled cargo service between the US and Latin America on October 17, 1947. ASA expanded its operations in 1961 to include contract passenger flights using ex-

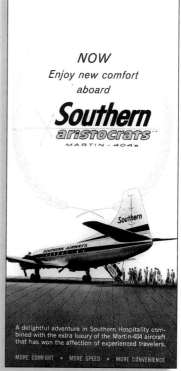

Southern Airways promoted its new fleet of 404s as 'Southern Aristocrats'.
(David H Stringer collection)

This 404 (N144S) operated Southern's last scheduled piston-engine passenger flight on April 20, 1978. (via Elliot H Greenman)

The small, but effective, van Zelm ailerons enabled the use of longer-span flaps as shown on this landing Southern Airways 404 (N142S).
(via Elliot H Greenman)

N454A at San Jose, California, in August 1961, resplendent in the attractive, but short-lived paint scheme of Aerovias Sud Americana which traded as ASA International Airlines. (William T Larkins)

Eastern 404s and Lockheed Constellations. Five 404s were acquired; however, it is not certain that all five were placed in service. After less than a year with ASA, two each went to Pacific Air Lines and East Coast Flying Service. The fifth remained in ASA service through late 1962, then it too was sold to East Coast Flying Service. ASA attempted to merge with Riddle Airlines during this period, but was frustrated in that effort by delays in receiving CAB approval. The company finally went into bankruptcy on May 12, 1965.

Meanwhile, East Coast Flying Service (ECFS) found a developing market for charter flights from the southeastern US to the Caribbean. One 404 was acquired from Eastern for this purpose in July 1960, and another from TWA a year later. From then on, its fleet was expanded to include about a half dozen 404s and some Convair 240s. (ECFS actually owned 13 different 404s over a period of about eight years; however, four were acquired for conversion and resale as executive airplanes. Others were leased to other operators.) Following Southern's initiative, EFCS was granted an exemption to fly its 404s in extended overwater service. Although three 404s remained for a couple more years, most were sold by the end of 1965.

EXECUTIVE 404S

In this age of sleek business jets and corporate liability, it is hard to remember that many top executives flew in converted North American B-25 Mitchell, Douglas A-26 Invader, and Lockheed PV-1 Harpoon bombers during the late 1940s and 1950s. The executive bomber fleet even included four highly modified examples of Martin's B-26 Marauder. Although the

bombers were fast for their day, they were cramped, noisy and of questionable airworthiness—plush interiors and gleaming exterior paint notwithstanding. Other companies were using Lockheed Lodestars or comfortable, but slow, DC-3s. Convair sold a few of its twins as executive airplanes, but the market was very limited because of their high cost. Martin was unable to sell any new 404s for this purpose; however, the Howard Hughes 404 was, for all practical purposes, a new airplane when it went into executive service after about two-and-a-half years of storage.

During the early 1960s, the market changed when the airlines began to dispose of their surplus Convair and Martin twins at affordable prices. There was no comparison of comfort between the spacious, pressurized cabin of a used Convair or Martin twin and that of a converted bomber. (Some A-26s and PV-1s were modified to include pressurization, but none of those conversions were particularly successful.) Furthermore, the direct operating costs were comparable as the Convair and Martin twins used essentially the same Pratt & Whitney Double Wasp engines as A-26s and PV-1s. The used Convair and Martin twins, therefore, found ready acceptance in the executive market. More Convair twins than 404s went into executive service simply because there were more Convairs available. Nevertheless, at least 14 ex-TWA or Eastern 404s are known to have been flown as executive airplanes in addition to the former Hughes 404 used by The National Supply Co. Other prominent executive operators of 404s included E F MacDonald, Federated Department Stores, ARMCO Steel, and Whirlpool. In the entertainment field, Frank Sinatra, Ray

Danny Davis purchased N404DD in 1972 from the Hubbard Broadcasting Co for travel with his orchestra, The Nashville Brass. A stylized horn appears on the nose and the name Lady Barbara *is just visible under the forward belly. This airplane is now used as an instructional airframe in Miami at the George T Baker Aviation School.* (John Wegg)

Charles, Cantiflas, and Danny Davis each used a 404. The Doobie Brothers, a rock band, also used 404s at different times.

The modifications for executive use varied considerably from one 404 to another; however, they typically included replacement of the airline passenger seats with a luxurious, low-density interior seating about 15 or 16 passengers. Although not required by the FAA for non-air carrier operation, weather radar was generally installed along with other modern avionics. An auxiliary power unit installation was available to make the airplane self-sufficient during ground operation, and a 991USg (3,740l) integral fuel tank could be installed in each wing. The resulting fuel capacity was sufficient to provide non-stop coast-to-coast range, albeit with very little payload. In the case of ex-Eastern 404s, the CB3 engines were usually replaced with or converted to CB16 engines to provide better altitude performance. Two 15,000lb (6,800kg)-second impulse Aerojet-General 15KS-1000-A1 jet assisted takeoff (JATO) units could also be installed to provide a greater performance margin if the 404 were to suffer an engine failure on takeoff. JATO was installed on E F MacDonald's airplane (msn 14135, N636) and probably on other executive 404s as well.

Generally, there were no external modifications to distinguish the executive 404s from their airline counterparts. Propeller spinners, probably the same as those used on Douglas DC-6s, were, however, installed on at least three airplanes (msns 14145, 14172, and 14235).

Frank Sinatra's 404 was a notable exception to the stately elegance that characterized most of the executive 404s. The forward portion of the cabin was the social center which included a piano, hi-fi system, and a curved bar complete with safety-belt equipped stools. (There was speculation at the time that inebriation of the guests rather than possible turbulence prompted the belt installation.) The main seating area separated the social center from Sinatra's private bedroom in the aft fuselage. For night flights, an artificial moon and twinkling stars were built into the ceiling. Lavatories were provided in both the fore and aft ends of the cabin. The exterior was equally flamboyant—except for the white cabin roof and brown trim, the entire airplane was painted pink.

Sinatra's 404 also served as a post-flight roulette wheel. As there were 18 possi-

Detail of propeller spinner and uncowled left-hand engine on msn 14235 (N3711K) at Chino, California, 1989. (Author)

ble positions in which the 18-cylinder Double Wasp engine could stop on shutdown, the cowl leading edge was painted with 18 numbered arcs. One of the three propeller blades was also marked. The winner for a particular flight was the lucky person who held the number of the arc on which the marked propeller blade stopped.

Popular as they were for awhile, the Convair and Martin twins proved to be interim equipment between the converted bombers and the executive jets of today. After a few years of glamorous executive service, some found their way back into the rigors of airline service.

COMMUTER 404S

Following their period of usefulness with Local Service airlines and executive operators, many 404s were passed down to the commuter airline industry. Florida, in particular, became the haven for 404s insofar as scheduled service was concerned.

Frank Sinatra's exotic N710E (ex N40434), photographed at Burbank, California, on November 24, 1962. By the forward entrance door are the name Christina *and the flags of 14 countries it had visited.* (Robert E Hufford)

Following retirement from Piedmont service, N40413 was acquired by Southeast Airlines for Florida intrastate service. (via Elliot H Greenman)

Southeast Airlines, apparently unrelated to an earlier Tennessee intrastate operator with the same name, first began air-taxi service in Florida in 1959 under the name Cat Cay Airways with Beech D18S equipment. In order to accommodate growing traffic, a Fairchild F-27 was added to the fleet in 1966. By the end of 1973, Southeast had evolved into a scheduled Florida intrastate operator with a fleet of four 202As and four ex-Piedmont 404s. Financial difficulties eventually forced Southeast to suspend operations in June 1976, although it was later revived for a few years with pure-jet equipment.

One of the oldest US commuter airlines was Provincetown-Boston Airline (PBA) which operated, as its name implied, between Boston and the Cape Cod city of Provincetown. During the winters, when there was little traffic to Cape Cod, the airline moved most of the fleet south and operated services in Florida under the name Naples Airlines. Following the demise of Southeast Airlines in 1976, PBA acquired its four 404s and added them to a large fleet that included such diverse types as DC-3s, NAMC YS-11s, EMBRAER Bandeirantes, and Cessna 402s. PBA eventually owned nine 404s; however, at least three were non-operational sources of spares. PBA's maintenance and operations were not above reproach, and the whole fleet was grounded by the FAA on November 10, 1984. Limited operations were

resumed with the turbine-powered airplanes two weeks later; however, a fatal Bandeirante crash in December proved to be the final blow to PBA. Just before the grounding, PBA had acquired Marco Island Airways which had operated a number of ex-Southern Airways 404s in Florida intrastate service since about 1973-74. That acquisition proved to be in vain as neither Marco Island's 404s nor its own were flown after the grounding.

Sarasota-based Florida Airlines began air-taxi service shortly after World War II. Services were entirely intrastate until 1975 when Orlando-based Shawnee Airlines and Atlanta-based Air South were acquired. With those acquisitions, Florida Airlines's service was expanded to include St Simon Island, Georgia, Hilton Head Island, South Carolina, and Nassau and Freeport in the Bahamas. By late in the 1970s, most of the passenger service was conducted with 404s obtained from Southern. Like Florida's

Following the demise of Southeast Airlines in 1975, N40424 was one of several 44-seat 404s purchased by Provincetown-Boston Airline, which marketed itself as 'America's oldest regional airline'. Five years later, this airplane had the distinction of serving John Anderson in his unsuccessful presidential campaign. (Gordon Reid)

Because of the length of Provincetown's runway, PBA's 404s were at first used solely by its Florida Division and were a familiar sight at Miami International Airport for many years.
(James P Woolsey)

other 404 operators, Florida Airlines eventually experienced financial difficulties; scheduled service was suspended in January 1980. Service was resumed a year later on behalf of Air Florida; however, that lasted only a few months until the airline was formally dissolved. The post-bankruptcy successor, Southern International Airways, also operated the 404s on behalf of Air Florida for awhile until it too went out of business.

Nevada Airlines used N40438 (msn 14173) for sightseeing flights from Las Vegas to the Grand Canyon beginning in 1978. That operation ended abruptly on November 16, 1979, with the crash of its sole 404.

During the winter months when there was little traffic to Cape Cod, Provincetown–Boston Airline operated Florida intrastate service under the name Naples Airlines, with or without the 'PBA' titles included in the tail logo.
(James P Woolsey (2), right, & Karl Krämer)

A Marco Island Airways 404 (N967M) on approach to Miami International Airport in February 1976. (Eddy Gual via Jean-Marie Magendie)

Five grounded Provincetown-Boston Airline/Marco Island Airways 404s at Naples, Florida, in September 1988. They would never fly again for PBA.
(Adolfo Tagliabue)

A JACK OF ALL TRADES

Some 404s were used to haul meat in Bolivia by Comercialisadora Aérea Mixta Boliviana Ltda (CAMBA) and Frigorifico Reyes—a definite contrast to the luxurious executive service for which 404s were used a decade earlier.

The 404s were also popular with miscellaneous non-airline operators such as air travel clubs, land promoters, and contract companies. There were two noteworthy accidents involving these operators, both particularly regrettable because they were caused by human carelessness.

The first occurred on May 30, 1970, when N40412 was forced to crash-land on a freeway median near Chamblee, Georgia, because it had been refueled in error with turbine fuel. The airplane, which was being used by Lehigh Acres Development to transport prospective purchasers to view property near Fort Myers, Florida, was destroyed. One person aboard was killed plus another five traveling in a car on the highway, and 30 received serious injuries.

The second occurred on October 2 of that year near Silver Plume, Colorado. Two 404s (N464M and N470M, respectively) had been chartered from Golden Eagle Aviation to fly the Wichita State University football team to a game at Logan, Utah. After a refueling stop at Denver, the flight crew of N464M elected to take a scenic detour through a mountain valley and crashed into the base of Mount Trelease. The airplane was destroyed, and 32 occupants were killed. The remaining eight persons aboard survived with serious injuries. There was strong disagreement among the three parties involved, Jack Richards Aircraft (the owner and lessor of the two 404s), Wichita State University, and Golden Eagle, as to which was the actual operator of the flight. Golden Eagle was considered by the FAA to have been the operator, an act for which it did not have FAA certification. Because the two 404s were operated in violation of the Federal Aviation Regulations, the other (N470M) was seized by the FAA on October 5, 1970, and held in custody pending payment of $10,000 in civil penalties and storage costs on January 5, 1972.

Although the airworthiness of N464M was not a factor in the crash, the activities of Jack Richards Aircraft and the condition of its remaining airplanes were under considerable suspicion. The FAA, therefore, ordered the company to present each of its other airplanes for inspection. Following the company's failure to comply, the FAA issued an emergency order on October 8, 1970, suspending the airworthiness certificate of each airplane until its airworthiness could be assured. In addition to its dozen 404s, the suspension included three DC-3s, three DC-6s, two Lockheed 1049Hs, a Grumman Mallard, and a North American

TWA's Skyliner Detroit *ended its days as CP-1570, hauling meat in Bolivia for CAMBA. It was involved in a fatal forced landing in 1987 following an engine failure.* (Rolf Larsson)

The rigors of Bolivian operations are illustrated by the remains of a Compañia Aérea Nacional 404 (CP-1704), which was demolished in a takeoff accident at La Paz in August 1985. (Michael Magnusson)

T-28A. In this respect, the author processed a Supplemental Type Certificate (No SA2288WE) which was issued on December 9, 1970, to legitimize an intermix of CB3 and CB16 engines on N462M (msn 14153).

Both RM-1Z/VC-3A airplanes were donated to The School of the Ozarks in 1972. The transfer agreement stipulated that msn 14290 was to be used for transporting ath-

Aggie 404s

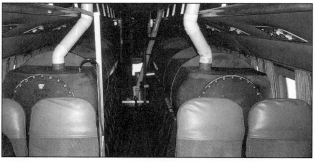

Two former Boeing KC-97 500USg (1,892l) fuel tanks installed in the cabin of the former Ray Charles 404 (msn 14143/N9234C), the first liquid sprayer conversion by Clayton Curtis. (Phil Brooks)

Patriotically painted N472M at Madera, California, in the bicentennial year of 1976. Howard Coones and his son, Rob, converted this ex-Basler 404 over a period of two years to a full-time agricultural applicator. A complicated strut arrangement was used to mount the spray bar under the wings. Other modifications included the installation of two 12ft (3.65m)-long stainless steel tanks in the cabin, mounted to the airplane's structure, not the floor, and the elimination of non-essential equipment such as wing de-icing and cabin heaters and pressurization. The electrically operated airscoops mounted in lieu of the first and eighth cabin windows provided positive pressure for the system, which could be used for wet or dry spraying, seeding, or fertilization.

A Supplemental Type Certificate was granted by the FAA on September 19, 1977, and Cooneses went on to convert N470M and N40408. All three conversions were used in California and Washington to seed areas devastated by forest fires. (John Wegg; details by William T Larkins)

As stenciled on the underside of msn 14143/N9234C, the Curtis 404s could carry almost five and a half tons of liquid in their spray tanks. The dump chutes for the spray system are just barely visible on the underside of the fuselage, adjacent to the trailing edge wing/fuselage fillet. (Author)

Clayton Curtis also converted msn 14153/N462M and msn 14228/N40443 with a liquid spray system, identical to that in msn 14143/N9234C, which featured a boom which ran inside the wings. This resulted in a much neater appearance than that of N472M, with seven spray nozzles protruding from the top of each wing. Two (N40443 & N9234C) were used for several years in Wyoming to spray grasshoppers, but N462M was not certificated until August 1987, a year after the fatal crash of N9234C which had brought Curtis's operation to an end. (Phil Brooks)

Five 404s at Madera, California, in September 1977, from left: N40443 (msn 14228), N40418 (14124), N461M (14227), N40445 (14230), and N40432 (msn 14167). All are converted to, or candidates for, conversion to aerial applicators—a use Martin definitely did not envision when the 404 was designed.

Three of the ex-Piedmont/Charlotte Aircraft 404s had been converted by Clayton Curtis with a 400cu ft (11.2m³) hopper in the cabin to disperse Mirex, a granular pesticide. They had been flown by Dothan Aviation on fire ant eradication programs.

(John Wegg)

Piedmont's once proud Great Smokies Pacemaker *in its final days at Sebring, Florida.*
(Karl Krämer)

letic teams and students, training in mechanical maintenance, and orientation and training in heavy aircraft. The other (msn 14291) was to be cannibalized to support the operation and was scrapped as stipulated; however, 14290 was resold in 1978. Its demise occurred a few months later in the Caribbean Sea off the coast of Venezuela.

In order to create a market for unsold ex-Piedmont 404s, Charlotte Aircraft Corporation had five airplanes converted in 1970 for aerial application—a use the Martin

Marco Island Airways purchased ex–Southern Fleet No 123 (msn 14138/N585S) as a source of spares. By October 1975, all that remained at Opa-locka, Florida, was the fuselage. (John Wegg)

designers had certainly not anticipated. Airplanes designed specifically for aerial application would obviously have been more efficient; however, none the size of 404s existed and, in any case, they would have been too expensive. In the case of the 404s, cheap airframes were available, they could haul large payloads, and they were relatively stable in low, slow flight. Although three were lost in accidents, the converted 404s were apparently successful as at least six others were converted for such use over the next 17 years. Probably their high hourly operating costs prevented them from being even more successful.

Basically, the 404s used two types of dispensing systems—spray systems for the application of liquid pesticides, or fertilizers, and hoppers for dispensing seeds and granular materials. The last 404 converted (N3711K, msn 14235) had a partially removable spray system with two tanks of 800USg (3,000l) total capacity. That airplane had a dual standard/restricted category airworthiness certificate so that it could operate in restricted category with the complete spray system installed, or in standard category with certain components removed.

Other unique modifications included the 1970 installation of infrared sensing equipment in the Atomic Energy Commission's N40409 (msn 14113) and approval granted a decade later to the late Art Scholl to remove the ventral stairs. The latter was a temporary modification to facilitate dropping an object from N404DD (msn 14132) during the filming of a movie.

Although the 404s were few in numbers, they were excellent in longevity of service. About two dozen saw scheduled passenger service more than three decades after the 202s first went into service. Today, there are only a handful of airworthy 404s. Their demise has finally come about, not because of the obsolescence one would expect of a half-century-old design, but simply because the airframes are tired. Few are particularly high-time airframes under today's criteria—probably no 404 has ever exceeded 65,000 hours of flying time. Most of the scrapped 404s were, therefore, victims of corrosion rather than fatigue. Adding to their demise is the lack of spares. The only sources of spares today are the scrapped sisterships. Under these circumstances, the 404s are simply too expensive to operate on a regular basis.

At the time of publication, the last Martinliner still working for a living was Rentavion's YV-145C which, after many years of storage, was brought back to life in 1996. It is based at Porlamar to carry tourists on day trips to Canaima National Park, the site of Angel Falls, the world's highest waterfall. (Ian P Burnett)

PBA was the last US airline to operate the 404 in passenger service (in November 1984); and, as a result of its brief 1989 service, Systems-International Airways has the distinction of being the last US company to use a 404 in cargo operations.

Latin America became the final destination for operational 404s. ADSA, of the Dominican Republic, flew a 404 on behalf of Aerovías Quisqueyana in May 1978—undoubtedly the last use of a 404 in scheduled international passenger service. A 404 used by Transportes Aéreos Samuel Selem (TASS) to haul meat in Bolivia was written off in April 1990. Rentavion of Venezuela was still operating at least one 404 for passenger charters as late as 1997 and is said to be interested in acquiring more aircraft, which could mean that the 404 will still be in regular service after the year 2000.

SAVE A MARTINLINER

Although Rentavion's 404 is the last Martinliner in commercial service anywhere, a number of organizations had recognized the need to preserve some examples before the type became extinct. Save A Connie, the group that restored a Lockheed Super Constellation for preservation as a flying show-piece, purchased N145S (originally Eastern's N451A) in 1990 for similar restoration. In 1991, the Mid Atlantic Air Museum, Reading, Pennsylvania, acquired—coincidentally—sistership N149S (ex-N450A) for restoration into Eastern's 'white-top' color scheme.

Jeff Whitesell acquired the former E F MacDonald 404 (N636X, msn 14135) in 1994 for restoration in Pacific Air Lines colors. Apart from being in excellent condition, that particular 404 holds considerable sentimental value as it was once used extensively by his father's company, Flying W Airways.

And, it is hoped, not last, and definitely not least, Sam Stewart and his son Ted have expressed interest in restoring their 404 (N3711K, msn 14235) to represent one of the Coast Guard airplanes.

While the working days of the 404s are almost over, these acquisitions should ensure that there will be at least a few examples flying for a number of years to come. Ironically, these preserved examples may outlast their competitors. Because the Convair-Liner is still in active service, no organization has made a similar effort to preserve a flying example. It is to be hoped that this omission will be corrected before an airworthy Convair in a passenger layout becomes extinct.

THE MARTIN TURBO 404

Concurrent with the development of the Model 404, Martin continued to investigate the possibility of turbine power for airplanes of this class. While the General Electric TG-100 engines were definitely out of the picture, Allison's 501 engines showed promise. Allison had acquired the prototype Convair 240 for use as an engine test-bed and was in the process of installing two 501-A4 engines. In addition, there was considerable interest in the T-38 military versions of the engines. Accordingly, the airframe of the Model 404 was designed for the eventual installation of those engines. Basically, that involved re-stressing the wings for greater bending moments, accounting for higher design speeds, and making certain changes to the fin and rudder. Although the resulting configuration was described as the 'Turbo 404', another model designation, such as '505', would probably have been assigned had Martin pursued the turbine installation.

(Would there have eventually been a Martin '707'?)

Martin also had a project group weighing the alternate possibility of installing turbine engines in an airframe of completely new design; however, the installation in the Model 404 airframe appeared to be the most cost-effective.

Unfortunately, tests with the Convair 240 showed that the Allison engines were not sufficiently developed at that time for dependable and economical airline use. After eight years of further development, the 501-D13 engines were finally ready for airline service in the Lockheed Electra; however, both the 404s and the competitive Convair-Liner were long out of production by then.

During the mid-1950s, there was some interest in producing a version of the Model 404 with turbine engines in West Germany. Napier Eland engines would probably have been used. Nothing came of that idea, and a later proposal to produce similar airplanes in South America was equally unsuccessful.

Although its engines were not ready in time to be used on new production Convair or Martin airplanes, Allison did consider the retrofit market potential sufficient to sponsor the conversion of existing Convair 340/440 airframes. A similar conversion of the 404 would probably have resulted in a fine airplane, but there were just too few airframes available for it to have been a financial success.

Finally, Convair reportedly considered offering a less costly installation of Rolls-Royce Dart engines in 404s using the nacelles of its 600/640 conversions. Slow sales of conversions of its own airplanes probably precluded any serious activity in that respect.

Although turbine power was considered right from the start, none of the Martin 202 or 404 variants were to enjoy that form of propulsion.

A Look Ahead! Martin Turbo 4-0-4s will set new airline standards of comfort, speed and reliability. Advanced studies indicate that the Allison T-38 Turbo-Prop engine will provide smooth, vibration-free power with unusually small specific fuel consumption.

Artist's impression and side-view of proposed Allison-powered Turbo 404. If it had gone into production, the nacelles, which are similar to those of the original Convair Turboliner testbed, would probably have been replaced with ones similar to those of the Convair 580 or Lockheed Electra.

(via John Wegg/Author)

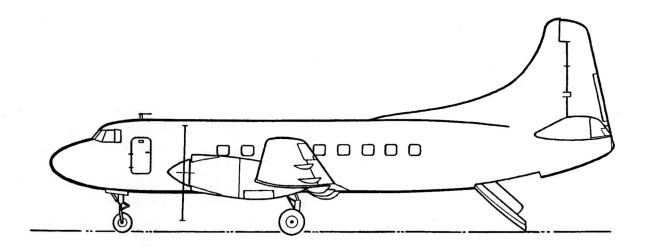

THE MARTINS IN RETROSPECT

Although the Martin 202s were acceptable by contemporary standards, they came into being during a period of very unfavorable economic conditions. Martin's closest competitor, Convair, was able to sell considerably more 240s, but it too was adversely affected by the prevailing economic situation. The 404 appeared on the airline scene later during improved economic conditions and provided Martin with an apparent competitive edge over Convair. That soon disappeared with the evolution of Convair's 240 into the 340.

Probably the most important single factor in Martin's lack of success was its failure to design the 202 with sufficient stability and controllability. The required redesign was not only costly and time-consuming, but in turn resulted in a structural flaw that led to the fatal crash of Northwest's NC93044. As a result, there was a general climate of distrust on the part of potential airline customers. This ruled out any further sales of 202s and, no doubt, had a negative effect on 404 sales a year or so later. To Martin's credit, the 202 redesign effort did result in a series of airplanes with flight characteristics that were considered satisfactory by their flight crews. Perhaps the greatest tribute to the Martin twins' flight characteristics was their successful use in the low, slow world of aerial application.

Although financial considerations were cited as the reason.s for the cancellation of United's 50-airplane 303 contract, the airline must have realized the hopeless situation caused by the stability problems. It would have been relatively simple to add the large dorsal fin ultimately used on the 202s. Increasing the dihedral in the wing of the Model 303 would have been another matter, however. Because of United's quest for additional cruise performance, Martin had designed a new wing of shorter span. With the one-piece tip-to-tip construction, it would have been extremely difficult to increase the dihedral of the new wing, either at the wing roots or outboard of the nacelles. Martin's only alternative, other than reverting to the 202 wing and losing the additional cruise performance, would have been a complete redesign of the 303 wing with adequate dihedral. This would have added considerable expense to the 303 development program and at least a year's delay. If it had not been faced with that dire prospect, United would probably have remained a Martin customer and, of course, would not have sponsored development of the Convair 240 into the 340. In that event, it is highly unlikely that the 340 would have been built; and Martin would have had the competitive edge.

Martin was generally in the unfortunate position of offering fewer passenger seats than Convair throughout the competition. Both the 202s and 240s were intended to be 40-passenger airplanes, but the 202s proved to be only 36-passenger airplanes in Trunk service because there was insufficient space for service areas and cargo or baggage compartments. When they were later relegated to Local Service operations, which demanded less cabin space, 40-passenger interiors were restored in some 202s. In contrast, Mohawk flew its 240s in Local Service with 46-passenger interiors. The 202s also lacked cabin pressurization and were no better, in that respect, than the prewar DC-3s. That deficiency was, however, mitigated somewhat in the early years by the fact that 240s frequently had to operate unpressurized as a result of pressurization system failures.

With the 404, Martin did respond with pressurization and a fuselage stretched to provide space for an additional row of seats. With encouragement from United, Convair countered with an even greater stretch and maintained its four-seat advantage. Martin should have recognized the increasing airline traffic and stretched the fuselage of the 404 much more than it did. It must be remembered, however, that Martin was certainly not the only aircraft manufacturer that erred in that regard. Potential airline customers may have misled Martin with inaccurate assessments of future needs.

Another significant factor was Martin's failure to receive the initial order from the US Air Force for T-29 airplanes. Once some of its airplanes were in the military inventory, Convair had a tremendous advantage over Martin in subsequent military procurements. Altogether, Convair sold more than 500 T-29, C-131, and R4Y airplanes in contrast to Martin's two RM-1Zs. Had Martin received those military orders, Convair would probably have fallen by the wayside, and Martin would have had the sustaining force to survive the cyclic nature of commercial airplane production.

With a reported total loss of $45 million on its commercial airplane programs, Martin elected to abandon such production altogether in the latter part of 1953.

It was unfortunate for Martin that it could not have kept its production line open longer. Convair faced a similar situation just a few months later but, with support from the military production, it elected to make some refinements in the 340 and continue production as the Model 440. Market conditions improved somewhat, and Convair was able to sell an additional 199 airplanes in spite of competition from turboprop types, such as the British Vickers Viscount. By the time 440 production was completed, the airlines were well into the turbine era. Had Martin been able to hold out longer, it could have stretched the fuselage of the 404 to provide cabin space comparable to that of the Convair airplanes and made refinements similar to those of the 440. The resulting model would probably have captured at least a portion of that market. By then, most of the 202 stigma had been overcome by the 404. Eastern Air Lines, in particular, was forced to turn to Convair in 1957 to supplement its 404 fleet with twenty 440s. Even Martin became a Convair customer that year by purchasing a 440 for its executive fleet. In a somewhat masochistic gesture, Martin chose the registration number N404M for its 440. This resulted in crews calling Air Traffic Control as 'Martin Convair November Four Zero Four Mike'!

How would Martin have fared if the Allison 501 turbine engines had been sufficiently developed for airline use during the 404 production period? This, of course, would not have offered Martin any particular advantage over Convair, as Convair would have been producing a similarly powered

model. In light of the eventual success of the converted Convair airplanes, it does appear though that *both* Convair and Martin would have enjoyed considerable additional sales at the expense of the Viscount. In its competition with reciprocating-powered airplanes, the Viscount's outstanding Rolls-Royce Dart turbopropeller engines more than compensated for its rather mediocre airframe and four-engine configuration. It would not have had that advantage if newly manufactured, Allison-powered Convair or Martin airplanes had been available. Trans-Canada Air Lines (TCA), for example, considered both the 340 and 404 to be promising prospects for its domestic route system. Even with its reciprocating engines, TCA was reported to be leaning toward the 340 in September 1952. TCA eventually purchased a large fleet of Viscounts; however, turbine engines in either the 340 or 404 would have probably been the deciding factor in luring the airline away from the Viscount. Although financing was a large factor in the purchase of Viscounts by Capital Airlines, it, too, would probably have chosen a turbine-powered 340 or 404 over the Viscount.

In this regard, one can also speculate that newly manufactured Martin or Convair twins would have been very competitive with the airplanes of this class of the 1980s, eg SAAB 340, British Aerospace ATP, Fokker 50, etc, if modern engines and avionics were installed and minor aerodynamic refinements were made.

The whole story of the Martin twins can be summarized by saying that the 202 paid the price of being designed with a fatal flaw, while the 404 was an excellent design that had the misfortune of being in competition with one that was outstanding. Undoubtedly, the 404 deserved much more success in sales than it achieved.

During the early 1960s, a Colorado-based element of Martin approached the FAA concerning the possible development of an airplane believed to have been similar in size and layout to the later Fokker F.28 Fellowship. An informal discussion of type certification requirements was held; however, Martin did not follow through with an application for a type certificate. Apart from any other doubts as to its viability, the lack of suitable engines probably precluded any significant activity on that project.

Ironically, Martin's fate in commercial airplane production also befell its victorious competitor only one airplane generation later. Neither name, Martin or Convair, appears today on the airlines's shopping lists.

Trans World Airlines Skyliner Baltimore, *the first of 103 Martin 404s built, was rolled out and flown in July 1951 in TWA's new 'brilliant white' color scheme. The white paint was added as a sun deflector.* (TWA via Jon Proctor)

Skyliner Cincinnati *at Newark, New Jersey, in June 1953. Some, if not all, of TWA's 404s were flown from Baltimore to Wilmington, Delaware—where TWA was incorporated—for handover. The airplane was then flown back to the Martin plant to drop off the contract personnel and attorneys. On occasion, the new 404 would be flown to Philadelphia and switched with a previously delivered 404 on a scheduled flight to New York-LaGuardia. The new 404 would then arrive in New York state as a 'used' airplane to avoid taxes.* (Robert Matthews)

TWA's Skyliner Wilkes-Barre *(N40441), the last of 40 Martin 404s delivered to TWA, undergoing an engine change.* (Tom Sheridan)

FLY EASTERN'S NEW SILVER FALCON

Labels: VERTICAL STABILIZER, HORIZONTAL STABILIZER, RUDDER, ELEVATOR, AILERON, LAVATORY, DRINKING FOUNTAIN, PASSENGER COATS, FLAPS, N440A, CABIN ENTRANCE DOOR, RACK FOR PASSENGERS' "CARRY-ON" BAGGAGE, FLIGHT ATTENDANT'S STATION, GALLEY, RADIO EQPT., PASSENGER BAGGAGE, FLIGHT DECK, LARGE PICTURE WINDOWS, PASSENGER CABIN, EASTERN, CARGO LOADING & GALLEY SERVICE DOOR, CARGO BINS, PRATT & WHITNEY ENGINES 2400 HORSEPOWER

SPECIFICATIONS

Wing Span	93' 3½'	Maximum Payload	9,300 lbs.
Fuselage Length	74' 7'	Engine Power	2400 horsepower each at take-off
Maximum Height	28' 2'	Maximum Speed	312 mph at 10,000 ft.
Empty Weight	(Approx.) 29,450 lbs.	Cruising Speed	270 mph at 16,000 ft.
Take-off Weight	43,650 lbs.	Maximum Range	1,270 miles*

*(at 52½% cruise power with one-hour fuel reserve and provision for 100 miles alternate.)

Cut-away drawing showing the interior details of Eastern's new Silver Falcons. Reputedly, Captain Eddie Rickenbacker, Eastern's colorful president, insisted that the 404s were not to be referred to by their designation in order to avoid comparison with the unlucky 202. (David Stringer collection)

An Ozark Air Lines 404 (N460M/msn 14162) photographed in December 1966. (Walt Redmond)

Eastern's 404s originally flew with bare metal fuselages under the class name 'Silver Falcon'. N460A (msn 14151) is seen on a cold, snow-covered ramp at Philadelphia, Pennsylvania, in February 1957. Unlike its sisterships in the background, Eastern's N457A (msn 14148) has just been painted with the same basic livery over a white fuselage. (both Harry Sievers)

A few of Eastern's 404s were repainted into new Silver Falcon livery. (David Lucabaugh via Clint Groves/Airliners America/ATP)

Compañia Panamena de Aviación (COPA), affiliated with Pan American at the time, flew Chiriqui (HP-302/msn 14170) on scheduled Panamanian service during the early 1960s. The basic color scheme was similar to that of Pan American. (Airliners America/ATP via John P Stewart)

The US Coast Guard's procurement of two executive-configured RM-1Zs saved Martin from a complete shut-out in military sales of 404 variants. The first, USCG serial number 1282, is seen here parked on July 3, 1966, in front of the Coast Guard's hangar at Washington–National Airport. By that time, it had been given the new military model designation VC-3A. (Larry Milberry/CANAV Books)

After service with the Coast Guard, the two VC-3As were transferred to Naval Air Reserve Training Unit VR-52 at nearby Andrews Air Force Base, Maryland. This airplane (msn 14290) as seen on June 8, 1969, has been given the new military serial number 158202. As their days of VIP transport were past, the 'V' had been dropped from their military model designation by then. (Dr Joseph G Handelman)

N40423 (msn 14133) at San Francisco, California, in October 1960. Pacific Air Lines had just placed the airplane in service, as evidenced by its lack of weather radar. (Clay Jansson via Walt Redmond) *N40428 (msn 14173) was flown briefly in an all-cargo configuration just before Pacific Air Lines retired its Martin 404 fleet altogether.* (Thompson via Jean-Marie Magendie)

A Piedmont Airlines 404 (N40407 Blue Grass Pacemaker/msn 14107) at Atlanta, Georgia, in November 1968. (Harry Sievers)

A Mohawk Airlines 'Cosmopolitan' 404, N471M Air Chief Manhanset (msn 14112), as seen in August 1963 from the New York-Idlewild passenger terminal of its former operator, Eastern Air Lines. (Harry Sievers)

Another Mohawk 404, caught turning on final approach at Toronto-Malton in June 1965. (Larry Milberry/CANAV Books)

A Southern Airways 404 (N147S) at Gulfport, Mississippi, in April 1964, in an elegant livery befitting its class name 'Southern Aristocrat'. (R Kessler)

Southern Airways was the last 'major' US airline to operate reciprocating-powered airplanes in scheduled service. Fleet Number 119 (N581S/msn 14247) appears pristine despite the fact that it would be retired from Southern service in December 1977, seven months after this photo was taken. (John P Stewart)

N454A (msn 14145) at San Diego, California, September 1961, in the complete markings of Aerovías Sud Americana (also known as ASA International Airlines). ASA used this same attractive livery on its DC-6A and DC-7; however, the military contract operator flew a Constellation and at least one other 404 in very abbreviated liveries without titles and pinstriping. (Clay Jansson via Walt Redmond)

Executive Martins

One of the earliest 404 executive operators was Max Houston of Houston Lumber Co. His nicely painted N333G Lumber Lady I (msn 14131) was photographed at a then almost deserted Orange County Airport, California, in July 1961.
(Clay Jansson via Walt Redmond)

Huber Investment Co (dba Huber Homes) used N3711K (msn 14235) to fly prospective purchasers to its various housing developments at Dayton, Columbus (where this photo was taken in January 1971), Cincinnati, Indianapolis, and Fort Lauderdale.
(Harry Sievers)

None of the 202/404 series airplanes were ever registered in Canada; however, US-registered airplanes did venture north occasionally. At Toronto-Malton, Ontario, on June 23, 1972, is Danny Davis's newly acquired msn 14132. The registration number N404Z would be replaced a year later with the more appropriate N404DD. (Larry Milberry)

N404DD received a new color scheme later in its service with Danny Davis and the Nashville Brass. The base color was apparently intended to represent the brass of the orchestra's instruments.
(John P Stewart)

The Doobie Brothers rock band also made use of the 404 as an executive and crew/equipment transport, with no less than four different airplanes so-employed over several years. This was the colorful logo applied to N467M (msn 14164). (John Wegg)

N40428 (msn 14134), at Orange County Airport, California, in October 1961, used as an executive transport by Outboard Marine's Evinrude Division.
(Clay Jansson via Walt Redmond)

Floridian Martins

Southeast subsequently dropped its nautical style fin decoration in favor of a more modern look, modeled by N40424 (msn 14130) at Miami, Florida, in October 1975.
(John Wegg)

Although it is not certain that Southeast ever used its 202As in scheduled service, four ex-Piedmont 404s were placed in scheduled service in 1972. N40424 (msn 14130) is shown at Marathon, Florida, in April of that year. (Harry Sievers)

N145S (msn 14142) is now with Save A Connie for preservation and airshow exhibition. Here, it is making a typical 404-style approach to Miami International Airport in February 1981 while in service with Florida Airlines. (John Wegg)

Provincetown–Boston Airline operated in Florida under the name Naples Airlines, although N40425 (msn 14131), seen on approach to Miami International Airport on February 20, 1983, retains PBA titles. (Patrick Gauthier via Jean-Marie Magendie)

N40407 (msn 14107) photographed in 1979 with 'Naples Airlines' titles. PBA avoided the winter slump in Cape Cod traffic by moving much of its fleet to Florida for winter service there under the name Naples Airlines. (John P Stewart)

Formerly N141S, N973M (msn 14156) was one of six ex–Southern Airways 404s used by Marco Island Airways for Florida intrastate and Caribbean service. (John P Stewart)

A Marco Island Airways 404 (N968M/msn 14159) on approach to Miami International Airport on February 24, 1983, while operating on behalf of Air Florida.
(Patrick Gauthier via Jean-Marie Magendie)

N257S (msn 14110) in the colorful paint of Shawnee Airlines, an affiliate of Florida Airlines.
(John P Stewart)

Resplendent in Air Florida Commuter colors, N144S (msn 14150) is actually operated by Southern International Airways, the short-lived successor to Florida Airlines.
(John P Stewart)

N144S (msn 14150) in the livery of its former operator, Southern International Airways, in January 1986. With the word 'Southern' replaced with 'Systems', this became the livery of its next operator, Systems-International Airways.
(via Jean-Marie Magendie)

This airplane (N40448/msn 14242), at Miami, Florida, in December 1972, was one of four 404s leased by Bahamas-based Flamingo Airlines.
(Jay Quintero via Jean-Marie Magendie)

N40450 (msn 14146) at Miami, Florida, March 1973, in the livery of short-lived Atlantic Southeast Airlines. This operator was not related to the later Atlanta-based commuter airline of the same name. (via Jean-Marie Magendie)

N474M (msn 14165) at Fort Lauderdale, Florida, in February 1971 while used by Colony Airlines for charters to the Bahamas. (Harry Sievers)

Ill-fated N40438 (msn 14173) of Nevada Airlines. A few months later, on November 16, 1979, this 404 was destroyed in a non-fatal accident near the Grand Canyon. (Elliot H Greenman)

Ocean Airways acquired five 404s, including N259S (msn 14233), from Florida Airlines in 1980 and attempted Georgia intrastate service on routes vacated by Florida Airlines's subsidiary Air South. Unfortunately, Ocean Airways also found no success on those routes. (John P Stewart)

N465M (msn 14152) of Interstate Airmotive at its home base, St Louis, Missouri, August 1971. (Harry Sievers)

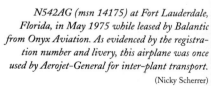

N542AG (msn 14175) at Fort Lauderdale, Florida, in May 1975 while leased by Balantic from Onyx Aviation. As evidenced by the registration number and livery, this airplane was once used by Aerojet-General for inter-plant transport.
(Nicky Scherrer)

Aero Virgin Islands (AVI) flew N40425 (msn 14131) in scheduled passenger service between St Thomas, USVI, and San Juan, Puerto Rico, beginning in 1987.
(John P Stewart)

One of two 404s used by Aerolíneas Dominicanas SA (ADSA, also known as Dominair), at San Juan, Puerto Rico, in November 1978. HI-285 (msn 14157) remained in Caribbean inter-island passenger service throughout the 1980s. (Stephen Piercey via John P Stewart)

Air Marianas was a planned inter-island service among the Pacific Mariana Islands. Although given the resplendent markings of Air Marianas, as seen at Oakland, California, in December 1982, N147S Flagship Saipan (msn 14161) is believed to be the 404 now derelict on Saipan. (Seymour Hills via Jean-Marie Magendie)

Air Travelers Club N40427 (msn 14133) at Long Beach, California, March 1973. (Harry Sievers)

One of the land developers that used 404s to transport prospective purchasers was Ocean Pines. N542AG (msn 14175) is seen at Baltimore in June 1969 in the basic livery of an earlier operator, Aerojet-General. (J Roger Bentley via Jean-Marie Magendie)

Despite the immaculate paint of Long Beach–based charter operator California Internationale, N302FA (msn 14128) seen here at Van Nuys in March 1976, was deemed to be unairworthy because of corrosion and scrapped later that same year. (John P Stewart)

The Voyager Travel Club's N460M flew far north of its Oklahoma City home on August 8, 1971, to Toronto. (Gary Vincent)

AIRSPEEDS (KNOTS) V₁ V₂							BOUNDRY SPEEDS	
WET T.O.			DRY T.O.					
GROSS WGT.	V₁	V₂		GROSS WGT.	V₁	V₂		GROSS
		GND	AIR			GND	AIR	WGT.	B.S.
44,900	98	100	106	41,500	104	104	110	43,000	91
43,650	96	98	104	41,000	100	100	106	41,000	90
42,000	92	97	103	40,000	96	96	102	39,000	89
40,000	90	95	101	38,000	92	94	100	37,000	86
38,000	88	94	100	36,000	90	94	100	35,000	84

A crew aide-memoire *placard in the cockpit of a Provincetown–Boston Airline 404 (N40413).* (Steve Hill)

Martinliner cockpits became well-used over time. This is the rather worn flight deck of N469M (14148), taken in August 1970, after 18 years of service with Eastern Air Lines, Mohawk Airlines, and Ozark Air Lines. (Gary Vincent)

The interior of a 44-seat Provincetown–Boston Airline 404 (N40413), looking aft to the rear stairs. (Steve Hill)

The penultimate 404 built, N255S is parked at Marathon, Florida, in September 1973 in the markings of air travel club Wings Away.
(Nicky Scherrer via Jean-Marie Magendie)

Three 404s were flown to Honolulu in March 1979 for a planned inter-island service by DHL Airlines. Although N471M (msn 14112) was appropriately re-titled on one side only (the only airplane so-graced), the service never began, and the 404s were eventually scrapped. (John Wegg)

N35JS (msn 14162) was associated with several vacation-travel related operators. It is seen January 1976 in the colors of Global Air Travel Club. (John P Stewart)

N40438 (msn 14173) of Kodiak Western Alaska Airlines at Anchorage, Alaska, in January 1977 with the yellow lower fuselage of a previous operator, Fiesta Air.
(Peter R Keating via Jean-Marie Magendie)

The "Mile Hi" Club appears to have simply painted over the green Ozark Air Lines livery on N456A (msn 14147) with red—even to the point of retaining the three swallows on the fin. (Harry Sievers)

After having once served as a luxurious executive airplane of Outboard Marine Corp, msn 14134 ended its days as a meat-hauler in the fleet of Bolivian carrier Comercializasdora Aérea Mixta Boliviana Ltda (CAMBA). (via John P Stewart)

Transportes Aéreos Samuel Selem's HP-1738 El Gordo (msn 14137) was another once-elegant executive airplane flown by Whirlpool Corporation. In contrast, it is seen at Cochabamba, Bolivia, in December 1989, hauling meat. (Nicky Scherrer)

Rentavion's YV-149C (msn 14247) was the last 404 built and appropriately one of the last 404s used in commercial passenger service. The Venezuelan operator is the last to use a Martinliner of any model as a working airplane. (Hanspeter Abt)

Preserved Martins

Aware that the 202 had become extinct and numbers of 404s were dwindling, Save A Connie purchased ex-Eastern Air Lines msn 14142/N145S in 1990. Delivered to Kansas City in December that year, it was repainted in SAC's TWA-look-alike red and white house colors in August 1992 and named Skyliner Kansas City. (Wilfred C Wann/Bob Shane)

Memories of the 404 and Eastern Air Lines will continue thanks to the excellent restoration of N450A (msn 14141) by the Mid Atlantic Air Museum. The museum acquired the airplane (as N149S) from Rover Sales in April 1991, and a year later had it repainted into full Eastern colors by the West Virginia Air Center. Its first public outing was to the Experimental Aircraft Association's Sun 'n Fun fly-in at Lakeland, Florida, in April 1992. (James P Woolsey (2) & Brian Lusk)

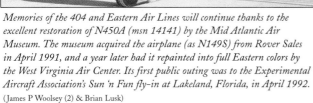

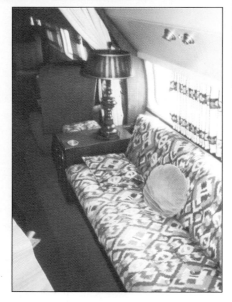

"Jeff Whitesell's Airliners of America recovered N636X (msn 14135, ex-TWA) from storage at Pueblo, Colorado, in 1994, and—after many months of hard work at Boeing Field—completed its restoration and painted it in Pacific Air Lines colors. Now based at Camarillo, California, the 404 appears regularly at West Coast air shows. (Bob Shane)

This 404 was converted for executive use for E F MacDonald with 16 seats, additional fuel capacity, and an APU, and the airplane was subsequently flown on charter work by Jeff's father, Bill Whitesell, owner of Flying W Airways. (John Wegg)

FLIGHT TESTING THE MARTINLINERS

by Jack L King

FLYING THE 'WORLD'S NEWEST AND MOST MODERN AIRLINER' was a major highlight of my early flight

career following World War II, and being assigned to the flight test certification program for the Martin

202 and 404 transports was icing on the cake.

After flying the lumbering tailwheel Douglas DC-3 and the tricycle-gear North American B-25 Mitchell, I recall the impressive contrast in available power and sleek design of the new Martin 202. It was apparent to me that the Martin design engineers had combined the best features of the famous high-speed B-26 Marauder with the latest technology, to meet the airlines's requirement for a new-generation of medium-range transport.

As speed and utility were the primary factors in the design of Martin's previous military aircraft, the original 202 did not meet the more strict CAA 04.6 certification requirements for flight stability and pilot control forces. Extensive CAA flight tests concluded that a larger tail and more wing dihedral were needed to comply with the new federal requirements. Thus it was back to the drawing board for design engineering which, in turn, required additional flight testing.

THE PRESIDENTIAL TAIL

During this era, founder and president Glenn L Martin was very much the final decision-

maker for the Martinliner program. As a confirmed bachelor, he lived with his mother and loved to spend time at his Eastern Shore home hunting ducks. Many people considered him to be somewhat eccentric, but he was well respected for his successful background as one of the US's great aviation pioneers.

When the design engineering group, headed by George Trimble, decided to construct three new vertical stabilizers for the 202—each one slightly larger than the other—it had planned to flight test the smaller one first to see if it would

The second prototype Martin 202 (N93002) after the type had been certificated. The photograph was taken at Baltimore (now BWI) before the airport was completed and was subsequently doctored by Martin's art department to depict a TWA 202A. Standing near the tail are (from left to right): George Rodney, Ed Crumpecker (flight test engineer), and Jack King.
(Martin P38332 via Jack L King)

comply with the stability test requirements. When Mr Martin was shown the three new designs under construction, he decided the larger design was more attractive and ordered it to be used. Thus, among the engineering groups, the huge new stabilizer became known as 'The Presidential Tail'.

FLYING WITH THE 'TOP GUN'

The Martin flight test department was headed by O E 'Pat' Tibbs, an excellent pilot who did not have an engineering degree but probably had more aeronautical savvy than most senior engineers. Other pilots assigned to the Martinliner program included engineering pilot George Rodney, who did most of the 202A and 404 flying. Earlier tests were flown by Tibbs, Bob Turner, 'Dutch' Gelvin, Ray Nessly, and Will Smith. Tibbs was a rather portly Texan and, when asked to appear on the television program *What's My Line?*, no one came close to guessing that he was a test pilot. I had an excellent relationship with Tibbs and we worked together to form a local QB (Quiet Birdmen) Pilots Hangar and, as a pilot, I considered him to be a 'top gun'.

Airport personnel referred to Tibbs as the 'old man', and on several occasions I was extremely pleased that he was in command. For example, during one flight in the 404 prototype, the aileron controls jammed immediately after takeoff. Tibbs told me that the control wheel would turn in one direction but would not return. Fortunately, he limited the amount of wheel displacement and told me to "inform the tower that we were doing a one-eighty and returning!" He did a wide shallow turn over the Chesapeake Bay and we briefly discussed the situation, which would be considered cockpit resource management (CRM) today. Tibbs had a tight grip with his left hand holding the displaced control wheel and his right hand on the power levers, and he directed me to lower the flaps just before touchdown. Fortunately for the downwind approach and landing, the light winds were not gusty.

The landing was normal and after taxiing to the ramp he was still holding pressure on the control wheel until mechanics could determine the cause. They discovered the jam was caused by a small quarter-inch (6mm) castellated nut, which had dropped from the spar-mounted flap unloader mechanism during an adjustment just before flight, and had lodged

between the large aileron cable pulley and the cable guard. The nut would roll against the pulley in one direction and jam in the other. Even now I shudder to think what would have happened if a less-experienced pilot had kept displacing the wheel to a greater arc.

PILOT TRAINING MANUALS

As I had done some previous aviation writing, Tibbs asked me to compile a pilots' familiarization manual for 202 and 404 airline customers. This was a rather comprehensive part-time assignment. When I was not flying, I had the opportunity to visit with various engineering and service groups in order to compile updated information covering all systems, and this was also very enlightening to me. Tibbs wrote the introduction to both manuals and for input on the chapter on flight characteristics I sat in with both Tibbs and engineering pilot George Rodney.

George Rodney (left) and Jack King in the cockpit of a 202A.
(Martin P38534 via Jack L King)

There was an ample supply of company photographs to illustrate the 202A manual; however, the 404 prototype was still being modified at the time and there were no photos available. In order to illustrate the 404 manual, I needed a selection of photos showing the 404 prototype paint design. In desperation I took a selection of 202 photos to the art department and asked them if they could apply fake 404 paint jobs. The retouched 202 photos were so realistic the art department decided to do a few more and add color for front covers of the company publication, *The Martin Star*.

I enjoyed meeting and working with the various airline pilots and representatives during the Martinliner program and was assigned to teach several training classes on the TWA Martins. I was also aboard on numerous airline pilot

The tufted wing of a 202 to show air flow over surface. The photograph was taken with flaps 45° and at a speed of 98mph (158km/h). (Martin A20335 via Jack L King)

'bounce drill' check-out flights, which were usually scheduled on weekends. Most pilots wanted to compare the Martins with their other equipment. For example, TWA captains would comment "this system is better than the Connie…" or vice versa. Several EAL captains complained that the 404 incorporated so many electrical solenoids it should be referred to as 'the flying solenoid'. One NWA captain commented that he was not sure what V_1 speed meant, but he sure knew what 'go-no go' speed meant!

SNOWED UNDER

Comprehensive icing tests had been conducted in Minneapolis during the initial CAA flight test program of the 202, but a priority schedule of retesting was initiated after Northwest Airline pilots began reporting severe icing encounters with very strange and unusual flight characteristics. Pat Tibbs had spent two weeks flying on various Northwest scheduled flights without encountering any unusual icing situations; however, the stories of strange icing encounters persisted after he returned to Baltimore.

Meanwhile, we were taking advantage of the winter weather to conduct some very unusual icing tests at the Martin Airport. We would encrust the wings and various exterior surfaces with ice by squirting a water hose during freezing weather. We also flew with various configurations of ice on one wing, football-sized obstructions anchored in the wing inboard fairing, and even large angles anchored to various locations of the wing without the violent results NWA had experienced.

In addition to a multitude of icing configurations, it was decided that we should also conduct some snow accumulation test flights for the record. On a bleak morning in February 1951, when snow began falling, we rolled the prototype 202A test ship out of the hangar to collect the ele-

On flight number 60, the 202's wings were intentionally iced to investigate the leading edge de-icer system. A fog nozzle was used to apply a rough coating of ice up to 0.5in (1.27cm) thick over the upper surface and leading edge of the left wing (top). The right wing had a thinner coat to simulate clear ice.

The takeoff was made without clearing the leading edges. About 35° of right wheel was required but no rudder was used. In a normal climb, 45–50° of right wheel was required and, with full trim tab applied, the forces were close to maximum that a pilot could apply for a continuous period.

With the left engine feathered, the right at 85% power, and flaps at takeoff setting, it was possible to hold wings level down to 120mph (193km/h). At this point the pilot had insufficient strength to apply the additional aileron that was available. In an approach to a clean stall, full right aileron was used at 110mph (177km/h). The landing approach was made at 108mph (174km/h) and the landing made without difficulty, although 90° of right wheel was used at touchdown.

During the flight, the leading edges were cleared by the use of anti-icing heaters (lower). There was little improvement noticeable in flight characteristics after the edges cleared. (Martin via Jack L King)

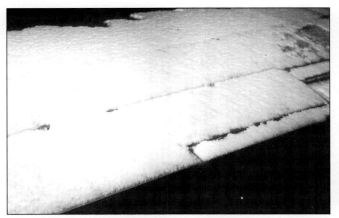

Photos taken after the 'Snowed Under' flight recounted in the text: Flight No 66 on February 7, 1951.
The top of the left wing and aileron, top of inboard portion of left wing, and the right side of the fuselage and fin.
(Martin A24243/A24244/A24245 via Jack L King)

ments. By late afternoon, there appeared to be from a half to an inch (13-25mm) of snow covering the entire aircraft. Tibbs then related that Jack LeClair, TWA's chief engineering pilot, would accompany us in the jump seat. I had great respect for Tibbs and was very pleased he would be in command during this questionable attempt to fly under these extremely adverse conditions.

We discovered that approximately 60lb (27kg) was required to hold the elevators in neutral without the engines running. We then fired up and noted the prop wash was not blowing the snow off the elevators, so Tibbs decided to make a high-speed taxi run. With the wing heaters on and taxi speeds up to 105mph (169km/h) there was still heavy wet snow on the elevators, so we had the ground crew sweep this off before taxiing back for takeoff.

The first takeoff was made to an altitude of about 5ft (1.5m) above the runway for a distance of 300ft (90m) to make sure there were no critical control conditions. Power was cut very soon after becoming airborne and we immediately taxied back for another takeoff which was made at about 105mph and a gross weight of 39,000lb (17,690kg).

By the time we became airborne, it was almost dusk and in addition to blowing snow, the air was rough as a cob as Tibbs continued to fight for control. Instrumentation indicated it took approximately 40lb (18kg) of force on the aileron control wheel for a normal turn. It was a rather wild ride and, after a few full aileron rolls were made in both directions, we returned to the airport. After landing and taxiing to the hangar it was almost dark, and when we inspected the aircraft we were surprised at the amount of snow still remaining after flight. Jack LeClair exclaimed, "Nobody— but nobody—will believe this without a photograph." So Tibbs called a company photographer.

DESTRUCTION OF THE 303

Although it was half a century ago, I still recall the mood of disbelief among employees when management announced that *everything* associated with the 303 program was being destroyed in order to take a tax write-off from the Internal Revenue Service. This covered all photographs as well as all engineering drawings, including the newly developed cabin pressurization system which would be needed later for the 404.

The new 303 one-piece straight wing had been designed for increased speed as well as to simplify production. When CAA flight tests revealed that the wing would need a complete redesign, the decision was made to scrap the project. It was later learned that other aircraft manufacturers had taken IRS tax write-offs simply by mothballing and storing unsold projects rather than ordering a complete destruction.

Before the welders moved in with their torches to start cutting up the two beautiful aircraft (only one of which had flown), a crew chief who knew I owned a gull-wing Stinson asked me if I could use some brand-new passenger belts. So I quickly unbolted quite an armload from the condemned 303 passenger cabin before the scrappers moved in.

AUTO FEATHERING WAS A HARD SELL

Most airline pilots were very apprehensive about some of the brand-new features of the Martinliners, especially automatic feathering. They expressed concern that an important function was being taken away when they lost command of the feathering button. Several airline chief pilots, including the president of ALPA, were very adamant on this new design until Pat Tibbs gave them a personal flight demonstration. It then became obvious that without engine power the huge paddle blades offered barn door-type resistance until feathered. Tibbs would demonstrate how much faster the automatic feature was than pilot response and showed how lost time, even seconds, could become extremely critical when an engine failed on takeoff.

As the Martinliners' auto feathering system was activated by only a major power loss indication from the BMEP torquemeter pressure—below 30psi (2.1kg/cm^2)—the likelihood of a false signal was much less than if activated by manifold pressure drop, when a backfire could activate the system. Although many airline pilots were still rather apprehensive about placing their trust in auto feathering, they seemed more receptive when they learned that user-friendly electrical 'remembering' circuits had been incorporated to prevent both engines from being feathered at one time.

The circuit deactivated the auto feathering system when a prop had been feathered either automatically or manually, and during the auto feathering the other prop manual feathering system was made inoperative to prevent an inadvertent feathering of the other engine.

Tibbs once made an impressive demonstration of the 202's single-engine performance at maximum gross weight with automatic feathering when he cut the left engine at V$_1$ taking off on Runway 32. He proceeded to climb out with ample altitude to clear the high tension wires at the boundary of the Martin Airport. The photo coverage made an excellent news release and helped to convince many pilots of the operational value of the automatic feathering feature.

Don Covington was chief flight test engineer on the original 202 and recalls the spectacular maximum gross single-engine takeoff demonstration at Martin. Covington was instrumental in many of the design changes and improvements to the original prototype. Unfortunately, following a serious accident in his personal aircraft, he decided to return to his family's lumber business, but he is still very active in the Martin Aviation Museum. Barney Meade took over as chief flight test engineer and directed the 202A and 404 flight test certification programs.

TIBBS MAKES A POINT

Pat Tibbs had a rather keen sense of humor and, as the director of flight test operations, seemed to enjoy resorting occasionally to unorthodox action in order to prove a point. For example, several airline pilots had complained to him about having engineering design and install a canvas curtain in the nose wheel compartment of the unpressurized 202, to prevent the rush of cold air in the cockpit during the winter when the gear was lowered. Engineering management had previously informed Tibbs that this was an unnecessary and cost-prohibitive item, so he decided he would have to take another approach.

As the chief engineer, Bill Bergen, seemed to thoroughly enjoy observing various flight test operations, Tibbs invited him along on one of the next scheduled flights to ride jump seat. It was a cold and blustery winter day and Tibbs made sure the cockpit temperature was warm and cozy as we climbed to altitude. Leveling off at about 12,500ft (3,800m), where the OAT (Outside Air Temperature) was substantially below freezing, he eased back on the power and dropped the gear. When the blast of frigid air swirled around the chief engineer he squirmed in the jump seat and blurted out, "What the hell is happening?"

Tibbs was grinning from ear to ear as he winked at me and inquired, "Jack, do you feel anything different?" By then Bergen recognized what had occurred and exclaimed, "OK, Pat, you made your point—we sure as hell need a nose wheel curtain!" Shortly after landing, Bergen placed a call to engineering at the main plant with orders to proceed with the nose gear curtain design—immediately.

PROP REVERSES IN FLIGHT

Another rather 'hairy dog story' involved a flight in which the left propeller reversed in flight while attempting to determine the single-engine minimum control speed of the 404 prototype at full gross weight. George Rodney was in command during this test, which was staged at 1,500ft (450m) over the Chesapeake Bay for smooth air and to obtain maximum power on the operating right engine. With the left propeller feathered, the minimum control speed was recorded at about 104mph (167km/h) and Rodney pulled out on the left feathering button to unfeather and resume flight.

Suddenly, a rather severe low-frequency vibration developed and I observed the prop windmilling slowly in reverse. Fortunately, the engine did not start. I told Rodney that the prop was turning in reverse and for a few moments he was not sure as he made circles with his finger to confirm the correct direction of rotation. Even with the high power we were still pulling on the right engine, we were slowly losing altitude and I was convinced we would be unable to make Martin Airport. I was familiar with the area and pointed out to Rodney there was a small private grass strip (Great Oaks Lodge) which was on the eastern shore and considerably closer than our home field.

Rodney agreed with this suggestion and we headed toward the northeast as I called the Martin tower and informed them of our intentions. Through the Unicom, I then informed our flight test engineers in the rear cabin, Barney Meade and Ed Crumpecker, and suggested they might jettison the rear step door and possibly throw out a few loose sand bags in the rear to help reduce the landing weight.

After the rear door, complete with steps, was dropped, it appeared that Rodney was already lining up on the grass strip, so I called the engineers to return to their seats. I noted from Rodney's expression that he seemed to still be in shock and his knees were shaking, but he did a remarkable job of landing the heavily loaded transport on the small grass strip with the left propeller still windmilling in reverse. After parking we noted the wheels had left their heavy footprints in the sod but, other than the missing rear door which had been jettisoned, there was no apparent damage.

A few minutes after parking we heard the distinctive rumble of the company North American AT-6 as Tibbs made a low pass over the strip. Before landing, he relayed a message to the Martin tower to send a prop specialist and a truck to haul the heavy load of lead ingots—used for ballast—back to the plant. The prop man soon discovered the discrepancy which had resulted in our close call. During a functional test that morning, a mechanic had inadvertently left a small jumper wire in the propeller junction box which was used to bypass the low-pitch electrical stops in the propeller. Thus, in flight, with this test jumper wire in place, as long as the feathering button was held out the feathering motor would continue to run, allowing the propeller to go past low pitch into reverse.

Fortunately, the huge rear door had landed in a nearby farmer's field of soft dirt and sustained no impact damage. After re-installing the rear door and removing the lead ballast, we made a ground test run and Tibbs and I flew the empty transport back to home base while Rodney ferried the AT-6. By the next day we were ready to resume the flight test program and everyone was elated that the left engine did not start in this configuration.

The CAB was very interested in the reverse prop incident as there had been several fatal airline accidents attributed to in-flight reversing, so Rodney and I were both subjected to extensive cross-examination. During my recounting of the incident, I referred to the 'forced landing' and the company lawyer came unglued. The legal expert informed me that if there was a choice of landing at any place other than the one field, the landing was 'precautionary'. So to conform, I changed my testimony accordingly.

ACCELERATE/STOP TESTS

One of the most difficult tests in the CAA 04.b certification tests of the Martinliners was establishing the minimum runway length requirements for landing, as well as stopping after an aborted takeoff after losing one engine at V_1. During this era there were no anti-skid devices, so it was extremely difficult to avoid a skid while applying maximum braking, and it took only a momentary wheel stoppage to go through several tire plys. We were averaging about only three to six stops before replacing scrubbed tires when flight test engineering developed a 'Rube Goldberg' fix.

This fix involved placing small studs about one inch (2.5cm) apart, extending from each outboard wheel rim and incorporating a small microswitch. This had an extension arm which would strike the studs as the wheels turned and illuminate lights in the cockpit. Thus, a blinking light indicated the respective wheel was turning and, if the light was either out or was full on, it was a signal to back off on the brake pressure. This crude, but workable, anti-skid indicator developed almost 50 years ago was probably another 'Martin first' and George Rodney was the first pilot to develop a foot feel for its use.

During the early accelerate/stop tests, there was a need to know the exact location of the aircraft when we reached V_1 speed and started maximum braking, so it was suggested that I try throwing a 5lb (2.3kg) bag of flour from the right cockpit window to mark the exact location on the runway. It does not take much imagination to visualize the ensuing fiasco. Flight test engineering then obtained theodolite instrumentation which photographed the takeoff and stopping on a grid. The V_1 location was marked by activating a photo flash bulb in a cabin window.

Braking tests confirmed that disc brakes held up better than brake shoes and, during several maximum braking efforts, I witnessed the metal brake disc turning from cherry red to almost transparent. During a couple of max stops we also experienced substantial fire in the landing gear caused by ruptured or melted hydraulic brake lines and, on the first incident, it was thought that the airport fire department may have ruined the heat treat of one gear assembly by using too much extinguishing fluid. Flight test engineers cautioned the fire departments that the fire would have gradually dissipated when the brake fluid was consumed; however, I thought their action appropriate as it appeared to me we could have lost the airplane.

Incidentally, we discovered that the favorable correction factor allowed by the CAA for conducting the landing and stopping tests downwind (up to 10kt/18km/h) was definitely to our advantage, so all tests were accomplished downwind and the data corrected accordingly.

SAWTOOTH CLIMBS

Many CAA certification flight tests involved repetitive performance flights under slightly different configurations. For example, single-engine performance required a vast number of tests to be conducted at various configurations of gross weight altitude, power, gear, and flap settings to determine the various segment and en route climb performance. With the left engine feathered, each climb of approximately 5min or 2,000ft (600m) was followed by a descent to the starting altitude for another run.

These tests were referred to as 'sawtooth climbs' as this was the way the tracings would appear on a VGTA flight recorder. As many climbs were based upon 'wet engine' performance, two additional ADI tanks were installed in the cabin to provide ample fluid for many repeat climbs.

The right engine was determined to be more critical to performance, so during all single-engine climb performance tests the left engine would be feathered while the right engine became the workhorse. On a typical program of repetitive sawtooth climbs, most of the climb performance would be based upon the right engine pulling maximum takeoff wet power, which required the extra ADI fluid.

Smooth air was a prime requirement for conducting most engineering performance and stability test flights. When calibrated airspeed was critical, we used a nose boom with a swiveling airspeed head and lowered a trailing airspeed bomb below the aircraft in undisturbed air. For extended periods we took off at 0500 to take advantage of the stable air. Pat Tibbs would always be present for our pre-dawn takeoff and usually would offer some comment about "flying the world's most modern aircraft to meet the sunrise." We did observe that he had a small cot installed next to his office and we suspected that while we were maneuvering on scheduled tests waiting for the sunrise, he was catching an early morning nap.

WALKING GEAR EASES TOUCHDOWN

Hard landing reports had been a complaint of many earlier 202 airline passengers and some pilots related that the CAA approved approach speed was too slow to allow for a proper flare. Several airline pilots discovered they could make much smoother landings in the 202 by increasing the 1.3 V_{SO} (1.3 times the stalling speed with flaps at landing setting) approach speed by some 10mph (16km/h) to allow more time for the touchdown flare; however, during routine CAA check rides this technique was not approved for obvious reasons. At the factory, Pat Tibbs developed a knack for making grease landings with the 202 through a combination of precise flare timing and the correct approach speed.

With the advent of the larger and pressurized 404, management decided to incorporate a new landing gear which had been used successfully for improving landings on the Lockheed Constellation. The new 'walking gear' not only moved up and down to cushion the landing, but also moved forward and aft so power and brakes had to be applied smoothly, especially during engine run-ups, to avoid lurching. I recall riding right seat with Tibbs while he developed a feel for using the exact combination of power and brakes to keep the gear where he wanted it without the 'walking' action.

FLIGHT TEST INSTRUMENTATION

One of the most important phases of flight testing is that of instrumentation. As the primary mission is that of collecting data, the test can only be as successful as the precision of the equipment used for measurement. Most of the basic principles of physics are involved, especially the science of applied aero-physics comprised of the units of measurement: length, mass, time, hydrostatics, fluids, pressures, temperatures, densities, velocities, acceleration and rate, as well as limited magnetism and gyroscopic principles.

Much of the data were displayed on a large, lighted instrument panel, located in the passenger cabin where flight test engineers could sequence a movie camera as needed. Practically everything that moves was connected to a position transmitter which provided a calibrated readout on the photo panel. During tests requiring temperature data, a Brown recorder could be activated to record thermocouples as needed. Pilot wheel forces were read directly from a hand-held force indicator reading in pounds/ounces, which was developed by the flight test engineering group.

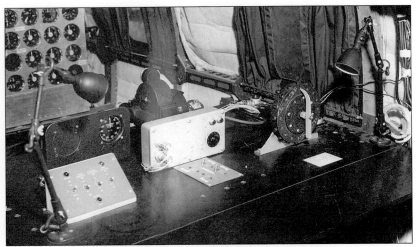

Photo panel of the 202 flight test engineer's position.
(Martin 98243, dated January 14, 1947, via Jack L King)

The Martin flight test engineering group designed and patented several highly specialized instrumentation equipment designs used in flight testing the company's airplanes. Before being assigned to the Martinliner flight group as engineering co-pilot/flight engineer, I worked with the flight test engineering laboratory group, where I developed several systems and patented two designs. I was awarded the prestigious Purple Martin Award for scientific achievement for patenting a jet engine thrust dynomometer and a direct geared autosyn position transmitter. A model of the position transmitter, along with the original $5 award check, is on display at the Martin Aviation Museum.

TWA ENGINE CRISIS

When the TWA 202As were being completed, the routine production flight test indicated that both engines on certain aircraft would become rough and misfire when power was reduced for the landing approach. As TWA already had several aircraft in service, there was an obvious urgency to correct the discrepancy and—after several days of round-the-clock testing—the Pratt & Whitney representative had not come up with an answer. Joining the witch-hunt, I stopped over at the main plant in the engine build-up section and questioned the mechanics about anything being different on the TWA series of engines. The lead man did recall that no one had specified what spark plugs to use, so they were using up some of their wartime surplus supply. I soon confirmed the 'popping' engines had BG plugs and the others had Champions.

I returned to the airport happy with my 'discovery' and

related the information to the flight test engineer, Barney Meade, and engineering pilot, George Rodney. It was late Friday afternoon and they both wanted to go sailing rather than make another test flight to confirm the discrepancy, so we agreed to wait until Monday. After they left I discussed what I had found with F O 'Fuzz' Furman, who headed ground test, and he was convinced enough without another flight test to call TWA in Kansas City and suggest the spark plugs were changed on the airplanes that had been misfiring on approach. The crisis was over.

When the first Martin 202A was delivered to TWA, I made the flight to Kansas City with a TWA senior captain and remember the enthusiastic reception the new aircraft received from the airline's employees. Apparently they moved everything that would move, including several systems which should not have been activated. The next day I rode jump seat on a scheduled TWA Connie back to Baltimore and received a first-hand briefing of how the big Lockheed compared to the Martin.

CG RANGE EXCEPTIONAL

Gross weight and center of gravity (CG) location were obvious key factors in all tests, so each flight was loaded accordingly. Large lead ingots were bolted to the floor at passenger seat locations and a few sand bags were carried occasionally to make minor changes in flight. Extensive tests indicated the 202 had an exceptionally wide CG range, from 12.4% to 37% MAC (Mean Aerodynamic Chord), which allowed passengers to sit anywhere during flight. On one occasion before flight when the 202 test ship had been loaded for an aft CG investigation flight at 37%, two engineers walked to the tail section to check on a project item and caused the aircraft to settle full nose up before the startled engineers hastily retreated.

THE 'LUNAL' SPOILER

Sometimes an unusual incident can help break the routine of day-to-day flight operations. After many stall tests indicated the need for a small inboard wing nose spoiler, engineering developed a rather simple section made up from sheet metal that helped meet the stall warning requirements. Pat Tibbs suggested the flight test engineers should provide a name for the new spoiler, so one of the engineers with an extensive vocabulary started searching his engineering reference book and came up with the name 'lunal', which means 'bent-up section'.

Soon the marketing department heard of this terminology and decided to add the lunal spoiler as a new feature of the Martinliners. As Eastern Air Lines was negotiating for a substantial 404 order, its chief executive, Captain Eddie Rickenbacker, was discussing the features of the airplane with his chief engineer when the lunal spoiler was mentioned.

Captain Eddie did not want to admit to his chief engineer that he was unaware of this new spoiler, so after the meeting was over he phoned Glenn Martin to ask, "Glenn, what the hell is this new lunal spoiler on the 404?" Mr Martin did not know either, so he asked Captain Eddie to hold while he called Tibbs for an explanation. Tibbs later enjoyed relating this story of the confusing lunal spoilers at pilot gatherings.

EPILOGUE

In addition to flying the 202 and 404, I was also assigned to the flight test crew of the XP4M-1 Mercator, a four-engine Navy patrol airplane with two large P&W R-4360 'corncob' radials plus two Allison jet engines. As the 404 test program was phasing out and when the prospect for new developments appeared dim, I took a position as chief pilot with a local construction company, operating DC-3 and Fairchild F-27 corporate transports (and later flew a Cessna Citation) and continued to operate from the Martin Airport for several decades.

Although all the senior pilots associated with the Martinliner flight test program have since 'Gone West', I still enjoy attending the monthly meetings of the Glenn L Martin Aviation Museum (in the basement of Hangar 5 at the now renamed Martin State Airport) and reminiscing with fellow members about the 'good old days'.

In retrospect, I have concluded that in more than 20,000 hours of transport flying the most enlightening and enjoyable experience was the time spent test flying the Martinliners. I recall what the legendary Capt Dick Merrill told me when I was writing his biography *Wings Of Man*: "It's not the destination but the journey which will be remembered."

(John Wegg)

FLYING THE MARTINS: THE AIRLINE PERCEPTION

COLD STATISTICS CAN INDICATE WHETHER AN AIRLINER HAS BEEN AN ECONOMIC SUCCESS; however, they do not tell the whole story. The missing ingredient is how the airplanes were perceived by the people who came in contact with them—the flight crews, the cabin attendants, the ground personnel, and the paying passengers. Unfortunately for the 202s and 404s, these perceptions were, in many instances, less than objective.

During the Northwest era, there were the accidents that gave the 202 a reputation for being accident-prone. (The contrasting trouble-free service with LAN and LAV was generally overlooked in that regard.) Although the Winona accident was caused by a major structural flaw, that deficiency was quickly corrected, and it would never again cause an accident. Some of the accidents were caused by operational or maintenance errors. Those were not the fault of the 202s, and they would probably have occurred regardless of whether the airplanes flown were 202s, Convair 240s, or any other type. Nevertheless, the 202s were perceived by flight crews and passengers as being unsafe airplanes. They were also associated later with the financial problems of California Central Airlines and Pioneer Air Lines.

The 404s were never burdened with a bad reputation, but they were less successful than the competing Convair 340s. Because they were second-best, some people tended to focus on their shortcomings and overlook the areas in which they were superior. Others reacted in just the opposite manner, viewing them as the underdog. The time-frame is also significant as far as the perceptions were concerned. During the early years, pilots who were thankful that they had finally worked up from DC-3s were undoubtedly more charitable than those who, 30 years later, regretted that they were not flying the latest in turbine-powered equipment.

Perceptions were also influenced in the early years by whether one worked for an airline that operated 404s or a competitor with Convair-Liners. In later years, perceptions were influenced by the make, Martin or Convair, with which a person first became familiar.

With these different perceptions in mind, it must be recognized that some will disagree with the following views; however, they seem to be the general consensus of the people involved with the 202s and 404s.

The first persons, other than Martin personnel, to come in contact with the 202s were the flight crews of Northwest Airlines. Some of the candidates for 202 type ratings may have had World War II military experience flying Boeing B-29s or Douglas C-54s. Most, however, were DC-3 pilots. For them, tricycle landing gears and reversible propellers were new experiences. All of the pilots were introduced to autofeather in the 202. Other unique features included hot air anti-icing systems, built-in control-system gust-locks, high-lift flaps, and a very respectable cruising speed of nearly 300mph (250kt/480km/h).

Initially, Northwest pilots were quite enthusiastic about the 202s. After all, they were the only line pilots flying modern, twin-engine airliners anywhere in the world. (That distinction was short-lived, however. LAN and LAV placed their 202s in service a short time later, and other airlines began service with Convair 240s.) Their early enthusiasm diminished somewhat as the typical service-introduction difficulties were experienced. Complaints included cockpit noise, excessive instrument panel vibration, an extremely stiff landing gear that made a smooth landing almost impossible, poor airframe anti-ice capability, and a host of other difficulties that ranged from nuisances to serious problems.

Ground personnel appreciated the design precautions taken to facilitate maintenance of the 202s, but they had the unenviable task of coping with all the early service difficulties. Although the outer wing panel attachment fitting problems were solved from a safety standpoint, the fittings remained a maintenance nuisance because they could not be sealed effectively and would collect moisture. At intermediate stops, the integral stairs, carry-on baggage compartments, and single-point refueling provisions were particularly appreciated. The underfloor cargo compartments were easy to reach from the ground, but this advantage was mitigated somewhat by the small size of their doors.

Flight attendants were quick to note that the original 40-passenger cabin arrangement of the 202s was inadequate insofar as the galley and lavatory installations were concerned. That was soon corrected, albeit with a loss of four revenue passenger seats.

TWA pilots were probably more objective about the 202As their company placed in service. Many of the early service difficulties had been corrected by then, and the 202As were expected to be interim equipment that would be returned to Martin just as soon as the 404s were delivered. Flying the 202As undoubtedly helped to foster an appreciation for the definitive 404s.

Although they were similar enough to enable flight crews to have common 202/404 type ratings, the 404s came on the scene with many improvements. In contrast to the 202s, pilots generally considered 404s to be excellent airplanes to fly. They were solid and stable in flight with well-balanced controls. Minimum control speed (V_{mc}) was down to about 100mph (85kt/160km/h), and rudder pedal forces were relatively light with one engine inoperative. Ground operation was good because of the excellent steering and cockpit visibility of the 404s. Pilots appreciated the fact that

it was possible to make respectable landings with 404s as a result of the redesigned landing gear shock strut assemblies. The pilots also liked the quiet, comfortable cockpits of the 404s. Cockpit visibility was improved; and the 404s were, of course, pressurized.

Ground personnel generally liked the 404s as well. They were easy to service on turnarounds, although the propeller blast made unloading and reloading the underfloor cargo compartments rather uncomfortable during quick turnarounds with one engine running. The underfloor compartments of the Convairs would present the same problem, but those airplanes also had externally accessed rear fuselage compartments that could be used instead. The outer wing panel attachment fittings continued to be a source of corrosion; however, they were greatly improved in that regard compared to those of the 202s.

There were, of course, the inevitable comparisons of the 404s with contemporary Convair 340s and 440s. Preferences in that respect varied considerably. Eastern flight crews and ground personnel apparently preferred the 404s to their later 440s. Mohawk flight crews, on the other hand, seemed to prefer the Convair twins in their fleet.

The 404s were especially appreciated by passengers because they were quieter than the Convair twins. An acquaintance, who was not particularly aviation-oriented, once remarked to the writer that the Eastern Air Lines 'Convair' with the passenger entry steps in the tail (obviously an erroneous reference to one of its 404s) was much quieter than those with the steps at the forward end of the cabin!

Popular as they were with passengers and ground crew members, the ventral stairs would prove to be a source of embarrassment for at least two Martin flight crews. One 404 captain was fined $100 in 1961 after taxiing from the gate with the ventral stairs dragging on the apron. While this was taking place, the flight attendant was left at the gate, waving and yelling for him to stop. The author witnessed an Aerojet-General crew commit a similar *faux pas* on the AiResearch apron of Los Angeles International Airport a few months earlier. Because that event happened at dusk, the sparks from the dragging stairs were quite spectacular.

COCKPIT CHECK LISTS & AIRPLANE FLIGHT MANUAL EXTRACTS

The following excerpt from the *CAA Approved Flight Manual for the Martin 202NW Airplane* is representative of the check lists for the Martin 202.

PRIOR TO STARTING ENGINES

a. Emergency brake - OFF

b. Emergency hydraulic pump - operative

c. Hydraulic pressure - 1500 psi

d. Parking brake - set

e. Hydraulic reservoir - full

f. Airspeed - static source

g. Pump selector - air speed

h. Fuel selectors - normal

i. Fuel quantity - per manifest

j. Master electrical switch - ON

k. External power light - ON

l. Battery switch - ON

m. Inverter power - ON

n. Generator warning light - ON

o. Generator field switch - ON

p. Cowl flaps - open

q. Oil cooler shutter - as desired

r. Booster pumps - OFF

s. Mixtures - idle cut off

t. Smoke and fire detectors checked - warning lights out

PRIOR TO TAKEOFF

a. Water pressure - OK

b. Mixture - auto rich

c. Fuel pumps - as desired

d. Fuel selector - normal

e. Props - automatic - 2800

f. Auto-feathering - ON

g. Supercharger - check and set low

h. Flaps - takeoff position

i. Hydraulic pressure - OK

j. Tabs - neutral

k. Battery light - ON

l. Generator warning light OUT - generator operating

m. Inverter power - ON

n. Carburetor air - DIRECT (COLD)

o. Oil cooler shutters - as desired

p. Gust lock - OFF

q. Cowl flap - in takeoff position

r. Anti-icers - as needed

s. Controls - free

PRIOR TO LANDING

a. Hydraulic by-pass - closed

b. Mixture - auto-rich

c. Fuel pumps - as desired

d. Carburetor air - DIRECT (COLD)

e. Gear down

f. Brakes checked and OFF

g. Supercharger low

h. Cowl flaps - as required

i. Oil cooler flaps - as required

j. Wing flaps - approach

k. Wing flaps - landing

l. Props full low pitch before touchdown

02.05.02
Jan-16-57

FORM 0-1105-M-404 (12-56)

MARTIN
FLEGHT CREW OPERATING MANUAL
CPCKPIT CHECK LIST - 404
M-404 CHECK LIST
BEFORE STARTING ENGINES

Necessary to only read "starred" items below at intermediate station if no crew change or mechanical delay.

1.	LOG BOOK (M-76) ....CK	
2.	CIRCUIT BREAKERS ....ON	
3.	HYD. QUANTITY ....CK	
4. *	BATTERY SEL ....EXT PWR	
5. *	GEN. SWITCHES ....ON	
6. *	LOAD CONTROL & ESS. RADIO SWS ....ON	
7. *	INVERTER ....CK & ON	
8. *	HORIZONS ....ERECT	
9. *	NAVIGATION LIGHTS ....CK	
10. *	ANTI-COLLISION LIGHTS ....OFF	
11. *	FIRE WARNING ....TEST	
12.	SEAT BELT - NO SMOKING ....ON	
13.	LANDING LIGHTS ....CK & OFF	
14.	AIR SCOOP HEATERS ....CK & OFF	
15.	PITOT HEATERS ....CK & OFF	
16. *	OIL COOLER FLAPS ....AS REQ	
17. *	COWL FLAPS ....OPEN	
18.	ENGINE BLOWERS ....LOW	
19. *	IGNITION SWITCHES ....OFF	
20. *	EMERG. SHUT-OFFS & CO$_2$ SEL ....IN	
21.	MIXTURES ....OFF	
22.	CARBURETOR AIR ....COLD	

23.	FUEL VALVES ....NORMAL
24.	AILERON BOOST ....ON
25.	HYD. BYPASS ....FORWARD
26.	WINDSHIELD WIPER FLOOR VALVE ....OPEN
27. *	PARKING BRAKE ....ON
28.	RMI HEADING SOURCE ....NORMAL
29. *	DEVIATION INDICATOR SEL ....CK
30. *	ADI QUANTITY ....CK
31.	STATIC SEL ....NORMAL
32. *	FUEL QUANTITY ....CK
33. *	OIL QUANTITY ....CK
34. *	ALCOHOL QUANTITY ....CK
35.	EMERG. FLAP SEL ....SAFETIED FORWARD
36.	EMERG. PUMP SEL ....SAFETIED NORMAL
37. *	COMP. POWER ....LOW
38. *	CABIN ALTITUDE ....RESET
39. *	AIRFLOW SELECTOR ....AS REQ
40.	OXYGEN PRESSURE ....980 MIN
41.	WARNING LIGHTS ....PUSH TEST
42. *	NAVIGATIONAL RADIO & SWITCHES ....ON & CK
43.	COMMUNICATION RADIO ....CK
44.	ALTIMETERS & CLOCKS ....CK
45. *	GROSS WEIGHT ...._____LBS

AFTER STARTING ENGINES

1.	DOOR LIGHTS ....OUT		4.	BATTERY SEL ....BATT
2.	COMP. OIL PRESSURE ....CK		5.	FUEL PUMPS ....OFF
3.	HYD. SYSTEM ....CK		6.	ANTI-COLLISION LIGHTS ....AS REQ
			7.	VENT. FANS ....AS REQ

BEFORE TAKE OFF

1.	FLUXGATE COMPASSES ....ERECT & CK		11.	FLAPS ................................T.O.
2.	GENERATORS ....CK		12.	BLOWERS ....CK & LOW
3.	HOR. EMERG. POWER ....CK & NORMAL		13.	COMPRESSOR POWER ....LOW
4.	TRIM TABS ....CK		14.	A.D.I. ....ON
5.	MIXTURES ....RICH		15.	FUEL PUMPS ....HIGH
6.	CARBURETOR AIR ....COLD		16.	AIR FLOW SELECTOR ....PRESS FLIGHT
7.	PROP GOV ....FULL INC		17.	RIGHT VENT FAN ....OFF
8.	AUTO FEA. SYSTEM ....ON & TEST		18.	FLIGHT CONTROLS ....FREE
9.	MANUAL FEA. SYSTEM ...PUSH-PULL-NEUTRAL		19.	V$_1$ & V$_2$ FOR GROSS WEIGHT ....CK
10.	ENGINE RUN-UP ....NORMAL		20.	COWL FLAPS ....FLUSH

AFTER TAKE OFF

1.	AUTO FEATHER ....OFF		4.	WING FLAPS ....UP (500-1200 FT.)
2.	COMPRESSOR POWER ....HIGH		5.	FUEL PUMPS ....OFF
3.	A.D.I. ....OFF		6.	SEAT BELT SIGN ....OFF
			7.	CABIN PRESSURE ....CK

POWER SETTINGS

TAKE-OFF WET 59.5" ....2800 RPM
DRY 55" ....2700 RPM
FIRST REDUCTION 48" ....2600 RPM
CLIMB - LOW BLOWER 172 BMEP ......2300 RPM
900 F/F
HIGH BLOWER 160 BMEP ....2300 RPM
820 F/F

V$_1$ & V$_2$ - WET POWER

G.W.	V$_1$	KTS	V$_2$	KTS
	S.L.	6000	GROUND	AIR
43650	96		98	104
42000	92	97	97	103
40000	90	92	95	101
38000	88	90	94	100

M-404 CHECK LIST

BEFORE LANDING - PRELIMINARY

1. LANDING GEAR LIGHTS . . . . TEST
2. SEAT BELT SIGN . . . . ON
3. PARKING BRAKE . . . . OFF
4. EMERG. BRAKE PRESSURE . . . . 1250#
5. TWI . . . . CK
6. DEVIATION IND. SEL. . . . . CK
7. STATIC SELECTOR . . . . NORMAL

8. ALTIMETERS . . . . SET
9. FUEL VALVES . . . . NORMAL
10. HYDRAULIC SYS. PRESS. . . . . 1200 MIN
11. ANTI-ICER HEATERS . . . . CK
12. ENGINE BLOWERS . . . . LOW
13. MIXTURES . . . . RICH
14. LANDING WEIGHT. . . . . CK
15. BOUNDARY SPEED. . . . . CK

BEFORE LANDING - FINAL

1. GEAR AND FLAPS. . . . . DOWN
2. PROPS . . . . AS REQ
3. A.D.I. . . . . AS REQ
4. CARBURETOR AIR . . . . AS REQ

5. CABIN PRESSURE . . . . CK
6. COMPRESSOR POWER. . . . . LOW
7. VENT FANS . . . . RT. FAN OFF
8. SEAT BELT - NO SMOKING SIGN . . . . ON

AFTER LANDING

1. FLAPS . . . . UP
2. PROPS . . . . FULL INC
3. COWL FLAPS . . . . OPEN

4. PROP DEICERS & ANTI-ICERS. . . . . OFF
5. A.D.I. . . . . OFF

SECURE COCKPIT

1. PARKING BRAKE . . . . ON
2. IDLE ENGINES . . . . 30 SEC
3. FLIGHT CONTROLS . . . . LOCKED
4. IGNITION . . . . OFF
5. ANTI-COLLISION LIGHTS . . . . OFF
6. PITOT & SCOOP HEATERS. . . . . OFF

7. INVERTER AND RADIO . . . . OFF
8. VENT FANS . . . . AS REQ
9. CABIN HEATERS . . . . OFF
10. WINDSHIELD VALVES . . . . OFF
11. BATTERY SWITCH . . . . EXT PWR
12. REPLACE NAV. KIT ITEMS

CABIN HEATER OPERATION ON GROUND AFTER FUELING

1. VENT FAN . . . . .ON
2. HEATER SWITCH .AUTO
3. FUEL SELECTION . . . . .L OR R

4. FUEL BOOST PUMP .LOW
5. WINDSHIELD CONTROL . . . . .DOWN

TAXI COOL

1. AIRFLOW SELECTOR . . . . TAXI COOL
2. VENT FANS . . . . BOTH ON

3. COMPRESSOR POWER . . . . HIGH
4. ENGINE RPM. . . . . BOTH 100 RPM

* * *

EASTERN AIR LINES INC.
AIRPLANE FLIGHT MANUAL   M404
C.A.A. APPROVED

OPERATING LIMITATIONS
OBSERVANCE OF THESE LIMITATIONS IS REQUIRED BY LAW

1. WEIGHT LIMITS

A. Maximum Take-Off Weight

The maximum take-off weights at sea level, with automatic propeller feathering operative, are:

  41,500 pounds with DRY engine rating.
  44,900 pounds with WET engine rating.

B. Maximum Landing Weight

The maximum landing weights at sea level are:
40,200 pounds with DRY engine rating.
43,000 pounds with WET engine rating.
Take-off and landing weights given above are maximum permissible but may be restricted by runway lengths or flight path obstructions. For maximum permissible weights at various altitudes see Section 3. In scheduled passenger flight operation operating weights are limited in accordance with Civil Aeronautics Regulations, parts 41 and 61.

C. Loading

This airplane is to be operated in accordance with the approved loading schedule.

D. Gross Weight - Zero Fuel

All weight in excess of 41,000 pounds must consist of fuel for structural reasons except that this value may be increased to 42,500 pounds if speeds V_{NE} and V_{NO} are properly reduced. (See Section 1-4B and C).

E. Fuel Distribution

All fuel must be distributed equally on both sides of the airplane within a tolerance of 200 gallons.

2. CENTER OF GRAVITY LIMITS

A. Loading. The airplane must be loaded at all times in accordance with the following limitations:

Condition	Gross Weight	Landing Gear	C. G. Limit % Mac	C. G. Limit Inches from Datum
Take-off	44,900	Down	19.8-37.5	440.2 - 461.4
Take-off and	43,000	Down	19.0-37.5	439.2 - 461.4
Landing	38,000	Down	17.0-37.5	436.8 - 461.4
Climb & Cruise	All Weights	Up	13.5-37.5	432.6 - 461.4

The datum for the above C. G. limits is fuselage station zero. (87 inches forward of nose).

Figure 1-1. Loading Limits

3. Power Plant
A. Power Limits

BLOWER	OPERATING CONDITION	BHP	RPM	MAP	ALT	MIX	TIME LIMIT
LOW	Take-Off Dry	2050	2700	55	SL	AR	2 Min.
	Take-Off Dry	2050	2700	53	6900	AR	2 Min.
	Take-Off Wet	2400	2800	59.5	SL	AR	2 Min.
	Take-Off Wet	2400	2800	59	5000	AR	2 Min.
	Maximum Continuous	1800	2600	48.5	SL	AR	None
	Maximum Continuous	1800	2600	46.5	9200	AR	None

Figure 1-2. CAA Approved Manufacturers Ratings

EASTERN AIR LINES INC.
AIRPLANE FLIGHT MANUAL M404
C. A. A. APPROVED

PAGE 2
SECTION 1
DATE 9-1-52

B. Engine

Manufacturer . . . . Pratt and Whitney
Model . . . . R2800 CB 3
Propeller Gear Ratio 0.450
Minimum Octane Fuel 100/130
Oil Grade. . . . . AN-0-8 Grade 1100/1120

C. Propeller

Manufacturer. . . . . Hamilton Standard
Model
  Hub 43E60
  Blade . . . . 6895A - 12
Pitch Settings (Sta. 42")
  Low . . . . +30.5°
  Feather. . . . . +95°
  Reverse. . . . . -11°
Governor Setting (Max)
  WET take-off power. . . . . 2800 RPM
  DRY take-off power . . . . 2700 RPM

D. Anti-Detonant System

Minimum ADI fluid for WET take-off is 11.2 gallons. Normal operating ADI fluid pressure is 21 - 23 PSI.
Discontinue WET take-off if ADI system malfunctions below speed V_1.

E. Instrument Markings

Tachometer   **RPM**
Maximum for WET take-off power
  Long radial red line. 2800
Maximum for DRY take-off power
  Short radial red line 2700
Precautionary range
  Yellow arc 2600-2800
Normal operating range
  Green arc 1400-2600

Manifold Pressure   **in/Hg.**
Maximum for WET take-off power
  Long radial red line 59.5
Maximum for DRY take-off power
  Short radial red line 55
Precautionary range
  Yellow arc. . . . . 48.5 - 55
Normal operating range
  Green arc 30-48.5

Cylinder Head Temperature   **°C**
Maximum for flight
  Radial red line 260
Maximum for ground
  Radial yellow line 202
Normal operating range
  Green arc 60-232

Oil Inlet Temperature   **°C**
Maximum
  Radial red line 100
Normal operating range
  Green arc 40-85

Carburetor Air Temperature   **°C**
Maximum low blower
  Low radial red line 38
Precautionary range
  Yellow arc. . . . . -5 to +10
Normal operating range
  Green arc . . . . 10 to 38

Oil Pressure   **PSI**
Maximum limit
  Radial red line 110
Minimum limit
  Radial red line 25
Normal operating range
  Green arc 75-100

Fuel Pressure   **PSI**
Maximum limit
  Radial red line. 23.5
Minimum limit
  Radial red line 17
Normal operating range
  Green arc . . . . 21 - 23

4. SPEED LIMITATIONS

All speed limitation values are in terms of calibrated airspeed.

A. Airspeed Indicator Markings   **KNOTS**
Maximum never exceed speed
  Radial red line 261
Range of V_{NE} depending on "gross weight - zero fuel"
  Red arc 247-261
Caution range extending from minimum V_{NO} to maximum V_{NE}
  Yellow arc 214-261
Normal operating range - extending from V_{S1} with flaps retracted to maximum V_{NO} value
  Green arc 91-230
Flaps extended speed - extending from V_{SO} with flaps in extended position to maximum V_{FE}
  White arc. . . . . 73 - 130

B. Never Exceed Speed (V_{NE})

Maximum limit up to 20,000 feet. . . . . 261 Knots
Above 20,000 feet, reduce maximum limit 5 Knots per 1000 ft. to maintain constant Mach Number.
V_{NE} varies with "Gross Weight-Zero Fuel" as shown in Figure 1-3.

Speeds in excess of these values may result in structural, flutter or control hazards.

PAGE 3
SECTION 1

DATE 3-28-52

EASTERN AIR LINES INC.
AIRPLANE FLIGHT MANUAL   M404
C.A.A. APPROVED

C. Normal Operating Speed (V_{NO})

Maximum limit up to 20,000 fee   230 Knots.
Above 20,000 feet reduce maximum limit by 5.0 Knots per 1000 ft.
to maintain constant Mach Number. V_{NO} varies with "Gross
Weight-Zero Fuel" as shown in Figure 1-3.

Speeds in excess of these values may result in excessive gust
loads whereas speeds below these values will reduce the loads
produced by severe gusts. These speeds should not be deliberate-
ly exceeded even during descent because of the possibility of
unexpected gusts. The speed range between V_{NO} and V_{NE} is to
provide for inadvertent speed increases.

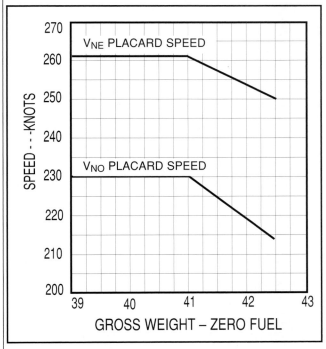

Figure 1-3 Speed Limitations

D. Maneuvering Speed (V_A)

Maximum deflection of primary controls must be confined to
speeds below 156 Knots.

E. Flaps Extended Speed (V_{FE})

Maximum speeds for operation with the wing flaps extended are
as follows:
0 to "TAKE-OFF"............................ 165 Knots
"TAKE-OFF" to "LANDING".................... 130 Knots

The upper limit of the white arc on the airspeed indicator corre-
sponds to 130 Knots.

F. Landing Light Extended Speed

Maximum speed with landing lights extended is 165 Knots.

G. Landing Gear Operating Speed (V_{LO})

The following speeds should not be exceeded during the landing
gear operation:
    Extension and Operation With
    Gear Extended (V_{LE}) .... 165 Knots
    Retraction .... 156 Knots
    Emergency Extension .... 113 Knots

5. CRITICAL CROSS WINDS

See Section 3.

6. FLIGHT LOAD ACCELERATION LIMITS

The positive limit load factors due to airplane structure are:

Gross Weight	Flaps Up	Flaps Down
44900	2.75g	2.00g
43000	2.85g	2.00g

7. TYPE OF OPERATION

As certificated, this airplane is eligible for operation
as follows:

a. Transport category, scheduled air carrier passenger operations.

b. Day and night, visual and instrument operations.

c. Overland operation. Overwater operation in accordance with
   the provisions of CAR 40.59 and CAR 43.30.

d. Icing conditions: - NACA light. (Equivalent to boot equipped
   airplanes for dispatching purposes).

8. MAXIMUM ALTITUDE

The maximum altitude at which this airplane has been demonstrated is 25,000 feet. Consequently, operation is limited to altitudes
not in excess of this value.

9. MINIMUM CREW

The minimum flight crew required for safe operation of this airplane is two, pilot and co-pilot.

10. ANTI-ICING HEATER LIMITATIONS

Due to structural limitations, the anti-icing heaters are to be used
in flight within the following limitations:

No. of Heaters in Operation	Maximum Outside Air Temperature
1	60ºC
2	29ºC
3	13ºC
4	2ºC

EASTERN AIR LINES INC.
AIRPLANE FLIGHT MANUAL   M404
C. A. A. APPROVED

PAGE 4
SECTION 1

DATE 9-10-51

11. AIR CONDITIONING, HEATING AND VENTILATING

A. Cabin Compressor Power Switch

Cabin compressor power switch in "LOW" for all take-offs and landings.

B. Maximum Cabin Pressure Differential

Maximum cabin pressure differential - - - - - - - - - 3.25 psi

C. Cabin Compressor Operating Limits

	Oil Pressure	Oil Temperature
Minimum	60 Psi	-6.7°C (20°F)
Normal	70-80 Psi	
Maximum	100 Psi	107°C (225°F)

D. Cabin Heaters

Do not operate heaters if airflow selector is in "TAXI-COOL" position.

E. Cabin Altimeter Marking

1. Radial Red Line denotes maximum pressurized cabin altitude - 14,000 ft.
2. Yellow Arc denotes cabin altitude range in which oxygen is required in accordance with CAR 61. - 10,000 feet to 14,000 ft.

12. STABILIZER - WING FLAP SYNCHRONIZATION

Do not initiate take-off if the stabilizer "OUT-OF PHASE" indicator light is on.

13. PLACARDS

The following placards are appropriate to this airplane.

A. Automatic Propeller Feathering

This placard is located on the overhead switch panel.

> **LIGHTS ON FOR ALL TAKE-OFF OPERATIONS**

B. Emergency Gear Extension

This placard is located on the access door in the bottom step riser to the flight compartment.

> **EMERGENCY GEAR EXTENSION DO NOT LOWER ABOVE 113 KNOTS.**

C. Landing Gear Control Handle

This placard is located on the pedestal adjacent to the landing gear control handle.

> **CAUTION: LEVER MUST RETURN TO NEUTRAL AFTER EACH OPERATION**

D. Cabin Door

This placard is located on pilot's side of forward cabin door.

> **THIS DOOR TO BE OPEN DURING ALL TAKE-OFFS AND LANDINGS**

E. Forward Entrance Door

This placard is located on the forward entrance door bar.

> **WARNING - BAR MUST NOT BE ACROSS DOORWAY DURING TAKE -OFF AND LANDING.**

PAGE 1
SECTION 2-1

DATE 7/29/57

EASTERN AIR LINES INC.
AIRPLANE FLIGHT MANUAL   M404
C. A. A. APPROVED

APPLICABLE AIRSPEEDS

APPLICABLE SPEEDS are shown in <u>knots, T.I.A.S.</u>

V_1 and V_2 **SPEEDS** are shown graphically in Section 3 of this manual. Tabulation below is for convenient reference, and is based on level runways at sea level airports under NO WIND conditions.

GROSS WEIGHT	M-404 WET T.O.	
	*V_1	*V_2
44,900	104	106
44,000	102	105
43,000	100	104
41,000	97	102
39,000	94	100
37,000	93	100

GROSS WEIGHT	M-404 DRY T.O.	
	*V_1	*V_2
41,500	110	110
41,000	106	106
40,000	102	102
38,000	98	100
36,000	96	100
34,000	94	100

*As pointed out in Section 3, Page 1, airspeed indicator reads 6 knots slow in the V_1 and V_2 speed range during ground run, due to ground effect.

CLIMB SPEEDS

Until flaps retracted . . . ·. 120-130

Enroute climb 140

Single engine climb (T.O. flaps, gear
up, METO power) 115*

*S. E. climb speed varies with gross weight, ranging from 110 knots at 35,000 lbs. to 120 knots at 44,900 lbs.

CRUISE AND DESCENT

Normal Operating Limit . . . . .225 (EAL Policy)

Never Exceed Speed (V_{NE}) . . . . .247* (EAL Policy)

*V_{NE} speed may be used in emergencies ONLY.

In turbulence
(in descent and slight turbulence) 180
(in severe turbulence) 150
(minimum in turbulence) 140

Single Engine Cruise
No Flaps . . . . .120 Minimum;
130-140 Desired

MAXIMUM SPEEDS FOR EXTENSION OF:

Take-off flaps 165
Approach flaps 130
Full flaps 105
Landing gear (normal extension) 165
Landing gear (emergency extension) 113
Landing lights 165

HOLDING SPEEDS

No flaps 130
With take-off flaps 130

PROCEDURE TURNS

2 engines 120
1 engine 120

FINAL APPROACH SPEEDS

No flaps 115
Take-off flaps 110
Approach flaps 105
Full flaps 100
ILS and RANGE (2 engines) 110
ILS and RANGE (1 engine) 115
Over the fence (Landing flaps) 95

POWER-OFF STALLING SPEED MOST FORWARD C.G. POSITION (See Flight Manual, Section 3, pages 6 & 9)

FLAPS	WEIGHT	APPROXIMATE SPEED
UP	44,900	98
UP	43,650	96
UP	42,000	95
T.O.	44,900	88
T.O.	43,650	87
T.O.	42,000	86
APPROACH	42,000	78
FULL	42,000	72

EMERGENCY SPEEDS

Flare Release (maximum) 109

Unfeathering (maximum) 130

Minimum Single Engine Control Speed 91

EASTERN AIR LINES INC.
AIRPLANE FLIGHT MANUAL   M404
C.A.A. APPROVED

PAGE 7
SECTION 2-5

DATE 1/14/55

NORMAL OPERATING PROCEDURES

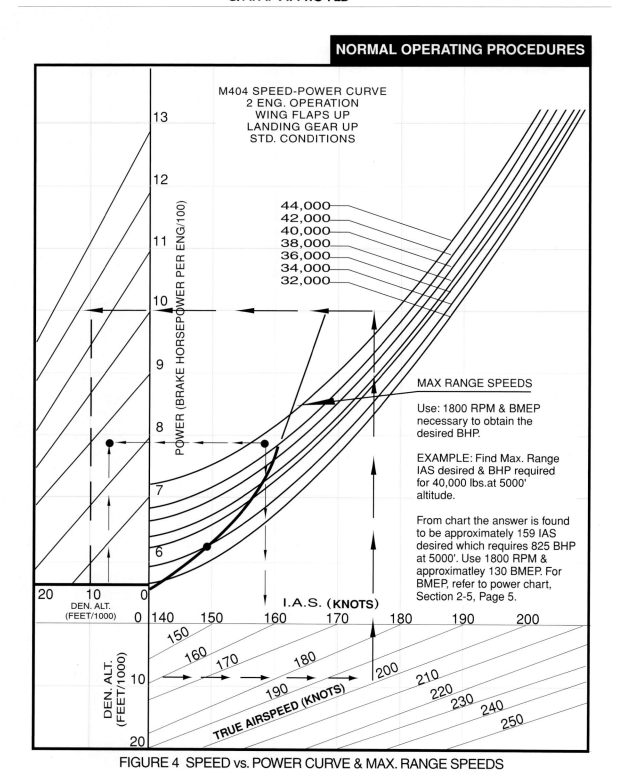

M404 SPEED-POWER CURVE
2 ENG. OPERATION
WING FLAPS UP
LANDING GEAR UP
STD. CONDITIONS

44,000
42,000
40,000
38,000
36,000
34,000
32,000

POWER (BRAKE HORSEPOWER PER ENG/100)

MAX RANGE SPEEDS

Use: 1800 RPM & BMEP
necessary to obtain the
desired BHP.

EXAMPLE: Find Max. Range
IAS desired & BHP required
for 40,000 lbs. at 5000'
altitude.

From chart the answer is found
to be approximately 159 IAS
desired which requires 825 BHP
at 5000'. Use 1800 RPM &
approximatley 130 BMEP. For
BMEP, refer to power chart,
Section 2-5, Page 5.

20   10   0
DEN. ALT.
(FEET/1000)

I.A.S. (KNOTS)

0   140   150   160   170   180   190   200

150
160
170
180
190
200
210
220
230
240
250

DEN. ALT.
(FEET/1000)

10

20

TRUE AIRSPEED (KNOTS)

FIGURE 4 SPEED vs. POWER CURVE & MAX. RANGE SPEEDS

1. EARLY DESIGNS (c1945) OF MARTIN AND ITS POTENTIAL COMPETITORS

	MARTIN 202-12	MARTIN 202-15	CURTISS CW-28	BOEING 431-16	BOEING 431-17	DOUGLAS DC-8	CONVAIR 110	MARTIN 228
DIMENSIONS								
Wing span, ft	81	93	100	96	101	110	91	93
Length, ft	72	72	73	72	72	78	71	69
Height, ft	27	27	27	26	26	26	25	25
Wing area, sq ft	765	860	875	738	NA	1,104	813	860
POWERPLANT								
Number	two	two	two	two	four	two	two	two
Make	Wright	P&W	Wright	P&W	unspec	Allison	P&W	Wright
Power, takeoff, hp	1,700	2,100	2,500	2,100	1,200	1,650	2,100	1,425
Fuel capacity, US gal	600	600	NA	NA	NA	NA	NA	650
WEIGHTS								
Maximum, lb	33,500	34,300	40,000	36,000	40,500	39,500	32,300	28,500
Empty, lb	22,381	23,400	27,000	24,600	28,000	23,915	22,000	20,000
PERFORMANCE								
Cruising speed, mph	254	270	288	252	253	270	275	244
Maximum speed, mph	314	306	NA	287	NA	NA	322	266
PASSENGER SEATS								
	30-36	30-36	32	30-40	30-40	34-48	30-47	26

NA - not available

The above information should be considered very tentative because the designs were in a state of evolution at that time.

2. PRODUCTION MODELS AND LATER PROJECTED DESIGNS COMPARED TO THE CONVAIR 240 & 340.

	MARTIN 202	MARTIN 303	MARTIN 304	MARTIN 202A	CONVAIR 240[1]	MARTIN 404	CONVAIR 340	MARTIN TURBO 404
DIMENSIONS								
Wing span, ft-in	93-3	89-4	89-4	93-3	91-9	93-3	105-4	93-3
Length[2], ft-in	71-4	71-4	71-4	71-4	74-8	74-7	79-2	74-7
Height, ft-in	28-5	28-5	28-5	28-5	26-11	28-5	28-2	28-5
Wing area, sq ft	864	NA	NA	864	817	864	920	864
Cabin length[3], ft-in	43-11	NA	NA	43-11	45-5	47-2	49-2	NA
Cabin width, ft-in	9-0	9-0	9-0	9-0	8-10	9-0	8-10	9-0
Cabin height, ft-in	6-5	6-5	6-5	6-5	6-7	6-5	6-7	6-5
POWERPLANT								
Number	two	two	two	two	two	two	two	two
Make	P&W	P&W	Gen Electric	P&W	P&W	P&W	P&W	Allison
Model	CA ser	CA ser	TG-100	CB ser	CA	CB ser	CB ser	501
Takeoff w/ADI, hp	2,400	2,400	—	2,400	2,400	2,400	2,400	—
without ADI, hp	2,100	2,100	2,200	2,050	2,100	2,050	2,050	2,750[4]
Max continuous, hp	1,800	1,800	NA	1,800	1,800	1,800	1,800	NA
Fuel capacity, USg	1,010	NA	NA	1,350	1,000	1,370	1,730	NA

continued overleaf

	MARTIN 202	MARTIN 303	MARTIN 304	MARTIN 202A	CONVAIR 240[1]	MARTIN 404	CONVAIR 340	MARTIN TURBO 404
WEIGHTS								
Takeoff w/ADI, lb	39,900[5]	36,750	—	43,000	40,500[6]	44,900[7]	47,000	—
without ADI, lb	39,000	NA	39,000	40,000	40,500	41,500	47,000	45,000
Landing w/ADI, lb	38,000[5]	NA	—	41,000	38,600[6]	43,000[7]	46,500	—
without ADI, lb	38,000	NA	34,000	40,000	38,600	40,200	46,500	NA
PERFORMANCE								
Max speed, mph	306	320[8]	385	310	NA	312	NA	NA
Cruising speed, mph	277	291[8]	365	280	270	280	284	325[8]
Rate of climb, ft/min	1,410	NA	NA	1,885	NA	1,250	NA	NA
Service ceiling, ft	25,900	NA	NA	24,000	NA	29,000	NA	NA
Takeoff w/ADI, ft	3,510	NA	NA	NA	NA	4,360	NA	NA
Landing w/ADI, ft	2,400	NA	NA	NA	NA	3,910	NA	NA
Range w/ADI & max payload, miles	565	NA	NA	NA	NA	925	NA	NA
Range w/ADI & max fuel, miles	1,560	NA	NA	NA	NA	2,525	NA	NA

NA - not available or, in the case of Convair 240s and 340s, not available under conditions directly comparable to those for which Martin data are shown. Great care should be exercised in comparing quoted performance figures for competing models as the manufacturers seldom use comparable conditions. For example, one model may have a much greater payload. If runway distances are compared at maximum payloads, the model with the greater payload may appear to have inferior takeoff performance. On the other hand, if the payload were reduced to the maximum payload of the other model, it may have superior takeoff performance. The only true way to compare competing models is to calculate performance under identical conditions using the FAA Approved Airplane Flight Manual for each model.

Notes:

1 The 240-0, as flown by American Airlines, is used for comparison as it was the most numerous variant. Later 240s had increased fuel capacity and weights.

2 Length of fuselage without radar added.

3 Cabin lengths of 34ft 8in, 37ft 11in, 33ft 5in, and 36ft 7in are generally quoted for the 202, 404, 240, and 340, respectively; however, these figures are not comparable because those for the Martin models include the service area, while those for the Convair models include only the passenger seating area. In order to provide a true comparison, the cabin lengths shown here include forward internal cargo compartments and service areas as well as passenger seating areas. The effective length of the Convair 240 or 340 cabin is actually longer yet, as 53in aft of the cabin was used for an externally-accessed cargo compartment.

4 The 501 series engines were producing 2,750hp at that time; however, it was correctly envisioned that they would eventually be rated at 3,750hp.

5 The 202 was approved initially without the use of ADI with takeoff and landing weights of 38,000 and 36,500lb, respectively.

6 The 240 was approved initially without the use of ADI with takeoff and landing weights of 39,000 and 37,619lb, respectively.

7 The 404 was approved initially with a maximum takeoff weight of 43,650lb with ADI and a maximum landing weight of 42,000 or 43,000lb depending on which of two main landing gear shock strut assemblies was installed.

8 Estimated speeds: Martin's estimate for the 303 appears to be overly optimistic while that for the Turbo 404 seems to be quite reasonable in light of the performance achieved later with the similarly powered Convair 580.

Several prominent identification features are visible in this view of Piedmont's Savannah River Pacemaker (msn 14120/N40402). Martin's Double Wasp engine installation (and that of the DC-6) was quite conventional compared to that of the Convair-Liners. Convair used an augmenter engine cooling system and, therefore, did not need cowl flaps as seen here. Unlike the flush-mounted scoops of the Convairs, Martin's induction air intake is prominent on the top of the nacelle. The scoop on the right underside of the 404 nacelle is used for oil cooling air. Engine exhaust is discharged on the lower left-hand sides of 404 nacelles while it is discharged above the wing trailing edges of Convair-Liners.

The large scoop on the left underside of the fuselage is part of the air-conditioning and pressurization system. It supplies ram air in flight to the secondary heat exchanger to cool the hot pressurized cabin air. The ellipse on the upper side between the service door and the letter 'P' is a light used to detect wing ice at night. The later addition of a nose radome has necessitated relocation of the pitot heads from the tip of the nose to both sides of the fuselage below the pilot's (and co-pilot's) side window. For the same reason, the landing light has been relocated on the nose gear.

Black areas on the propeller blade leading edges are boots for the electric anti-ice system. (George W Hamlin)

Uncowled right-hand engine installation on msn 14235/N3711K at Chino, California, in December 1990, with a non-standard propeller spinner. (Author)

The almost closed ventral stairs of Allegheny's msn 9166/N171A. The lack of aerodynamic balance on the rudder tip is a distinguishing feature between 202s and 404s. (Howard Smeltzer)

This view shows the two features that most prominently distinguish Martins from Convair-Liners—the stabilizer dihedral and the pronounced additional wing dihedral outboard of the nacelles.

The ventral stairs generally distinguish 202s and 404s from Convair-Liners; however, the 240s delivered to Western Air Lines, Trans-Australia Airlines, and Orient Airways did have this feature as well. (George W Hamlin & John Wegg)

The single-wheel of the nose gear distinguishes it from Convair-Liners, while the gear's aft slant contrasts with the forward slant of Douglas DC-4/DC-7 nose gears. (John Wegg & Terry Love)

The use of smaller van Zelm ailerons enabled Martin to use relatively large wing flaps as seen in this view of a 404. (Terry M Love)

Like all other post-World War II transports, Martin 202s and 404s used dual-wheel main landing gears. (John Wegg)

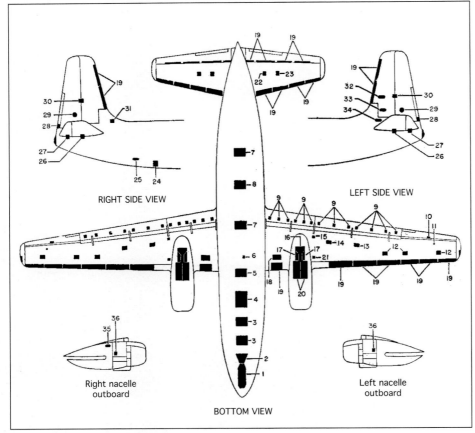

RIGHT SIDE VIEW

LEFT SIDE VIEW

Right nacelle
outboard

Left nacelle
outboard

BOTTOM VIEW

Martinliner access panels (shown for the 202 prototype). (Aviation)

Shown here are various servicing and maintenance access provisions on Martin 202: (1) nose wheel forward doors, (2) aft door, (3) heater hatch, (4) radio hatch, (5) electrical hatch, (6) power receptacle, (7) fuselage hatch, (8) cargo hatch, (9) flap inspection doors, (10) aileron actuator rod cover, (11) access hole cover, (12) outer wing door, (13) outboard tank door, (14) inboard tank door, (15) rear spar splice gap cover, (16) main gear strut door, (17) nacelle access door, (18) leading edge access door, (19) removable leading edge, (20) main gear doors, (21) front spar splice cover, (22) elevator tab torque tube connection door, (23) tab actuating gear box door, (24) lavatory hatch, (25) ramp mechanism door, (26) stabilizer panel, (27) stabilizer rear spar and elevator torque rod panel, (28) tab panel, (29) rudder spring tab rod door, (30) fin-to-rudder hinge plate, (31) heating duct connection door, (32) tab gear box door, (33) rudder tab torque tube connection door, and (34) fin front spar bolt door. Nacelle details: (35) oil tank filler door and (36) fire extinguisher nozzle insertion door. Left nacelle (not shown) has similar details.

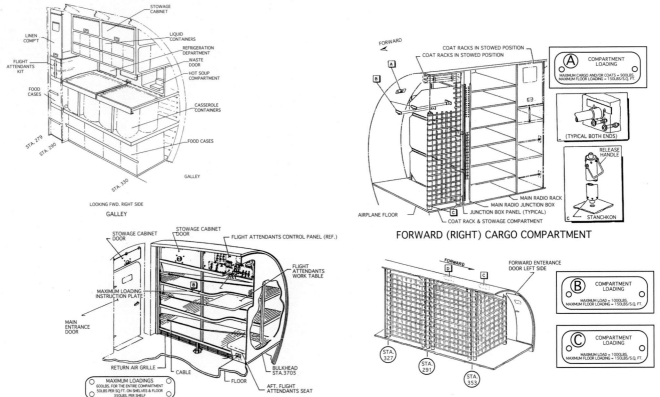

GALLEY

LOOKING FWD. RIGHT SIDE

FORWARD (RIGHT) CARGO COMPARTMENT

Galley and cargo compartment details, as illustrated in an Eastern Air Lines Flight Manual for a 404. (courtesy Capt Jerry Frost)

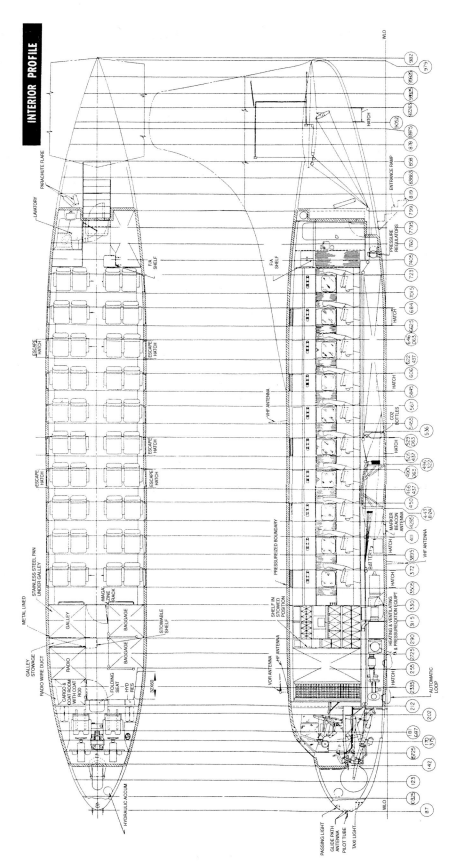

Interior profile of an Eastern Air Lines 404. (courtesy Capt Jerry Frost)

⊷ ⊶⊰◈⊱⊷ ⊶

COMMERCIAL OPERATORS and WOULD-BE OPERATORS

As a supplement to information in the main text and as an additional reference, brief details plus complete fleet listings are given here for all operators that used Martin 202s or 404s on a commercial basis. 'Commercial', as used here, refers to any passenger or freight service, charter or scheduled. It is difficult in some instances to ascertain that operations were really conducted as the owner or lessee operated under a different name from that shown in the registration records or on the lease. Nevertheless, such owners or lessees are shown unless there is little doubt that no revenue service ever took place.

Also included in this section are the operators that placed and later canceled orders for 202s or 404s, and those that engaged in unsuccessful negotiations to acquire them.

Quasi-commercial operators, such as travel clubs, real estate promoters, and agricultural applicators can be found under the heading **OTHER FLEET OPERATORS**. Companies whose use of 202s or 404s was incidental to another primary activity (such as using them for logistics or research and development) can also be found under that heading. The balance of Martinliner operators are located under **MILITARY OPERATORS** and **EXECUTIVE OPERATORS**.

The tabulation is generally in the order of registration number with manufacturer's serial number (msn), model, fleet number (FN), dates owned or operated, individual aircraft name, and remarks. The abbreviations LF and LT are used for Leased From and Leased To. More information on specific airplanes can be found in the **INDIVIDUAL AIRPLANE HISTORIES** section.

ADMIRAL AIR SERVICE
OAKLAND, CALIFORNIA

Jim Sorthun operated one 202 under this name.

N93047　9133　　Nov62 - Sep64

ADMIRAL AIRWAYS, INC
PHILADELPHIA, PENNSYLVANIA, & BURBANK, CALIFORNIA

Formerly Quaker City Airways, Admiral was active in 1961 and 1962 with a fleet of leased Douglas DC-6As and Lockheed Constellations. A 202 was reportedly leased from Martin Air Leasing during 1961 as well; however, it is doubtful whether Admiral made much use of it. The Civil Aeronautics Board canceled Admiral's operating certificate shortly thereafter.

N93049　9132　　　61 -　　61

ADSA—SEE AEROLÍNEAS DOMINICANAS SA

AERO SIERRA DE DURANGO
VICTORIA DE DURANGO, DURANGO, MÉXICO

In 1989, this company intended to acquire a number of ex-PBA/Marco Island 404s to start operations. Although a fleet of NAMC YS-11s was obtained instead, all operations stopped after a short while.

AERO VIRGIN ISLANDS (AVI)
ST THOMAS, US VIRGIN ISLANDS

AVI leased a 404 from Borinquen Air Leasing to supplement its DC-3s in scheduled passenger service between St Thomas and San Juan, Puerto Rico, beginning in 1987. The 404 was also operated occasionally on behalf of Taino Airways. After several years of storage, in 1992 it was painted in the colors of Tol-Air, a local cargo airline owned by Jorge Toledo, and used as an attraction for an airport restaurant/bar.

N40425　14131　　87 -

Aero Virgin Islands (AVI) leased this former Provincetown-Boston Airline 404 (msn 14131/N40425) for scheduled service between San Juan, Puerto Rico, and St Thomas, USVI. It is seen at San Juan on October 30, 1987, and after serving as an attraction at an airport bar/restaurant, is now abandoned. (Tommy Lakmaker)

AEROLÍNEAS DOMINICANAS SA—ADSA
SANTIAGO, DOMINICAN REPUBLIC

Using the name Dominair, ADSA flew two 404s in scheduled service connecting with affiliate Puerto Rico International Airlines (PRINAIR) at San Juan, Puerto Rico, and for scheduled domestic services. Charter service was also provided to other points in the Caribbean. One airplane (HI-285) was leased to Aérovias Quisqueyana from January to May 1978 for scheduled Santo Domingo–San Juan services. ADSA was the last operator to use the 404 in international scheduled (albeit often unpredictable) passenger service.

HI-285　14157　　Oct76 - Jan90

HI-334　14241　　Mar79 -

Aerolíneas Dominicanas SA (ADSA) operated two 404s in domestic service and for flights to San Juan, Puerto Rico. Msn 14241, seen here, spent most of its post–Eastern Air Lines life as an executive airplane, then became HI-334. It was scrapped at Santo Domingo in 1983. (MAP)

AEROPOSTA ARGENTINA, SOCIEDAD MIXTA (SM)
BUENOS AIRES, ARGENTINA

Aéroposta was one of the airlines that evolved into Aerolíneas Argentinas. Five 202s were ordered in October 1946, to supplement or replace its seven Douglas DC-3s and five Junkers-Ju 52/3ms. Msns 13907-13911 were assigned; however, the order was canceled before they were built.

AEROPROVEEDORA LTDA—PROA
BOGOTÁ, COLOMBIA

Proa was a Colombian operator involved primarily in freight charters. The 202 was used in a cargo configuration; however, the 404, which crashed on a training flight shortly after it was purchased, did retain a passenger interior. Some flights were operated on behalf of TAC Colombia.

HK-1484	9167	Sep73 -	77
HK-1485	14237	Apr74 -Aug74	

Aeroproveedora's 202 freighter (msn 9167/HK-1484), still in the basic livery of its previous operator, Central American Airways. (Norbert Oertel)

AEROTRANSPORTES DEL LITORAL ARGENTINO SA (ALA)
BUENOS AIRES, ARGENTINA

In 1964, this privately owned airline was reported to be negotiating with US aircraft brokers for a small number of 404s but was experiencing difficulty in obtaining sufficient funding for the purchase. Apparently the obstacles were insurmountable as ALA continued flying DC-3s.

AEROVÍAS DEL CESAR LTDA—SEE TAC COLOMBIA

AEROVÍAS QUISQUEYANA
SANTO DOMINGO, DOMINICAN REPUBLIC

Following the revocation of its permit to carry passengers with Lockheed Constellations in January 1978, Quisqueyana leased a 404 from Aerolíneas Dominicanas (ADSA) to operate its scheduled Santo Domingo–San Juan, Puerto Rico, services. All operations ceased four months later.

HI-285	14157	Jan78 -May78

AEROVIAS SUD AMERICANA, INC—ASA INTERNATIONAL AIRLINES
MIAMI, FLORIDA

Originally established in 1947 as a cargo carrier, ASA expanded its operations in 1961 to include military contract passenger service using ex-Eastern 404s, Lockheed Constellations, and at least one Douglas DC-7. Five 404s were leased from Falair for that purpose, but perhaps not all were placed in service. Because of financial difficulties, ASA suspended all services in May 1965 and filed for bankruptcy.

N444A	14121	Jun61 -May62	FN 444
N452A	14143	Jun61 - Jan62	FN 452
N454A	14145	Jun61 - Jan63	FN 454
N455A	14146	Jun61 -May62	FN 455
N456A	14147	Jun61 - Jan63	FN 456

Aerovias Sud Americana (ASA International Airlines) used a few ex-Eastern Airlines 404s briefly for military contract passenger flights, including msn 14121/N444A. The Stratocruisers in the background indicate that it was photographed at Oakland, California, in 1966. (Larry Smalley via Peter M Bowers)

AIR ATLANTIC
DANVERS, MASSACHUSETTS

This company leased a 202A from Modern Air Transport for charters.

N93206	14076	68 -

Air Atlantic leased 202A msn 14076/N93206 from Modern Air Transport around 1968 for charters. This photo was taken at Miami on May 3, 1969, and by then the airplane may have already been returned to Modern. (John P Stewart)

AIR BORNE CARGO LINES, INC
NEW YORK, NEW YORK

This operator ordered some all-cargo 202s to supplement or replace its eights DC-3s, but it ceased operations in 1947.

AIR FLORIDA (AIR FLORIDA COMMUTER)
MIAMI, FLORIDA

Air Florida started operations as an intrastate carrier in 1972 and embarked on a massive expansion in 1978 under the freedom of deregulation. To feed and extend its greatly expanded route system, Air Florida contracted with Marco Island Airways in spring 1980 to operate a Miami–Key West 404 service on its behalf. Under the Air Florida Commuter banner, Florida Airlines (qv) also started 404 service to the Bahamas in April 1981, and later added intrastate service on behalf of Air Florida. Southern International Airways, the successor to Florida Airlines, took over the Air Florida Commuter services until it ceased operations in December 1981. The contract was then assumed by Marco Island Airways. With the demise of Air Florida, all Air Florida Commuter operations were halted in July 1984. Four 404s (N144S, N145S, N147S, & N259S) were painted in full Air Florida Commuter colors; however, other 404s of Florida Airlines and Marco Island Airways were also used as required. For full fleet details, see entries for Florida Airlines and Marco Island Airways.

AIR FRANCE
PARIS, FRANCE

Manufacturer's serial numbers (msns) 9130, 9131, 9133, 9135 and 9137-9141 were assigned during negotiations for the sale of 202s to an undisclosed French customer—undoubtedly Air France as Convair was also in negotiations with the French flag carrier at the time. Those unsuccessful negotiations were probably the closest Martin came to penetrating the European market with either 202s or 404s. Of the nine airplanes, msn 9130 and 9131 were eventually delivered to Línea Aéropostal Venezolana; 9133 and 9135 went to Northwest; and 9137-9141 were placed in storage uncompleted.

AIR HYANNIS
HYANNIS, MASSACHUSETTS

This scheduled commuter carrier leased an unidentified 404 from Florida Airlines in July 1980 for its Boston–Nantucket route. Scheduled operations terminated early in 1981.

AIR MARIANAS
SAIPAN, NORTHERN MARIANAS

Air Marianas was the name under which Ray Elliot Jr of Richmond, California, intended to conduct charter and contract services. The 404 was painted in full Air Marianas colors at Oakland and ferried to Saipan, but it is uncertain whether operations ever started. A 404 seen derelict in 1990 at Isley Field, Saipan, was undoubtedly the same airplane.

N147S	14161	Nov82 - Aug83	*Flagship Saipan*

AIR OMNI
SARASOTA/BRANDENTON, FLORIDA

Air Omni was the tentative operating name for a proposed merger of Florida Airlines and Marco Island Airways (qv) in 1981. Although the merger was never completed, Air Omni titles and logo were applied to two airplanes (N145S msn 14142 and N257S msn 14110).

Air Omni was to have been the operating name of a merged Florida Airlines and Marco Island Airways. The merger never took place; however, msn 14142/N145S was painted in the planned livery of Air Omni. (via John P Stewart)

AIR SOUTH—SEE FLORIDA AIRLINES

AIRLINE TRANSPORT CARRIERS—SEE CALIFORNIA CENTRAL AIRLINES

ALA—SEE AEROTRANSPORTES DEL LITORAL ARGENTINO SA

ALLEGHENY AIRLINES
WASHINGTON, DISTRICT OF COLUMBIA, LATER PITTSBURGH, PENNSYLVANIA

All American Airways began mail-carrying operations before World War II using a unique in-flight mail pick-up system. Eventually, the company evolved into the Local Service passenger airline known as Allegheny Airlines (later USAir and now US Airways). Ex-California Central and Pioneer 202s with 40-passenger interiors were acquired and placed into service on June 1, 1955, with the class name 'Martin Executive'. Pittsburgh–Johnstown–Philadelphia–Atlantic City, and Pittsburgh–Johnstown–Harrisburg–Newark routes were served initially. Eventually, 202s were used on the entire Eastern US route system. The 202s, which were erroneously referred to as '202Bs', were later supplemented with most of the ex-TWA 202As. Three 202s (N171A, N175A, & N176A) were converted to an all-cargo configuration as 'Allegheny Cargoliners' after being retired from passenger service. Three others were written-off in accidents, one minor and one fatal. All surviving 202s and the 202As were retired in March 1966 and sold to Fairchild Hiller in trade for F-27Js.

N170A	9163	Mar55 - Apr66	FN 170, *The Atlantic Shore*
N171A	9166	Mar55 - Nov66	FN 171, *The New Yorker*
N172A	9142	Mar55 - Nov55	FN 172, *The Ohio Valley*
N173A	9136	May55 - Feb66	FN 173, *The Pennsylvanian*
N174A	9159	Jan56 - Dec59	FN 174, *The Clevelander*
N175A	9145	Jan56 - Aug66	FN 175, *The Pittsburgher*

One of Allegheny's 'Martin Executives', The New Yorker (msn 9166/N171A) at Philadelphia in 1960. (via Walt Redmond)

With the introduction of its Napier Eland-powered Convair 540s, Allegheny adopted a new paint design. The Eland-powered airplanes did not last long, but the new paint, seen here on one of the 202As (msn 14073/N93203), remained until Allegheny resumed turbine operations with Convair 580s.

(Dave Lucabaugh via Walt Redmond)

ALLEGHENY AIRLINES (CONTINUED)

N176A	9128	Dec56 - Oct66	FN 176, *The Detroiter*
N177A	9147	Jul57 - Nov63	FN 177
N93201	14071	Apr58 - Aug66	FN 178
N93203	14073	Nov58 - Aug66	FN 179
N93204	14074	Jul61 - Jun66	FN 184
N93205	14075	Aug61 - Aug66	FN 185
N93206	14076	Jun59 - Aug66	FN 183
N93207	14077	Sep61 - Aug66	FN 186
N93208	14078	Jun59 - Aug66	FN 182
N93209	14079	Jun61 - Aug66	FN 187
N93210	14080	Nov58 - Aug66	FN 180
N93212	14082	Dec58 - Jun66	FN 181

ASA INTERNATIONAL AIRLINES—SEE AEROVIAS SUD AMERICANA

ATLANTIC SOUTHEAST AIRLINES, INC (ASA)
MIAMI, FLORIDA

Atlantic Southeast Airlines, which was not related to the later Atlanta-based commuter airline with the same name, acquired several ex-Piedmont 404s in the mid-1970s. Of the six, only one (N40450) appears to have ever been operational. It was also leased to Kwin-Air for a period in 1975.

N40401	14106	Mar72 - 79
N40417	14123	Aug74 - Oct76
N40421	14127	Mar72 - Aug72
N40430	14136	Mar72 - Aug79
N40433	14168	Mar72 - Aug79
N40440	14166	Mar72 - Oct76
N40450	14146	Aug74 - Nov76

This Atlantic Southeast Airlines (ASA) was unrelated to the later Atlanta-based commuter airline of the same name. This airplane, msn 14146/N40450, was its only operational 404. The legend 'SO-241C' on the fin is believed to have been the company's FAA operating certificate number. (via John Wegg)

AVI—SEE AERO VIRGIN ISLANDS

AVIATECA—EMPRESA GUATEMALTECA DE AVIACIÓN
GUATEMALA CITY, GUATEMALA

Martin attempted to sell AVIATECA 20 Model 202s from the canceled Pennsylvania-Central Airlines order. Reportedly, two were sold to AVIATECA in September 1948, but neither one was delivered.

BAJA AIR LINES—SERVICIO AÉREO BAJA
TIJUANA, BAJA CALIFORNIA, MÉXICO

Formed by Capt Francisco Muñoz in 1956, Baja leased a 40-seat 202 from Caltex Air Parts for scheduled service linking Tijuana and Puerto Vallarta with the small communities of Bahia de Los Angeles, Gurrero Negro, Mulegé, Novojoa, and Los Mochis. The 202 was also used to supplement its Cessna 195, Beech C-45, and Lockheed 18 on charter work. Although repainted with Baja titles and the Mexican registration XA-SOX, the ex-Ozark Air Lines 404 remained in storage at Las Vegas, Nevada. The airline obtained a Convair 240 (msn 120) instead and used SOX for that airplane.

XA-SEX	9143	Feb66 - Jan68	
N456A	14147		XA-SOX NTU

Servicio Aéreo Baja, or Baja Air Lines, leased msn 9143 for service to small communities in Baja California, México. The owner and chief pilot became quite adept at operating the 202 in and out of very small, unimproved airports.
(Clay Jansson via Walt Redmond)

BALANTIC
FLORIDA

Balantic, which may have been a real estate promoter rather than a commercial operator, leased one 404 from Onyx Aviation.

N542AG	14175	75 -

Msn 14175/N542AG while leased by Balantic from Onyx Aviation.
(via John Wegg)

BASLER FLIGHT SERVICE, INC
OSHKOSH, WISCONSIN

Basler conducted 404 charter flights as Basler Airlines. The first 404 (N467M) was originally registered to Business Aircraft Corp, an affiliated company.

N467M	14164	Feb72 - Aug75
N472M	14234	Oct68 - Aug75

Basler Flight Service used two 404s (msn 14164/N467M and 14234/N472M) for charter flights under the name Basler Airlines. (Karl Krämer)

BRANIFF AIRWAYS
DALLAS, TEXAS

Braniff was one of several customers that first chose Martin products, then later obtained a fleet of Convair 340s and 440s as its DC-3 replacements. Eighteen 202s (msns 9203-9220) were ordered in January 1946 (bringing the 202's order book to 155 aircraft), and 12 303s (msns 13776-13787) were ordered in January 1947, but all were canceled before delivery.

Braniff, however, did operate various Eastern Air Lines 404s on interchange flights linking Miami and Atlanta with the Braniff route system at St Louis. The 404s replaced DC-4s on the interchange service in May 1953, and served until they, in turn, were replaced by Convair 440s four years later.

CALIFORNIA CENTRAL AIRLINES
BURBANK, CALIFORNIA

Airline Transport Carriers was an Irregular carrier owned by the redoubtable Colonel Charles C Sherman and his wife, Edna K. Following the CAB's drastic curtailment of service by Irregular carriers, Sherman escaped CAB control in January 1947 by forming a separate company to continue operating the low-cost California intrastate service. As flights were flown entirely within the state of California where the CAB had no jurisdiction, California Central's operations were under the authority of the California Public Utilities Commission. (Limited Irregular carrier operations were continued as California Hawaiian Airlines under CAB cognizance.) The three Douglas DC-3s used initially for the California service, plus two DC-4s, were traded in 1951 to Northwest for five 202s.

As there was no need for a galley and little need for coat stowage in the prevailing California weather, 44-seat interiors were installed before their entry in service on August 31, 1951. California Central promoted the 202s as 'Martinliner 300s', an optimistic reference to their cruising speed. At various times, the service—which linked Los Angeles and Burbank with San Diego, Oakland, and San Francisco—was also promoted as the 'California Air Lounge' and the 'California Commuter'. Those titles were applied prominently to the rear stairs in full view of boarding customers. The service was extremely popular; however, the fares were simply too low for the airline to be profitable. As a result, the airline ceased operations and

filed for bankruptcy in February 1954. The four 202s (one had been sold back to Martin four months earlier) were stored for a year, then sold to Allegheny and Southwest.

N93042	9163	Aug51 - Mar55	FN 042, *City of Oakland*
N93045	9166	Sep51 - Mar55	FN 045, *City of Burbank*
N93047	9133	Jun51 - Mar55	FN 047, *City of San Diego*
N93052	9142	Sep51 - Mar55	FN 052, *City of San Francisco*
N93057	9135	Sep51 - Sep53	FN 057, *City of Los Angeles*

California Central Airlines operated five 202s in scheduled California intrastate service. City of San Diego *(msn 9133/N93047) in the foreground has just arrived at Burbank, while* City of Oakland *(msn 9163/N93042) is starting its engines.* (Bob Steele via Jukka Kauppinen)

CALIFORNIA INTERNATIONALE
LONG BEACH, CALIFORNIA

This charter company leased a 404 from Universal Applicators to supplement its Douglas DC-3.

N302FA	14128	75 - 76	

California Internationale leased msn 14128/N302FA in 1975 to supplement its DC-3s in charter work. This photo was taken at Van Nuys in March 1976. (via John Wegg)

CALIFORNIA TIME AIRLINES, INC
BURBANK, CALIFORNIA

California Time, formed by H C Buckland, began intrastate passenger service to Palm Springs and San Jose from Burbank in October 1964 using a former Pacific Air Lines's 202. The company was acquired by Fifth Avenue Coach Lines of New York in 1965 and, although there were plans to acquire a second 202 and a Douglas DC-7B, it ceased operations shortly thereafter.

N93059	9148	Dec63 - Sep65

California Time Airlines acquired msn 9148/N93059 late in 1963 for an unsuccessful attempt to provide intrastate passenger service from Burbank to Palm Springs and San Jose. (Clay Jansson via Walt Redmond)

CAMBA—SEE COMERCIALIZADORA AÉREA MIXTA BOLIVIANA LTDA

CAN—SEE COMPAÑIA AÉREA NACIONAL

CAPITAL AIRLINES—SEE PENNSYLVANIA-CENTRAL AIRLINES

CENTRAL AMERICAN AIRWAYS FLYING SERVICE
LOUISVILLE, KENTUCKY

Owned by W L 'Will' Paris, this Bowman Field-based operator used a 202 for general charters, such as college sports teams and rock band tours. For example, British rock star Joe Cocker used this aircraft for one of his US tours. CAA also used a similarly registered Douglas DC-3 (N272R) and Lockheed 749A Constellation (N273R). The 202 was sold to Colombian operator Aeroproveedora (Proa).

N71R	9167	Jul65 - Sep73	

Central American Airways kept this 202 (msn 9167/N71R) in general charter work for several years. The company's specialties included sports teams and rock band tours. (A R Krieger)

CHICAGO & SOUTHERN AIRLINES (C & S)
MEMPHIS, TENNESSEE

C & S ordered 10 202s (msns 9193-9202) and took options on an additional seven, but the order was canceled before the airplanes were built. The 202s were scheduled to enter service on July 1, 1947, on routes serving Chicago, New Orleans, Detroit, and Houston. Convair 340s were ordered later, but C & S had merged with Delta Air Lines by the time they were delivered.

COASTAL AIRWAYS, INC—SEE PRO AIR SERVICES, INC

COLONIAL AIRLINES, INC
NEW YORK, NEW YORK

Colonial ordered 20 Martin 202s in December 1945. At the time, Colonial was operating Douglas DC-4s on its New York, Washington, and Bermuda route and DC-3s on its Ottawa–New York–Washington route. Presumably, the 40-seat 202s were intended for the latter service. In any event, Colonial elected to cancel the 202s and acquire additional DC-4s. Colonial was absorbed by Eastern Air Lines in June 1956, but it continued to operate as the Colonial Division of that airline until 1961 when the New England routes were sold to Mohawk Airlines. Although Colonial never received any 202s, the routes were eventually served by a Martin product after all.

COLONY AIRLINES (AIR SECO, INC DBA)
FORT LAUDERDALE, FLORIDA
Operating as Colony Airlines, Air Seco briefly used a 404 for charter flights from Florida to the Bahamas.

N474M	14165	Oct69 -	70

Air Seco, dba Colony Airlines, used msn 14165/N474M around 1969 for charter flights from Florida to the Bahamas. The aircraft still appeared in fading Colony titles at Fort Lauderdale in August 1973. (Karl Krämer)

COMERCIALIZADORA AÉREA MIXTA BOLIVIANA LTDA (CAMBA)
LA PAZ, BOLIVIA

One of the famed *carniceros* (meat-haulers), CAMBA used 404s and a sole 202A to carry perishables, including meat, to communities throughout Bolivia. Because of accidents—routine in the rugged high-elevation terrain—and later purchases, the fleet never exceeded three aircraft at any one time. The 202A was passed to Compañia Aérea Nacional (qv), and CAMBA ceased operations in June 1987 after losing its last 404.

CP-1317	14163	Nov76 -	77
CP-1318	14134	Jul77 -	Jul81
CP-1440	14114	Jan79 - Dec79	
CP-1441	14075	Oct79 -	81
CP-1570	14167	Jul80 - Jun87	

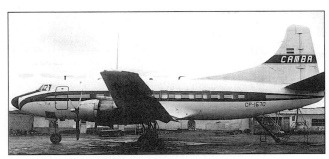

CAMBA regularly used 404s to haul fresh meat in Bolivia. Msn 14167/CP -1570 was operational in this capacity into the late 1980s.

(Michael Magnusson)

COMMANDER AIRLINE—SEE WILLIS AIR SERVICE

COMPAÑIA AÉREA NACIONAL (CAN)
LA PAZ, BOLIVIA

CAN started operations in 1981 with a 202A acquired from fellow meat-hauler Comercializadora Aérea Mixta Boliviana (CAMBA). The ex-Howard Hughes 404 was purchased from México around 1981. Although it was repaired following a landing accident in January 1984, its luck ran out in a takeoff accident from La Paz in August the following year. The 202A is believed to have crashed in 1984. After several years in limbo, CAN was revived with a DC-6 in 1988 but has since ceased operations.

CP-1441	14075	81 -	84
CP-1704	14172	81 -	Aug85

COMPAÑIA PANAMENA DE AVIACIÓN (COPA)
PANAMA CITY, PANAMÁ

COPA, the first non-US operator of the model, used an ex-TWA 404 on scheduled Panama City–David service from fall 1961 until late 1965 when it was replaced with a Hawker Siddeley HS 748. The 404 had a color scheme similar to that of Pan American, which held 33% of COPA at the time.

HP-302	14170	Feb61 -	Sep65

CRUZEIRO (SERVICOS AEREOS CRUZEIRO DO SUL, LTDA)
RIO DE JANEIRO, BRAZIL

Cruzeiro is reported to have ordered 10 Model 202s in June 1946, but possibly only options were held. None were built for Cruzeiro and the Brazilian airline later acquired a fleet of Convair 340s, 440s, and used 240s.

DELTA AIR LINES
ATLANTA, GEORGIA

Based on a verbal agreement to purchase ten, Martin assigned msns 9221 plus 13767-13775 to a fleet of 202s for Delta. The 'order', which also included options for ten more, was canceled before a contract was signed. Delta later acquired a fleet of Convair 340s and 440s.

Delta passengers did fly on Martinliners, however, through an interchange agreement with Trans World Airlines. TWA held authority for the Detroit–Cincinnati route, and Delta the Cincinnati–Atlanta route, therefore an interchange agreement was made and one aircraft made a single flight number trip between Atlanta and Detroit. Delta operated the Cincinnati–Atlanta segment, but its crews never flew TWA 404s; TWA crews, on the other hand, did fly Delta's Convair 340s and 440s (and DC-3s and DC-4s) between Cincinnati and Detroit when a Delta aircraft was assigned to the route.

An impression of a Delta Air Lines 202. An order for twenty 202s was announced in June 1946. (The Martin Star)

DHL AIRLINES
HONOLULU, HAWAII

DHL Airlines, a subsidiary of the DHL Corp, was formed in 1978 to operate three 404s transferred from affiliate Petroleum Air Transport (Pat Air) (qv) on inter-island passenger services. Although DHL titles were applied to one airplane and the service was briefly advertised, it was never started. Following storage at Honolulu, still in Pat Air colors, the three airplanes were scrapped. DHL Airlines was to have been a separate entity from DHL Island Airways, which operated Beech 18s and DC-6s on inter-island cargo services.

N465M	14152	Mar79 - Sep79
N471M	14112	Mar79 - Sep79
N473M	14224	Mar79 - Sep79

Now well-known as a world-wide small-package carrier, DHL attempted unsuccessfully to start a Hawaiian inter-island passenger service in 1979 with three 404s, including msn 14112/N471M, the only aircraft to carry 'DHL Airlines' titles. (John Wegg)

DIAMENTE AIR
CARACAS, VENEZUELA

An unidentified 404 was reported with this company in 1996, although it is believed the aircraft is not active.

YV-878C

DODERO (COMPAÑIA ARGENTINA DE AERONAVEGACIÓN DODERO)
BUENOS AIRES, ARGENTINA

Dodero, a subsidiary of the Dodero shipping company, ordered four 202s in mid-1946, the first overseas airline to do so. Negotiations were also in progress for the sale of 202s to affiliate Flota Aérea Mercante Argentina (FAMA), but FAMA eventually chose the Convair-Liner. The subsequent cancellation of the 202s for Dodera may have been related to FAMA's selection. Both Dodera and FAMA were predecessor companies of Aerolíneas Argentinas to which the 240s were eventually delivered.

The first overseas airline to order 202s, in June 1946, was Dodero. The shipping company planned to carry passengers between ports and inland cities in Argentina. (The Martin Star)

DOMINAIR—SEE AEROLÍNEAS DOMINICANAS SA

EAST COAST FLYING SERVICE
MARTINSBURG, WEST VIRGINIA

East Coast Flying Service used 404s and a couple of Convair 240s for charter flights early in the 1960s. Board chairman S Ross Lipscomb also operated under the name East Coast Leasing. Some of the 404s were non-operational airplanes acquired for resale, etc.

N442A	14111	Jul60 -May65
N442D	14143	Jan62 - Jul62
N442E	14102	Jun61 -Feb65
N446A	14137	Nov62 - Jan63
N447A	14138	Nov62 -Aug65
N456A	14147	Jan63 -Feb65
N458A	14149	Nov62 -Aug65
N474M	14165	Sep65 - Jan68
N478A	14226	Nov62 - Apr68
N493A	14241	Jan63 - Jul63
N497A	14245	Jun64 -Sep65
N542AG	14175	Sep65 -Feb69

East Coast Flying Service did not believe in promoting its name prominently on its airplanes. The small lettering on the nose of N442E (msn 14102) is in marked contrast to the 'billboard' livery of some of today's operators.

(via Peter R Keating)

EASTERN AIR LINES
NEW YORK, NEW YORK

Eddie Rickenbacker, then president of Eastern, signed a contract with Martin in November 1945 to purchase 50 202s including msns 9168-9192. The 36-seat 202s were scheduled to be delivered between April and November 1947 to supplement the airline's DC-3 fleet, but the order was canceled before any were built.

Following development of the 202 into the 404, and an improved economic environment, Eastern entered into a new contract for 60 Model 404s (35 firm plus 25 options). The options were later exercised, making Eastern the largest operator of the 202/404 series. Eastern received the first and last 404 with deliveries made from October 1951 through February 1953. The 404s, flown under the class name 'Silver Falcon', with standard 40-passenger interiors, were first used as extra sections backing up Constellation flights. Scheduled Silver Falcon service started on January 5, 1952, and from January 15, the following routes had dedicated 404 service: New York (LaGuardia)–Baltimore–Washington–Richmond–Charleston–Jacksonville; New York (LaGuardia)–Baltimore–Columbia; New York (LaGuardia)–Philadelphia–Raleigh/Durham–Jacksonville–Miami; and Newark–Washington–Atlanta–Tampa–Miami. Subsequently, they were used on the shorter segments of the entire domestic route system.

The fleet was supplemented with 20 Convair 440s in 1957, then retired in 1962. Just before their retirement, four 404s were assigned as extra sections to supplement Eastern's Lockheed Super Constellations on the Air-Shuttle, then in its second year. Originally finished with Eastern colors on polished aluminum fuselages, the 404s later appeared with their markings over a white fuselage background. A handful were repainted in a revised Falcon livery in 1961. Despite suffering four accidents during their ten-year service with the airline, the 404s became the first type in Eastern's history to operate that long without a single passenger fatality.

N440A	14109	Oct51 -Sep62	FN 440
N441A	14110	Nov51 -Dec62	FN 441
N442A	14111	Nov51 - Jul60	FN 442
N443A	14112	Dec51 -Sep62	FN 443
N444A	14121	Dec51 - Jun61	FN 444
N445A	14122	Dec51 -Feb56	FN 445
N446A	14137	Dec51 -Nov62	FN 446
N447A	14138	Dec51 -Nov62	FN 447
N448A	14139	Jan52 - Oct61	FN 448
N449A	14140	Jan52 -Dec62	FN 449
N450A	14141	Jan52 -Dec62	FN 450
N451A	14142	Jan52 -Sep61	FN 451
N452A	14143	Feb52 - Jun61	FN 452
N453A	14144	Feb52 -Mar57	FN 453
N454A	14145	Feb52 - Jun61	FN 454
N455A	14146	Feb52 - Jun61	FN 455
N456A	14147	Feb52 - Jun61	FN 456
N457A	14148	Mar52 -Feb62	FN 457
N458A	14149	Mar52 -Nov62	FN 458
N459A	14150	Mar52 - Oct61	FN 459
N460A	14151	Mar52 -Aug61	FN 460
N461A	14152	Mar52 -Sep61	FN 461
N462A	14153	Mar52 -Aug61	FN 462
N463A	14154	Mar52 -Dec62	FN 463
N464A	14155	Apr52 -Aug61	FN 464
N465A	14156	Apr52 - Jul61	FN 465
N466A	14157	Apr52 - Jul61	FN 466
N467A	14158	Apr52 -Dec62	FN 467
N468A	14159	Apr52 -Dec62	FN 468
N469A	14160	Apr52 -Sep62	FN 469
N470A	14161	Apr52 -Aug62	FN 470
N471A	14162	Apr52 -Aug61	FN 471
N472A	14163	May52 -Sep61	FN 472

As represented by msn 14162/N471A, the large fleet of Eastern Air Lines 404s was delivered with bare aluminum cabin roofs. They were flown under the class name 'Silver Falcon', a name revealed at a meeting of the airline's advisory and field board of directors in Miami on October 9, 1951, when EAL's first airplane was delivered. (via John Wegg)

EASTERN AIR LINES (CONTINUED)

N473A	14164	May52 - Sep61	FN 473
N474A	14165	May52 - Dec62	FN 474
N475A	14223	Sep52 - May62	FN 475
N476A	14224	Sep52 - Oct62	FN 476
N477A	14225	Sep52 - Oct62	FN 477
N478A	14226	Oct52 - Nov62	FN 478
N479A	14227	Oct52 - Aug61	FN 479
N480A	14228	Oct52 - Aug62	FN 480
N481A	14229	Oct52 - Dec62	FN 481
N482A	14230	Oct52 - Dec62	FN 482
N483A	14231	Oct52 - Dec62	FN 483
N484A	14232	Oct52 - Dec62	FN 484
N485A	14233	Nov52 - Dec62	FN 485
N486A	14234	Nov52 - Sep62	FN 486
N487A	14235	Nov52 - Dec62	FN 487
N488A	14236	Nov52 - Dec62	FN 488
N489A	14237	Nov52 - Nov61	FN 489
N490A	14238	Nov52 - Dec62	FN 490
N491A	14239	Nov52 - Dec62	FN 491
N492A	14240	Nov52 - Nov57	FN 492
N493A	14241	Dec52 - Nov62	FN 493
N494A	14242	Dec52 - Dec62	FN 494
N495A	14243	Dec52 - Dec62	FN 495
N496A	14244	Jan53 - Mar58	FN 496
N497A	14245	Jan53 - Dec62	FN 497
N498A	14246	Jan53 - Dec62	FN 498
N499A	14247	Feb53 - Dec62	FN 499

Later, Eastern applied the same basic trim over a white cabin roof, as seen on msn 14157/N466A. (MAP)

Eastern normally applied the class name 'Silver Falcon' on each side of the rear fuselage by the ventral stairway; however, this particular 404 (msn 14234/N486A) also has this legend on the nose. (Howard M Svendsen)

EDDE AIRLINES
SALT LAKE CITY, UTAH, & LONG BEACH, CALIFORNIA

William and Joseph Edde's Supplemental, Intrastate, and Contract carrier used an ex-Pacific Air Lines 202 for charter flights in the mid-1960s, supplementing its fleet of Lockheed Constellations, a Douglas DC-3, and a Curtiss C-46. The company, associated with Edde Aircraft, ceased operations in 1969.

N93053	9143	Mar64 - Feb66

Edde Airlines used msn 9143/N93053 for charter flights during the mid-1960s. (Clay Jansson via Walt Redmond)

FIESTA AIR
LONG BEACH, CALIFORNIA, & SCOTTSDALE, ARIZONA

Charter operations were conducted under this name by the Prairie Avenue Gospel Center (also known as Hawthorne Christian Schools) beginning in June 1976. In addition to the 404s, Fiesta Air also operated a Lockheed 188A Electra and a Beech D50 Twin Bonanza.

N302FA	14128	Mar70 - Apr75	
N463M	14155	Jun71 - Aug74	spares use
N40432	14167	Apr71 - Aug71	
N40438	14173	Oct71 - Apr75	

FLAMINGO AIRLINES
NASSAU, BAHAMAS

Flamingo leased four 404s from Charlotte Aircraft Corp for Caribbean inter-island service. Although the aircraft flew under US registry, Flamingo was actually based in the Bahamas. The 404s were replaced with leased Convair-Liners; however, the airline was absorbed by Bahamasair in 1973.

N9234C	14143	72 -	72
N40411	14115	72 -	72
N40421	14127	71 -	71
N40448	14242	Aug71 -	72

Bahamas-based Flamingo Airlines leased four 404s, including msn 14115/N40411, from Charlotte Aircraft Corporation for Caribbean inter-island service early in the 1970s. (John P Stewart via Peter R Keating)

FLORIDA AIRLINES
SARASOTA/BRADENTON, FLORIDA

Florida Airlines, previously a Florida intrastate operator, took over Shawnee Airlines (qv) in 1976 and gained control of Air South of St Simons Island, Georgia. In the same year, the airline leased a 404 from Dolphin Aviation—the first of what became one of the more prominent latter-day 404 fleets. Points served with 404s under the Florida Airlines name included Tampa, Sarasota/Bradenton, Fort Myers, Miami, and Fort Lauderdale. Air South operations included Atlanta and St Simons Island, Georgia, and Hilton Head Island, South Carolina. A Fort Lauderdale–St Simons Island route connected the two systems. Those served under the Shawnee name included Orlando, Fort Lauderdale and West Palm Beach. A scheduled Fort Lauderdale–Freeport service was flown in 1977, and charters were also operated to the Bahamas and various other Caribbean destinations.

Florida Airlines ceased scheduled operations on January 11, 1980, because of competition and rising fuel costs but continued its Miami–Havana charter flights (started in 1979) and contract services for Bahamasair. On February 1, 1980, it resumed the Sarasota–Miami route which was later modified with the addition of Fort Myers. After reorganization, Miami–St Petersburg service started on November 1, 1980. The new owners considered the acquisition of Marco Island Airways and merging the two companies with the name Air Omni (qv)

The Air South operation was sold to Ocean Airways (qv) along with five of its seven 404s in January 1980. Following that operator's demise a few months later, the 404s were purchased from bankruptcy court and returned to service with Florida Airlines.

Florida Airlines started 404 service on behalf of Air Florida on April 1, 1981. The first such Air Florida Commuter service was between Miami and the Bahamas, and intrastate flights were added later. Following several months of operations under Chapter 11 bankruptcy protection, Florida Airlines was reorganized on August 7, 1981, as Southern International Airways (qv).

N144S	14150	Jun78 -Aug81	Sanibel Island, later City of Sarasota/Bradenton
N145S	14142	Jun78 -Aug81	Hilton Head Island, later City of Fort Myers
N147S	14161	Mar78 -Aug81	Longboat Key, later City of Miami
N255S	14246	Sep77 -Aug81	City of Macon
N257S	14110	Mar78 -Aug81	Sea Island
N258S	14232	79 -Aug81	St Simons Island, later City of Atlanta
N259S	14233	May76 -Aug81	City of Ft Lauderdale

Florida Airlines used seven ex-Southern Airways 404s in scheduled Florida intrastate service, including City of Ft. Lauderdale, *msn 14233/N259S.* (Ben Ullings)

Florida Airlines transferred some of its 404s, including msn 14246/N255S, to routes served by its Georgia-based affiliate Air South. (John P Stewart)

Msn 14110/N257S is seen with Air South titles and the startling yellow and pink color scheme of Shawnee Airlines, another Florida Airlines affiliate. (John P Stewart)

FLOTA AÉREA MERCANTE ARGENTINA (FAMA)—SEE DODERO

FLYING TIGERS—SEE NATIONAL SKYWAYS FREIGHT

FLYING W AIRWAYS, INC
MEDFORD, NEW JERSEY

Commercial operator Flying W Airways used a 202 and two 404s for charter work. Also included in the fleet was a very rare Lockheed 14 Super Electra. The former E F MacDonald executive 404 (N636X) was later repurchased by Jeff Whitesell, the son of Flying W's owner, for restoration in the colors of Pacific Air Lines. The executive interior installed more than 35 years earlier remains in excellent condition.

N93046	9167	Nov64 -Nov64
N474M	14165	Jan68 - Mar69
N636X	14135	Apr63 -Nov65

FRIGORIFICO REYES (FRI REYES)
LA PAZ, BOLIVIA

At one time the most prominent of the meat-haulers, Fri Reyes flew mostly Convair twins and Douglas DC-4s; however, at least two 404s were also used. Both 404s were leased from or operated on Fri Reyes's behalf by Transportes Aéreos Samuel Selum (TASS).

| CP-1738 | 14137 | 84 - Apr90 |
| CP-1917 | 14146 | Jun84 - |

GOLDEN EAGLE AVIATION, INC
OKLAHOMA CITY, OKLAHOMA

Golden Eagle leased two 404s from Jack Richards Aircraft Sales to fly the Wichita State University football team to a game at Logan, Utah. During a scenic detour through a mountain valley, N464M crashed on October 2, 1970, killing 32, most of whom were team members. One of the survivors was the co-pilot, Golden Eagle president Ronald G Skipper.

| N464M | 14151 | 70 - Oct70 |
| N470M | 14146 | 70 - Oct70 |

INTERNATIONAL TRANSFER CORP—SEE PRO AIR, INC

INTERSTATE AIRMOTIVE, INC
ST LOUIS, MISSOURI

Commercial operator Interstate Airmotive flew three 404s, two DC-3s, and a Lockheed Lodestar for charters, etc. All operations were suspended on July 4, 1972, because of financial difficulties.

N465M	14152	May70 - Oct72
N471M	14112	Nov67 - Oct72
N473M	14224	Aug67 - Oct72

St Louis-based Interstate Airmotive Corp used two ex-Ozark Airlines 404s, including msn 14112/N471M, in the late 1960s and early 1970s for charter service. (John T Wible via George W Pennick/via Elliot H Greenman)

JAPAN AIR LINES CO, LTD (*NIHON KOKU KABUSHIKI KAISHA*)
TOKYO, JAPAN

As all aviation activity by Japanese nationals was prohibited after World War II by the Allied occupational forces, the newly formed, privately owned Japan Air Lines contracted with Northwest Airlines to provide airplanes and crew for a period of one year. Transocean Air Lines, flying five 44-seat 202s and a 69-seat DC-4 under sub-contract from Northwest, inaugurated postwar service on October 25, 1951, on the Sapporo– Tokyo–Nagoya–Osaka–Iwakuni–Fukuoka route. There is an unconfirmed report that N93046 (msn 9167) was also used—possibly as a replacement for N93043 which crashed before completion of the contract. The 202s were all named after planets.

N93041	9162	Oct51 - Oct52	*Suisei*	(Mercury)
N93043	9164	Jan52 - Apr52	*Mokusei*	(Jupiter)
N93049	9132	Oct51 - Oct52	*Kinsei*	(Venus)
N93060	9149	Oct51 -Sep52	*Dosei*	(Saturn)
N93061	9150	Oct51 -Sep52	*Kasei*	(Mars)

As all aviation activity by Japanese nationals after World War II was prohibited by the Allied powers, during the early postwar recovery period Northwest was approved by the Allies to operate domestic flights on behalf of a new Japan Air Lines. In turn, Northwest sub-contracted with Transocean—which was responsible for the whole operation, including flight dispatch—to use five 44-seat 202s (N93043 Mokusei *illustrated) and a DC-4.* (JAL via Richard J Hurley)

KNIGHT AIRLINES
MIAMI, FLORIDA

A charter and contract services operator, Knight flew a scheduled Miami–Lakeland route for a brief period.

N40430	14136	Aug79 - Apr83	not operated
N40450	14146	Nov76 -May84	
N40433	14168	Aug79 - Apr83	not operated

KODIAK WESTERN ALASKA AIRLINES
KODIAK, ALASKA

KWA purchased N302FA from Universal Applicators in 1976; however, it was found to be unairworthy because of extensive corrosion. In renegotiating the sale, the seller agreed to include N40438 which had a sound airframe, but run-out engines. The latter was then rebuilt using the engines and other components from N302FA. (An engine failure would cause the demise of N40438 three years later in service with Nevada Airlines.) KWA briefly used N40438 for the Anchorage–Kodiak–King Salmon–Dillingham route, then leased it on July 10, 1976, to Kachemak Seafoods, Inc.

N302FA	14128	Mar76 - 76	spares use
N40438	14173	Apr76 - Jan77	

Kodiak Western Alaska Airlines purchased msn 14128/N302FA but found it to be damaged beyond repair by corrosion. As part of the settlement agreement, msn 14173/N40438 was substituted and made airworthy using some components removed from 14128. (Peter R Keating via Denis Goodwin)

KWIN-AIR
OPA-LOCKA, FLORIDA

Kwin-Air used an Atlantic Southeast 404 briefly for charter flights to the Caribbean.

N40450	14146	75 -	75	

Kwin-Air leased msn 14146/N40450 in 1975 for Caribbean charters. The airplane still has the livery of the owner, Atlantic Southeast Airlines, including 'SO-241C' on the fin. (John Wegg)

LAN-CHILE—SEE LINEA AÉREA NACIONAL

LANSA—SEE LINEAS AÉREAS NACIONALES SA

LAUSA—SEE LINEAS AÉREAS UNIDAS

LINEA AÉREA NACIONAL (LAN-CHILE)
SANTIAGO, CHILE

The first of LAN-Chile's four 40-seat 202s (CC-CLR) arrived in Santiago on November 13, 1947, to supplement a fleet of aging Lockheed 10-A Electras, Lockheed Lodestars, and Douglas DC-3s. Options for four more were not taken up, but those delivered served as the flagships of the LAN fleet until 1955 when DC-6Bs were acquired. The 202s were used initially on domestic services from Santiago to Antofagasta and Arica. In 1949, they replaced Lodestars on trans-Andean service to Buenos Aires (extended to Montevideo in February 1951). The 202s were also used on flights to Tacna (Perú), and La Paz (Bolivia).

During their career with LAN, the 202s were re-registered twice and converted to 36-passenger airplanes. Although they had apparently given good service with LAN, their lack of pressurization was a definite disadvantage, particularly on flights over the Andes. Four Convair 340s were, therefore, acquired from Allegheny Airlines beginning late in 1960 and the 202s were relegated to the Santiago–Valdivia route. Following unsuccessful attempts to sell them at an advertised bargain price of $30,000 each, the 202s were retired and scrapped in 1962. Their uneventful 15-year career with LAN was in marked contrast to the troubles experienced by Northwest.

CC-CLR	9125	Nov47 -	62	FN 0299, RR CC-CLMA/FN 261, then CC-CCK
CC-CLS	9126	Nov47 -	62	RR CC-CLMB/FN 262, then CC-CCL
CC-CLT	9127	Aug48 -	62	FN 0058, RR CC-CLMC/FN 263, then CC-CCM
CC-CLU	9129	Aug48 -	62	RR CC-CLMD/FN 264, then CC-CCN

LÍNEA AÉROPOSTAL VENEZOLANA (LAV)
CARACAS, VENEZUELA

Although faced with numerous cancellations, Martin was able to find a buyer for two of the airplanes originally assigned to an undisclosed French customer—undoubtedly Air France. LAV ordered two 36-passenger 202s in October 1947 to replace its remaining Lockheed 18 Lodestars and supplement a fleet of 16 Douglas DC-3s. A third Air France 202 was also reassigned to LAV, but only the first two were delivered. Initially, the 202s were operated between Caracas and Barbados, and domestically from Caracas to Barcelona, Maturin, Ciudad Bolivar, and Maracaibo. Following the addition of Vickers Viscounts to the LAV fleet in 1956, the 202s were relegated to the less demanding Maracaibo–Panama City, Caracas–Barcelona, and Caracas–Barbados routes. One 202 was damaged beyond economical repair in October 1958, and the other was placed in storage a month later. Eventually the survivor was sold to California Airmotive and scrapped at Fox Field, near Lancaster, California.

YV-C-AMB	9130	Dec47 -	63	*Rafael Urdaneta*
YV-C-AMC	9131	Dec47 - Oct58		*Andres Bello*
???	9133			not delivered

Martin's misfortunes in 202 sales were mitigated to a minor degree when Línea Aéropostal Venezolana purchased two, including msn 9130/YV-C-AMB Rafael Urdaneta. (Martin via William T Larkins)

LÍNEAS AÉREAS NACIONALES, SA (LANSA)
BARRANQUILLA, COLOMBIA

LANSA ordered three 40-passenger 202s in 1948 to supplement a fleet of 15 Douglas DC-3s. Colombian registrations C-300, C-301 and C-302 were assigned; however, none were delivered.

All of the Latin American customers that placed orders early in the 202 development program canceled except Linea Aérea Nacional (LAN Chile). Msn 9126/CC-CLS, seen at the Martin factory, was the second of its four airplanes.

(Martin via Peter M Bowers)

Shortly after delivery, Linea Aérea Nacional adopted a revised color scheme and used four-digit fleet numbers. The identity of 0060, seen here in company with a de Havilland Dove, is unconfirmed. (via R E G Davies)

LAN 202s had to cross the Andes at 17,000ft (5,200m) on eastbound flights from Santiago to Buenos Aires, and at 26,000ft to 27,000ft (7,900-8,200m) on their return.

LÍNEAS AÉREAS UNIDAS, SA (LAUSA)
MEXICO CITY, DF, MÉXICO

LAUSA obtained one 202A in 1960 for its regional routes from Mexico City; however, it was repossessed by California Airmotive because of non-payment. The name of the company was changed to Líneas Aéreas Unidas Mexicanas, SA (LAUMSA) in 1962.

XA-NEK   14075   Jan60 -Dec60

Msn 14075 was leased early in 1960 to Líneas Aéreas Unidas SA and re-registered XA-NEK. Although seen here in service at Mexico City, it was quickly returned to the lessor, California Airmotive Corporation, because of lease payment problems. (via Gary Kuhn)

LINEE AEREE ITALIANE (LAI)
ROME, ITALY

LAI tried to replace its DC-3s with a fleet of 404s, but it had to settle for used Convair 240s after attempts to obtain financing from the Italian government failed.

LLOYD AIRLINES
MIAMI, FLORIDA

Lloyd acquired a 202 in 1960, but went out of business shortly thereafter.

N93046   9167   Nov60 -Mar61

LONE STAR AIRLINES
DALLAS, TEXAS

This Texas intrastate airline operated three 44-seat 202A 'Customliners', leased from California Airmotive, for a few months in 1960. Its 12-daily, 75-minute shuttle flights between Dallas-Love Field and Houston-Hobby featured 'Texas-Belle' cabin service. Operations started on or around March 1 but stopped before the end of the year. Fares were $10.80 (plus tax) one-way and 'commuter tickets' could be purchased in books of ten with a 5% discount. Lone Star offered 'commuter passengers' ten seats on each flight on a first-come, first-served basis, which could be reserved by calling its ticket office one hour before departure. (This innovation preceded Eastern's no reservations Air-Shuttle by a year.)

N93204	14074	60 -	60
N93207	14077	59 -	61
N93209	14079	60 -	61

Lone Star Airlines attempted a shuttle service between Dallas and Houston in 1960 using three 202As leased from California Airmotive Corp. Returned to the lessor, msn 14074/N93204 is seen in storage on July 14, 1961, with its orange trim gleaming in the Las Vegas sun. (Author)

MARCO ISLAND AIRWAYS
MARCO ISLAND, FLORIDA

Owned by the Deltona Corp, Marco Island Airways acquired 44-seat ex-Southern 404s to link Marco Island with Miami beginning October 1972. In spring 1980, the service was extended to Key West under contract to Air Florida, and a Miami–Tampa route added on November 15, 1980. In that year, the company upgraded from Part 135 to become a Part 121 carrier, adopted a revised color scheme, and shortened its name to Marco Airways. Subsequently, scheduled international service was flown from Miami to Eleuthera, Freeport, Marsh Harbour, Rock Sound, and Treasure Key, in the Bahamas. On December 2, 1981, Marco Airways became the Air Florida Commuter on that route, replacing the defunct Southern International Airways. These flights were continued until parent Air Florida ceased operations on July 3, 1984. Marco Airways was subsequently acquired by Provincetown-Boston Airline on October 5, 1984.

On July 22, 1982 a 404 operating Flight 39 between Miami and Key West was hijacked to Cuba by two men who poured gasoline on the floor of the aircraft.

N585S	14138	Sep73 -Sep75	spares use
N967M	14149	Sep73 - Oct84	
N968M	14159	Oct73 - Oct84	
N969M	14231	May74 - Oct84	

N973M	14156	76 - Oct84
N974M	14158	Oct77 - Oct84
N982M	14247	Dec77 - Oct84

Marco Island Airways flew ex-Southern Airways 404s in Florida intrastate service. Msn 14149/N967M is seen in the characteristic nose-low approach attitude. (MAP)

MARK AERO—SEE MISSOURI COMMUTER AIRLINES

MARTIN AIR TRANSPORT
MIAMI, FLORIDA

J Patrick Soltes, president of Martin Air Transport, acquired a 202A in 1975. The airplane, which had been stored for two years, was being restored to flying condition in 1976, but it is unclear how much, if any, use Martin Air Transport made of it.

N93205	14075	Jul75 - Jun79

MID AMERICA AIRLINES
TULSA, OKLAHOMA

N93209	14079	Nov67 -Aug69

Msn 14079/N93209 was used briefly by Mid America Airlines in red and black trim until it was repossessed in 1969. (Ronald C Hill)

MISSOURI COMMUTER AIRLINES
ST LOUIS, MISSOURI

Mark Aero, an associate of Petroleum Air Transport, leased three 404s in 1973-1974 for planned Missouri intrastate operation, but service never began. Negotiations were underway for a fourth 404 but, like the Missouri Commuter Airlines operation itself, never completed.

N302FA	14128	NTU
N465M	14152	74 - Jul76
N471M	14112	Jan74 -Dec76
N473M	14224	74 - Jul76

Mark Aero leased three 404s, including msn 14224/N473M, for a planned intrastate operation under the name Missouri Commuter Airlines. (Karl Krämer)

MODERN AIR TRANSPORT
TRENTON, NEW JERSEY; BALTIMORE, MARYLAND; & MIAMI, FLORIDA

A Gulf American Corp subsidiary, Modern Air Transport acquired five 202As in August 1966 for domestic supplemental and charter operations. Modern also held authority for charters to Canada and México, but the 202As do not appear to have ventured that far. The airline ceased all operations in September 1975.

N93205	14075	Aug66 - Oct69
N93206	14076	Aug66 - Oct69
N93208	14078	Aug66 - Jan70
N93209	14079	Aug66 -Nov67
N93212	14082	Aug66 - Jan70

One of five 202As (msn 14078/N93208) acquired by Modern Air Transport for domestic supplemental and charter operations. (Doug Olsen via Walt Redmond)

MOHAWK AIRLINES
UTICA-ROME, NEW YORK

Local Service carrier Mohawk acquired former Colonial Airlines routes in eastern New York and Vermont in 1961 from Eastern Air Lines. In order to supplement its Convair 240s, 340s, and 440s, and thereby serve its considerably expanded route system, Mohawk also obtained 15 404s from Eastern in the deal. The first 404 entered service on August 14, 1961; by the end of September, eight 404s were on routes primarily serving New York state, such as New York–Albany. As were its 240s, the 404s were flown under the class name 'Cosmopolitan'. Mohawk increased the seating capacity of its 404s from 40 to 44. One of those acquired from Eastern was used for parts and never placed into service. Another was leased but lost in a fatal accident. The 14 serviceable airplanes were sold to Ozark Air Lines in trade for more Convair 240s. Mohawk operated its last 404 service in September 1965.

N449A	14140	Jun63 - Jul63	LF Charlotte Acft
N460M	14162	Aug61 -Aug65	*Air Chief Delaware*
N461M	14227	Aug61 -Dec64	*Air Chief Manhattan*
N462M	14153	Aug61 -Mar65	*Air Chief Abnaki*

N463M	14155	Aug61 -Aug64	
N464M	14151	Aug61 -Dec65	*Air Chief Huron*
N465M	14152	Sep61 -Sep65	*Air Chief Sauk and Fox*
N466M	14164	Sep61 -Dec62	*Air Chief Ottawa*
N466M	14163	Dec62 -May65	*Air Chief Potawatomi* (regn switch with 14164)
N467M	14163	Sep61 -Dec62	*Air Chief Potawatomi*
N467M	14164	Dec62 - Oct64	*Air Chief Ottawa* (regn switch with 14163)
N468M	14139	Oct61 - Apr65	*Air Chief Montauk*
N469M	14148	Feb62 -Dec64	*Air Chief Susquehanna*
N470M	14109	Sep62 - Jun65	*Air Chief Montagnais*
N471M	14112	Sep62 - Oct65	*Air Chief Manhanset*
N472M	14234	Sep62 - Jul65	*Air Chief Powhaten*
N473M	14224	Oct62 -Aug65	*Air Chief Micmac*
N474A	14165	Dec62 -Sep65	spares use

Mohawk Airlines operated a large fleet of Martin 404s and Convair 240s, 340s and 440s. Air Chief Micmac (msn 14224/N473M) is seen taxiing past one of its 240s. Mohawk's 404s and 240s operated under the class name 'Cosmopolitan', while its 340s and 440s were 'Metropolitans'. (via Author)

MUTUAL AVIATION, INC
BUFFALO, NEW YORK

Mutual Aviation, a domestic scheduled all-cargo operator, ordered some 202s in 1946 for its services from New York, Newark and Buffalo. The order was canceled before their delivery, and Mutual ceased operations in 1948.

NAPLES AIRLINES—SEE PROVINCETOWN-BOSTON AIRLINE

NATIONAL SKYWAYS FREIGHT—THE FLYING TIGER LINE
LONG BEACH, CALIFORNIA

Flying Tiger ordered some all-cargo 202s in 1946; however, the order was canceled before their delivery. The airline used the slogan 'The Flying Tiger Line', then adopted it as the official name in 1947 after a move to Burbank, California.

NEVADA AIRLINES
LAS VEGAS, NEVADA

Air-taxi operator Nevada Airlines (owned by Stanley Booker) used a 404 for flights between Las Vegas and Grand Canyon. The airline was grounded by the FAA for safety violations on June 4, 1980, following the destruction of the aircraft in a crash in November 1979.

N40438	14173	May78 -Nov79

Ill-fated msn 14173/N40428, used by Nevada Airlines for sightseeing flights from Las Vegas to the Grand Canyon. The airplane crashed at Tuscavan, Arizona, in 1979 following an unwanted autofeather just after takeoff— fortunately without any loss of life. (A J Hickey via Peter J Marson)

NIHON KOKU KABUSHIKI KAISHA—SEE JAPAN AIR LINES CO, LTD

NORTHWEST AIRLINES
MINNEAPOLIS, MINNESOTA

Northwest ordered 25 Martin 303s (msns 13727-13751) plus 15 options in June 1946, with ten 202s (msns 9158-9167) to be leased pending delivery of the 303s. When the Model 303 was canceled, the ten 202s were converted to a firm sale. Service with 202s was started by October 12, 1947, on routes between Minneapolis-St Paul and Chicago, and between Chicago and Winnipeg via Minneapolis-St Paul, Fargo, and Grand Forks. Fifteen additional 202s were also ordered—three on December 23, 1947, and 12 on February 10, 1948). Most of the additional 202s were originally assigned to the canceled Pennsylvania-Central Airlines contract; however, two (msn 9133 & 9135) had been slated for delivery to an undisclosed French customer (undoubtedly Air France). As more airplanes were delivered, 202 service was extended east to New York and west to Seattle. Some 202s were delivered with 40-passenger interiors, but the fleet was subsequently standardized with 36-seat configurations. Following five fatal accidents in three years, all 20 surviving 202s were withdrawn from service on March 17, 1951.

NC93037	9158	Aug47 - Oct50	FN 537, *The Province of Alberta*
NC93038	9159	Aug47 -Mar51	FN 538
NC93039	9160	Sep47 -Mar51	FN 539
NC93040	9161	Sep47 -Nov50	FN 540
NC93041	9162	Oct47 -Mar51	FN 541
NC93042	9163	Oct47 -Mar51	FN 542
NC93043	9164	Oct47 -Mar51	FN 543
NC93044	9165	Nov47 -Aug48	FN 544
NC93045	9166	Nov47 -Mar51	FN 545
NC93046	9167	Nov47 -Mar51	FN 546, *Topliner North Star*
NC93047	9133	Dec47 -Mar51	FN 547
NC93048	9128	Dec47 -Mar51	FN 548
NC93049	9132	Dec47 -Mar51	FN 549
NC93050	9134	May48 -Mar50	FN 550
NC93051	9136	May48 -Mar51	FN 551
NC93052	9142	May48 -Mar51	FN 552
NC93053	9143	May48 -Mar51	FN 553, *Minneapolis*
NC93054	9144	May48 - Jan51	FN 554
NC93055	9145	Jun48 -Mar51	FN 555
NC93056	9146	May48 -Mar51	FN 556
NC93057	9135	Jun48 -Mar51	FN 557

NC93058	9147	Jun48 - Mar51	FN 558
NC93059	9148	Jun48 - Mar51	FN 559
NC93060	9149	Jun48 - Mar51	FN 560
NC93061	9150	Jun48 - Mar51	FN 561

N144S	14150	Jan80 - Oct80	
N145S	14142	Jan80 - Oct80	
N147S	14161	Jan80 - Oct80	
N149S	14141	79 - 79	LF Vero Monmouth
N257S	14110	Jan80 - Jan81	non-operational
N259S	14233	Jan80 - Oct80	

Northwest evaluated several different experimental liveries before adopting the scheme shown on msn 9144/NC93054 at Pittsburgh in 1948 as its standard. This airplane would later crash following an unexplained loss of control in cruise. A venerable TWA Boeing Stratoliner is partially visible in the background. (Howard Smeltzer)

Ocean Airways acquired five 404s in 1980, including msn 14161/N147S, from Florida Airlines and began service on Georgia routes abandoned by the latter's affiliate Air South. The operation was unsuccessful, and the 404s were returned to Florida Airlines in less than a year. (Jay L Sherlock)

Northwest's msn 9133/NC93047 with a slight variation in the logo. Northwest purportedly adopted its traditional red fin for enhanced air-to-air visibility.
(via John Wegg)

OZARK AIR LINES
St Louis, Missouri

Local Service carrier Ozark traded its Convair 240 fleet to Mohawk for 404s which were placed in service in December 1964, on routes from St Louis to Milwaukee, Minneapolis, and Chicago. The 404s only served about two years pending delivery of Fairchild Hiller FH-227s.

N456A	14147	Mar65 - Aug67
N460M	14162	Aug65 - Sep67
N461M	14227	Dec64 - Jul67
N462M	14153	Mar65 - Dec66
N463M	14155	Aug64 - Jul67
N464M	14151	Dec65 - Jun67
N465M	14152	Sep65 - Aug67
N466M	14163	May65 - Jun67
N467M	14164	Oct64 - Mar67
N468M	14139	Apr65 - Mar67
N469M	14148	Dec64 - Apr68
N470M	14109	Jun65 - Jul67
N471M	14112	Oct65 - Jul67
N472M	14234	Jul65 - Jan67
N473M	14224	Aug65 - Aug67

Like most airlines of that era, Northwest eventually added a white top as shown here on msn 9145/N93055, taxiing at General Mitchell Field, Milwaukee, Wisconsin, on July 29, 1950. (Leo J Kohn)

OCEAN AIRWAYS
New Haven, Connecticut, & St Simons Island, Georgia

Known as Monmouth Airlines until May 1979, this commuter airline leased a 404 from its sister company, Vero Monmouth Airlines (qv) for an Atlantic City–Baltimore–Washington route. In 1980, the Mid-Atlantic states operation was discontinued in favor of 404 service on the Georgia routes vacated by Florida Airlines-affiliate Air South. Five 404s, which were previously leased to Florida Airlines and acquired by Ocean Airways in January, were placed in service on March 15 on St Simons Island–Macon–Atlanta and St Simons Island–Atlanta routes. In August 1980, Macon–Atlanta was dropped but Atlanta–Montgomery was added. The airline suspended its southern division service by October 1980 because of poor revenues and the expenses of introducing 404s, and filed for Chapter 11 bankruptcy protection. The 404s were parked at Orlando and eventually purchased by the owner of Florida Airlines.

N469M, seen here preparing to depart from Minneapolis-St Paul in August 1964, was part of the fleet of 404s that Ozark Air Lines received from Mohawk in exchange for its former fleet of Convair 240s. (Howard M Svendsen)

PACIFIC AIR LINES
SAN FRANCISCO, CALIFORNIA

Following completion of the contract with Japan Air Lines, Transocean Air Lines offered the four 40-passenger 202s flown on behalf of that airline for sale. Southwest Airways, the predecessor of Pacific Air Lines, purchased them in fall 1952 for $1 million. After refurbishment, two were placed in service on April 17, 1953, supplementing Douglas DC-3s on Southwest's San Francisco–San Jose–Monterey/Carmel–Paso Robles–Santa Barbara–Los Angeles route. On March 15, 1954, one (N93061) made a belly-landing at Oxnard, but was quickly returned to service. One of the original 202s was destroyed in a hangar fire, but Southwest acquired four more, one from California Central and three from Pioneer, to bring its fleet to seven by 1956. Pacific Air Lines, as the carrier was known after March 6, 1958, expanded Martin service north to Medford, and conducted contract flights on behalf of the US Navy. The 202s were also used extensively for charter service.

As an interim measure, the 202s were supplemented in 1958 and 1959 with three 202As leased from TWA and one leased from California Airmotive (the latter was only used for ten days before it was written-off in a ground accident). Beginning late in 1959, Pacific began to replace the 202s and 202As with ex-TWA 404s. In addition to returning the leased 202As, Pacific also sold five 202s to TWA in trade for 404s.

Pacific received Supplemental Type Certificate (STC) SA4-1042 to increase the passenger capacity of its 404s to 44. One 404 was converted later to an all-cargo configuration. Pacific operated its last scheduled 404 passenger service in April 1967, when Fairchild F-27s took the shorter routes over completely. Pacific merged with Bonanza and West Coast Airlines on April 9, 1968, to form Air West. As the five remaining 404s were retired and awaiting sale, none were repainted in Air West colors.

N93041	9162	Oct52 - Jun60	FN 041
N93047	9133	Mar55 - Jun60	FN 047
N93049	9132	Oct52 - Jun60	FN 049

N93053	9143	Jan56 - Mar64	FN 053
N93056	9146	Jan56 - Jun60	FN 056
N93059	9148	Jan56 - Dec63	FN 059
N93060	9149	Oct52 - Jun60	FN 060
N93061	9150	Sep52 - Dec55	FN 061
N93202	14072	Aug59 - Aug59	FN 202, LF Calif Airmotive
N93205	14075	Apr58 - Jun59	FN 205, LF TWA
N93206	14076	Jan59 - May59	FN 206, LF TWA
N93208	14078	Dec58 - May59	FN 208, LF TWA
N444A	14121	May62 - Aug68	FN 444
N455A	14146	May62 - Jul66	FN 455
N40408	14108	Sep60 - Apr66	FN 408
N40409	14113	Apr60 - Sep64	FN 409
N40422	14128	Sep60 - Aug68	FN 422
N40427	14133	Apr60 - Aug68	FN 427
N40432	14167	Nov59 - Aug68	FN 432
N40436	14171	Jan60 - Jul67	FN 436
N40438	14173	Jan60 - Aug68	FN 438, later all-cargo
N40441	14176	Nov59 - Sep67	FN 441

Note: The 202As also retained TWA fleet numbers in some cases.

Southwest eventually dropped 'Airways' from the titles as seen at San Francisco on msn 9148/N93059. (Clay Jansson via Walt Redmond)

In 1958, Southwest changed its name to the more geographically appropriate Pacific Air Lines, as shown on msn 9143/N93053. (Clay Jansson via Walt Redmond)

Southwest Airways operated N93061 for about only a month in this DC-3 era paint scheme. Msn 9150 was later damaged beyond repair late in 1955 in a hangar fire at San Francisco. (William T Larkins)

N93060 is seen at San Francisco, California, in October 1952 in the definitive Southwest Airways 202 paint design. A United DC-6 Mainliner is caught taking off in the background. (William T Larkins)

Except for 'Four O Four' that appears on the fin of msn 14133/N40427, Pacific retained the same basic livery as used on its 202s. (William T Larkins)

N93053 is seen at Los Angeles in January 1963 after the addition of FAA-required weather radar. (Clay Jansson via Walt Redmond)

N40408 is also seen after the addition of weather radar. 'Four O Four' has been removed from the fin—as the 202s were all gone, there was no longer any point in emphasizing that it was an improved 404. (via Alex Reinhard)

PAN AMERICAN-GRACE AIRWAYS INC (PANAGRA)
NEW YORK, NEW YORK

PANAGRA, which was jointly owned by Pan American Airways and steamship operator W R Grace and Co, ordered seven 303s (msns 13788-13794) in 1946 to replace DC-3s. The order was later canceled.

PANAGRA's order for seven 303s was announced in June 1946. (The Martin Star)

PAT AIR—SEE PETROLEUM AIR TRANSPORT

PBA—SEE PROVINCETOWN-BOSTON AIRLINE

PENNSYLVANIA-CENTRAL AIRLINES (PCA)
WASHINGTON, DISTRICT OF COLUMBIA

PCA was the launch customer for the 202, ordering 35 aircraft in November 1945, plus 15 more the following January. Seating capacity was to have been 40, with delivery scheduled from early in 1947. Of the 50 202s, all but 20 (msns 9128, 9132, 9134, 9136, and 9142-9157) were canceled by the time the 202 received its type certificate. Those too were canceled in mid-September 1947. Some were completed for Northwest; others were placed

in storage partially completed. Because of its association with the nation's capital, PCA used the advertising slogan 'The Capital Airline' during that period and later adopted Capital Airlines, Inc, as its corporate title. Although the attempt to modernize its fleet with 202s was unsuccessful, the airline later became the US pioneer in turbine power with Vickers Viscounts.

PETROLEUM AIR TRANSPORT (PAT AIR)
ST LOUIS, MISSOURI, & LAFAYETTE, LOUISIANA

Petroleum Air Transport (Pat Air) was owned by Mark G Morris who also owned Mark Aero (later Jet Way), and operated a fleet of passenger 404s (plus Douglas DC-3s and DC-6s) on oil industry personnel charters out of Louisiana. Pat Air was acquired by DHL Corp in 1978, and the three 404s then operated were transferred the following year to DHL Airlines in Hawaii. Pat Air was declared bankrupt in February 1980.

N465M	14152	Jul76 - Mar79
N471M	14112	Jul76 - Mar79
N473M	14224	Jul76 - Mar79
N40436	14171	Jan76 - Sep76

PIEDMONT AIRLINES
WINSTON-SALEM, NORTH CAROLINA

Piedmont acquired one of the largest fleets of 404s, mostly ex-TWA, beginning late in 1961. The first two aircraft were introduced on January 1, 1962, on Knoxville–Tri Cities (Bristol/Kingsport/Johnson City)–Roanoke–Lynchburg–Charlottesville–Washington, and Knoxville–Asheville–Charlotte–Winston-Salem–Greensboro–Highpoint–Raleigh-Durham–Rocky Point–Elizabeth City–Norfolk routes. All were operated with 44-passenger interiors. The 202 was used only for spares. All surviving 404s were sold to US Aircraft Sales Co in trade for NAMC YS-11s.

N40400	9123	65 -	65	spares use
N462M	14153	Jun67 -	Jul68	FN 462, *Long Island Pacemaker*, LF Fairchild Hiller
N467M	14164	May67 -	Jun68	FN 467, *Cherokee Pacemaker*, LF Fairchild Hiller
N468M	14139	May67 -	Jun68	FN 468, *Brazos River Pacemaker*, LF Fairchild Hiller
N472M	14234	May67 -	Jul68	FN 472, *Fox River Valley Pacemaker*, LF Fairchild Hiller
N40401	14101	Jan62 -	Aug62	FN 401, *Tidewater Pacemaker*
N40401	14106	Feb65 -	Dec69	FN 401, *Great Smokies Pacemaker*
N40402	14102	Feb65 -	Nov72	FN 402, *Savannah River Pacemaker*
N40403	14174	May65 -	Oct68	FN 403, *Mount Mitchell Pacemaker*
N40405	14105	Feb62 -	Jan70	FN 405, *Ohio Valley Pacemaker*
N40406	14170	Sep68 -	Nov66	FN 406, *Appomattox Pacemaker*
N40407	14107	Dec61 -	Mar72	FN 407, *Blue Grass Pacemaker*
N40408	14108	Apr66 -	Jan73	FN 408, *Rappahannock Pacemaker*
N40410	14114	Feb62 -	Dec68	FN 410, *Shenandoah Pacemaker*
N40411	14115	Feb62 -	Jan70	FN 411, *Tennessee Valley Pacemaker*
N40413	14117	Jan62 -	Jun72	FN 403, *Sand Hills Pacemaker*
N40414	14118	Oct61 -	Jan73	FN 414, *Commonwealth Pacemaker*
N40415	14119	Jan62 -	Oct72	FN 415, *Yadkin Valley Pacemaker*
N40417	14123	Dec61 -	Oct68	FN 417, *Piedmont Pacemaker*
N40418	14124	Jan62 -	Dec68	FN 418, *Hampton Roads Pacemaker*

N40419	14125	Dec61 - Feb72	FN 419, *Kanawha River Pacemaker*
N40420	14126	Dec61 - Apr69	FN 420, *Tarheel Pacemaker*
N40421	14127	Jan62 -Nov69	FN 421, *Appalachian Pacemaker*
N40423	14129	Feb62 - Jan72	FN 423, *Pamlico Pacemaker*
N40424	14130	Feb68 - Oct68	FN 424, *Pee Dee Pacemaker*
N40425	14131	Apr66 -Dec68	FN 425, *Manassa Pacemaker*
N40430	14136	Dec61 -Dec68	FN 430, *Chesapeake Pacemaker*
N40433	14168	Jan62 - Jan70	FN 433, *Peach Tree Pacemaker, Tidewater Pacemaker*
N40440	14166	Nov64 - Oct68	FN 440, *Santee Pacemaker*
N40442	14225	Oct62 -Nov69	FN 442, *Blue Ridge Pacemaker*
N40443	14228	Oct62 - Oct69	FN 443, *Tidewater Pacemaker*
N40444	14229	Dec62 -Nov69	FN 444, *West Virginia Centennial 1863-1963 Pacemaker, New River Pacemaker*
N40445	14230	Dec62 - Feb70	FN 445, *Potomac Pacemaker*
N40446	14238	Apr64 - Jul66	FN 446, *Buckeye Pacemaker*
N40447	14239	Aug64 -Nov64	FN 447
N40448	14242	Aug64 - Oct68	FN 448, *Albemarle Pacemaker*
N40450	14146	Jul66 -Dec69	FN 450, *York River Pacemaker*

Two of Piedmont's 404s (N40414 Commonwealth Pacemaker *and N40418* Hampton Roads Pacemaker, *respectively) at Atlanta on April 30, 1966. The '404' legend on the fins appears in different styles.* (Robert E Hufford)

PIONEER AIR LINES
HOUSTON, TEXAS

Essair, the predecessor of Pioneer Air Lines, was the first Local Service operator to be certificated. After upgrading from an initial fleet of Lockheed 10-A Electras to 11 Douglas DC-3s, Pioneer, as it was known by then, recognized a need for modern postwar airplanes to replace the DC-3s. Nine 36-seat 202s were purchased from Northwest and flown under the class name 'Pacemaster' from June 2, 1952, until their CAB-forced retirement a year later. Routes served included Houston–Austin–San Angelo–Midland Odessa–Lubbock– Plainview–Amarillo, Dallas/Ft Worth–Abilene–Lubbock–Clovis, and Santa Fe–Albuquerque. Five new Convair 340-60s (msns 170,179, 180, 185, & 186) were also ordered at the time of the 202 pur- chase; however, they were later delivered to United Air Lines when Pioneer failed to obtain government approval for their acquisition. The 202 fleet was transferred to Pioneer Aeronautical Services and stored at Dallas-Love Field then other locations, including Oakland, California.

N93038	9159	Apr52 - Jan56	FN 038, *Pacemaster Stephen F Austin*
N93046	9167	Mar52 -Nov60	FN 046, *Pacemaster Sam Houston*
N93048	9128	Apr52 -Dec56	FN 048, *Pacemaster David Crockett*
N93051	9136	Apr52 -May55	FN 051, *Pacemaster Ben Milam*
N93053	9143	Mar52 - Jan56	FN 053, *Pacemaster William B Travis*
N93055	9145	Apr52 - Jan56	FN 055, *Pacemaster Kit Carson*
N93056	9146	Mar52 - Jan56	FN 056, *Pacemaster James Bowie*
N93058	9147	Apr52 -Dec57	FN 058, *Pacemaster Mirabeau B Lamar*
N93059	9148	Mar52 - Jan56	FN 059, *Pacemaster James Fannin*

Pioneer Air Lines had expected to obtain nine 202As and used this retouched photo of N93201 for promotional purposes. The deal fell through when TWA decided to keep them, forcing Pioneer to settle for nine ex-Northwest 202s. (via Jim Babcock)

Pacemaster Kit Carson *(N93055), one of Pioneer's nine 202s. The ex-Northwest 202s were overhauled at Greenville, Texas, by TEMCO, which had originally modified 202s.* (Doug Olson via Peter M Bowers)

PROA–SEE AEROPROVEEDORA LTDA

PRO AIR SERVICES, INC (PROAIR)
MIAMI, FLORIDA

Proair, an affiliate of International Transfer Corp, operated scheduled service between the Bahamas and Fort Lauderdale and Miami, plus passenger and cargo charters. Besides the 404, which was first registered to Coastal Airways, at the same address, Proair also used Douglas DC-3s, Beech 18s, and an Aero Commander 500.

| N255S | 14246 | Mar84 -Dec85 | |

One of the last 404 operators in the US was Pro Air Service, an affiliate of International Transfer Corp. Msn 14246/N255S was used in scheduled service between the Bahamas and Miami. (Tommy Lakmaker)

PROVINCETOWN-BOSTON AIRLINE (PBA)
PROVINCETOWN, MASSACHUSETTS, & NAPLES, FLORIDA

Founded in 1949, PBA operated scheduled service in the New York–Maine–Massachusetts market during the summer under the PBA title and in Florida during winter months under the division name Naples

Airlines. In 1976, PBA acquired a fleet of 44-seat 404s from defunct Southeast Airlines to add to its Douglas DC-3s and Cessna 402s. Initially, the 404s were used only in Florida because Provincetown's runway was too short. Even after the runway was extended, the 404s were not used regularly on the Northeast network until June 1979, when PBA took over from defunct Nor'East on the Boston–Hyannis route. PBA experienced unprecedented growth from 1981 to 1984, adding 24 destinations and 50 aircraft—including turbine-powered Bandeirantes and NAMC YS-11s—and buying several airlines. Marco Island Airways (qv) was acquired in October 1984; however, the FAA revoked PBA's operating certificate on November 10, 1984, for maintenance and management violations. Full service was restored by December 2, but the airline suffered a fatal Bandeirante crash four days later. Although the crash was attributed to an aircraft design defect, rather than PBA's operation, the loss of passenger confidence led to a Chapter 11 bankruptcy filing on March 13, 1985. PBA was acquired by PEOPLExpress a year later. None of PBA's 404s, nor those acquired from Marco Island Airways, were returned to service after the FAA certificate revocation.

N967M	14149	Oct84 -Sep88	grounded Nov84
N968M	14159	Oct84 -Dec88	grounded Nov84
N969M	14231	Oct84 -Sep88	grounded Nov84
N973M	14156	Oct84 -Dec85	spares use only
N974M	14158	Oct84 -May86	grounded Nov84
N982M	14247	Oct84 -May86	non-operational
N40403	14174	Apr77 - 87	spares use only
N40407	14107	Jan76 -Sep88	grounded Nov84
N40413	14117	Jan76 -Sep88	grounded Nov84
N40415	14119	Dec76 -Sep88	grounded Oct77
N40417	14123	Feb78 - 87	spares use only
N40420	14126	May77 - 87	spares use only
N40423	14129	Jan77 -Feb87	grounded Nov84
N40424	14130	Nov75 -Sep88	grounded Nov84
N40425	14131	Nov75 -May86	grounded Nov84
N40440	14166	Feb78 - 88	spares use only

Provincetown-Boston Airline (PBA) began service in 1949 linking the tip of Cape Cod with Boston, then expanded to include service to other areas in New England. When Southeast Airlines folded in 1976, PBA acquired its four 404s, including msn 14107/N40407. (MAP)

During the winter months when there was little traffic to Cape Cod, PBA followed the vacation traffic to Florida and operated intrastate service there under the name Naples Airlines. (John P Stewart)

RAPSA—SEE RUTAS AÉREAS PANAMENAS SA

RED BARON CHARTER
CLAYTON, MISSOURI

N69RB	14114	Mar73 -Feb75

RENTAVION, CA
CARACAS, VENEZUELA

Based at Caracas-Maiquetia, Rentavion, a Douglas DC-3 operator, acquired three 404s, although to date only one aircraft has been used at any time. The 48-seat 404s have been used mostly for tourist charters to Caribbean islands and for day-trips between Porlamar and Canaima National Park, the site of Angel Falls. Rentavion is the last commercial operator of the Martinliner anywhere, and plans to make a second aircraft operational. Evidently, at one time it also planned to acquire more ex-PBA 404s as well.

YV-145C	14129	May89 -	active
YV-149C	14247	Sep88 -	stored
YV-150C	14171	Oct88 -	being made operational

ROYAL HAITIAN HOTEL
PORT-AU-PRINCE, HAITI

The Royal Haitian Hotel used a 404 for charters between Haiti and Florida. It was later registered HH-RHH in Haiti and reputedly used for state transport by the dictator in power at the time.

N40419	14125	Mar77 - Jan87

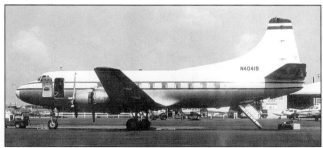

N40419 was operated on behalf of the Royal Haitian Hotel from the mid-1970s for charters between Florida and Haiti, and was eventually re-registered in Haiti as HH-RHH. The trim lines were red (top) and blue (lower), and these colors were repeated (in reverse order) on the fin, and on the wing tips (blue at the tip). (John Wegg)

RUTAS AÉREAS PANAMENAS SA (RAPSA)
PANAMA CITY, PANAMÁ

RAPSA, an associate of Aerovías Panama SA (APASA), started charter operations in September 1958. From February 1965 through May 1970, RAPSA used three 202s (plus three DC-3s) for scheduled service in competition with COPA between Panama City and David. The three 202s are believed to have been scrapped at Panama City around 1972.

HP-398	9133	Sep64 -Feb72
HP-427	9136	Mar66 -Feb72
HP-431	9163	Jul66 - 72

HP-431 was one of three 202s used by Rutas Aéreas Panamenas SA (RAPSA) for scheduled service between Panama City and David. (Dan Hagedorn via Gary Kuhn)

RAPSA later adopted a much brighter red and white livery, as shown by HP-398. (VIP Photoservice)

SANTIAGO FREIGHT CARGO, CXA
SANTIAGO, DOMINICAN REPUBLIC

This operator, also known as Santiago SA, obtained an ex-PBA 404 in 1987 and then an ADSA 404, but neither may have been operated. Both airplanes were sold to Rentavion, Venezuela and the company no longer exists.

HI-501	14129	Mar87 -May89
HI-285	14157	-Sep89

SERVICIO AÉREO BAJA—SEE BAJA AIR LINES

SHAWNEE AIRLINES
ORLANDO, FLORIDA

Shawnee Airlines flew scheduled services from July 1968 to December 1972 when it ceased operations. Operations were resumed in April 1973 after a reorganization, with services from Orlando to West Palm Beach and Fort Lauderdale, and to Freeport and Nassau.

Following its acquisition of Orlando–based Shawnee Airlines, Florida Airlines operated some of its 404s, including msn 14233/N259S, on former Shawnee routes with Shawnee titles and livery. (John P Stewart)

The yellow and rose color scheme of the 404s rivaled that of TWA aircraft in brightness, if not aesthetic qualities. Shawnee was acquired by Florida Airlines (qv) in 1976, but continued operations under its own name until the following year.

N255S	14246	Feb77 -Sep77	
N257S	14110	Jan76 - Mar78	
N259S	14233	Feb76 -May76	
N468M	14139	76 - 76	non-operational
N469M	14148	Nov76 - 76	non-operational

SOCIÉTÉ NATIONAL DE TRANSPORT
PORT-AU-PRINCE, HAITI

One 404 was acquired in 1980 but apparently not placed in service as it retained its US registry and was resold a couple of months later.

N40436	14171	Jun80 -Aug80

SOUTHEAST AIRLINES
MIAMI, FLORIDA

Southeast was formed in 1958 as Cat Cay Airlines and started charter operations the following year. After it had changed its name, the company moved into scheduled intrastate service and, early in the 1970s, used ex-Piedmont 404s with 44-passenger interiors for service between Miami, Key West, Marathon, and Opa-locka, and Freeport, Bahamas. The four 202As acquired earlier from Modern Air Transport were apparently used only for charter operations as all flight schedules referred to 404s. Operations were suspended because of financial difficulties in June 1976, and the 404s were sold to PBA. The company was subsequently revived and acquired by MCA Leasing but ceased all activity in 1981.

N93205	14075	Oct69 -Mar75	
N93206	14076	Oct69 - Jan72	
N93208	14078	Jan70 - Jan72	spares use
N93212	14082	Jan70 - Jan72	
N40407	14107	Apr72 - Jan76	
N40413	14117	Jun72 - Jan76	
N40424	14130	Dec71 -Nov75	
N40425	14131	Apr72 -Nov75	
N67097	14145	Dec75 - Jul76	spares use only

One of the earliest Florida intrastate operators was Southeast Airlines. Following initial service with Fairchild F-27s and smaller airplanes, Southeast Airlines acquired a fleet of former Allegheny Airlines 202As, including msn 14075/N93205. (Peter R Keating)

Southeast Airlines replaced its F-27s and all but one 202A in 1972 with four ex-Piedmont 404s which it flew until all operations were suspended in June 1976. (MAP)

SOUTHERN AIRWAYS
ATLANTA, GEORGIA

Local Service airline Southern Airways acquired a fleet of ex-Eastern 404s and introduced the type in service on October 29, 1961, on Atlanta–Dothan–Eglin AFB, Atlanta–Huntsville–Muscle Shoals, and Atlanta–Columbus–Dothan–Panama City routes with the class name 'Aristocrat'. Southern was the last 'major' US scheduled airline operating 404s (or any other reciprocating engine-powered transport for that matter) when N144S made Southern's last 404 flight on April 30, 1978. The former Federated Department Stores executive 404 was only owned for one day in what appears to be a paper transaction for its sale from Lockheed Aircraft to Piedmont.

N141S	14156	Jul61 - 76	FN 101
N142S	14157	Jul61 -Sep63	FN 102
N143S	14237	Nov61 - Apr74	FN 103
N144S	14150	Oct61 -May78	FN 104
N145S	14142	Sep61 -May78	FN 105
N146S	14223	May62 - 70	FN 106
N147S	14161	Aug62 -Mar78	FN 107
N148S	14160	Sep62 - 70	FN 108
N149S	14141	Dec62 -Aug75	FN 109
N251S	14243	Dec62 - Jan68	FN 110
N252S	14154	Dec62 - 70	FN 111
N253S	14158	Dec62 - Oct77	FN 112
N254S	14159	Dec62 - Oct73	FN 113
N255S	14246	Aug63 -Mar72	FN 114
N256S	14236	Jun64 - Feb72	FN 115
N257S	14110	Jun64 - Jan76	FN 116
N258S	14232	Jun64 -Dec77	FN 117
N259S	14233	Jun64 - Jan76	FN 118

The last 'major' US scheduled airline to operate Martin 404s was Southern Airways. Heading the four pictured at Atlanta in September 1968 is msn 14110/N257S (formerly Eastern's N441A). There are differences in livery and radar installations—the latter probably dependent on whether the radar was installed before retirement from Eastern service. (Gordon Reid)

N581S	14247	Oct64 -Dec77	FN 119
N582S	14239	Nov64 - 76	FN 120
N583S	14111	May65 - Jun76	FN 121
N584S	14149	Aug65 -Sep73	FN 122
N585S	14138	Aug65 -Sep73	FN 123
N586S	14245	Sep65 - 71	FN 124
N587S	14231	Jan66 -May74	FN 125
N671L	14174	May65 -May65	non-operational

Note: Southern originally used the three numbers of the registration as fleet numbers.

SOUTHERN INTERNATIONAL AIRWAYS
SARASOTA/BRADENTON, FLORIDA

Southern International was formed on August 7, 1981, as the post-bank-ruptcy successor to Florida Airlines (qv). By the end of the year it operated solely as an Air Florida Commuter with some of the 404s in full Air Florida Commuter livery. It operated its last Air Florida Commuter flight on December 1, 1981, and ceased operations.

N144S	14150	Aug81 -Feb85
N145S	14142	Aug81 -Feb85
N147S	14161	Aug81 -Nov82
N255S	14246	Aug81 - Jan83
N258S	14232	Aug81 -Aug83
N259S	14233	Aug81 -Feb85

Three Southern International Airways 404s were acquired by Wheeler Systems Inc for cargo service. Although Systems-International Airways did use a sistership, msn 14142/N145S remained in storage at Bartow, Florida, as seen here, until it was obtained in 1990 by Save A Connie Inc for preservation.
(Karl Krämer)

SOUTHWEST AIRWAYS—SEE PACIFIC AIR LINES

SYSTEMS-INTERNATIONAL AIRWAYS, INC (SIA)
WASHINGTON, DISTRICT OF COLUMBIA

Systems-International Airways received three ex-Southern International Airways 404s from parent Wheeler Systems, Inc, in February 1985 and was subsequently FAA-certificated as a cargo carrier. One 404 (N144S) was used briefly in this service; however, it eventually joined the other two, which had retained their passenger interiors, in storage at Bartow, Florida. Sistership N145S was later stored at Fort Lauderdale, Florida, then acquired by Save A Connie for preservation.

N144S	14150	Apr89 -
N145S	14142	Apr88 -Sep90
N259S	14233	Apr88 -

TAC COLOMBIA
BOGOTÁ, COLOMBIA

Aeroproveedora operated some flights on behalf of TAC Colombia using its 202.

HK-1484   9167

TAINO AIRWAYS
SANTO DOMINGO, DOMINICAN REPUBLIC

Aero Virgin Islands (AVI) operated its sole 404 on behalf of Taino Airways occasionally.

N40425   14131

TRANS GLOBAL AIRLINES
Jet Power, dba Trans Global Airlines, owned a 404 for just one month.

N40450   14146   Nov76 -Nov76

TRANS WORLD AIRLINES (TWA)
KANSAS CITY, MISSOURI

Formerly known as Transcontinental & Western Air, TWA—then under the control of Howard Hughes—operated a fleet of 12 202As and 40 404s with standard 36-and 40-passenger interiors, respectively, under the class name 'Skyliner'. The 202As (Fleet numbers 211-222) replaced Boeing 307 Stratoliners on a Pittsburgh–New York route, and Douglas DC-3s on Kansas City–Chicago–Dayton– Columbus–Pittsburgh–Philadelphia–New York, and Kansas City–Chicago–Pittsburgh–Philadelphia–New York routes effective September 1, 1950.

TWA operated its first commercial service with the 404 (Fleet numbers 401-441) on January 15, 1952, and Martinliner service was gradually extended to the shorter segments of TWA's entire domestic route system. The last 404 service was operated on April 29, 1961. Routes served just before retirement included St Louis–Terre Haute–Indianapolis–Dayton–Washington–Baltimore; Kansas City–St Louis–Louisville–Cincinnati; Chicago–Dayton–Columbus–Pittsburgh; and Chicago–Dayton–Columbus–Wheeling–Washington–Baltimore. Baltimore, the birthplace of the Martinliner, was appropriately one of the last cities served. Following retirement, the 19 surviving aircraft were stored at St Louis, Kansas City, and Chicago, but all were disposed of by early 1962.

TWA also took five 202s from Pacific in trade for 404s; however, they were placed in storage and not operated.

Reg	Msn	Dates	Notes
N93041	9162	Jun60 -Sep60	non-operational
N93047	9133	Jun60 -Nov61	non-operational
N93049	9132	Jun60 -Nov61	non-operational
N93056	9146	Jun60 -Nov61	non-operational
N93060	9149	Jun60 -Nov61	non-operational
N93201	14071	Jul50 - Apr58	FN 211, *Skyliner San Francisco*
N93202	14072	Jul50 - Jul59	FN 212, *Skyliner Oakland*
N93203	14073	Jul50 -Dec58	FN 213, *Skyliner Fresno*
N93204	14074	Aug50 - Jul59	FN 214, *Skyliner Burbank*
N93205	14075	Jul50 - Jul59	FN 215, *Skyliner Los Angeles*
N93206	14076	Aug50 - Oct59	FN 216, *Skyliner Phoenix*
N93207	14077	Aug50 - Jul59	FN 217, *Skyliner Las Vegas*
N93208	14078	Aug50 - Oct59	FN 218, *Skyliner Albuquerque*
N93209	14079	Sep50 - Jul59	FN 219, *Skyliner Santa Fe*
N93210	14080	Sep50 -Dec58	FN 220, *Skyliner Amarillo*
N93211	14081	Sep50 - Jan55	FN 221, *Skyliner Lancaster*

Msn 14076/N93206 at New York-LaGuardia on August 14, 1950, as originally delivered with TWA markings applied over a bare metal fuselage.

(Leo J Kohn)

Reg	Msn	Dates	Notes
N93212	14082	Sep50 -Dec58	FN 222, *Skyliner Hannibal*, later *Skyliner Denver*
N40401	14101	Feb52 - Jan62	FN 401, *Skyliner Baltimore*
N40402	14102	Jan52 - Jun61	FN 402, *Skyliner Indianapolis*, later *Skyliner Chicago*
N40403	14103	Nov51 - Apr56	FN 403, *Skyliner Pittsburgh*
N40404	14104	Nov51 -Nov56	FN 404, *Skyliner Philadelphia*
N40405	14105	Dec51 - Feb62	FN 405, *Skyliner New York*
N40406	14106	Dec51 - Feb60	FN 406, *Skyliner Washington DC*
N40407	14107	Dec51 -Dec61	FN 407, *Skyliner Indianapolis*
N40408	14108	Dec51 -Sep60	FN 408, *Skyliner Columbus*
N40409	14113	Dec51 - Jun60	FN 409, *Skyliner Dayton*
N40410	14114	Dec51 - Feb62	FN 410, *Skyliner Cincinnati*
N40411	14115	Jan52 - Feb62	FN 411, *Skyliner St Louis*
N40412	14116	Jan52 - Mar60	FN 412, *Skyliner Wheeling*
N40413	14117	May52 - Jan62	FN 413, *Skyliner Louisville*
N40414	14118	May52 - Oct61	FN 414, *Skyliner Boston*, later *Skyliner Dayton*
N40415	14119	May52 - Jan62	FN 415, *Skyliner Albany*
N40416	14120	May52 - Feb55	FN 416, *Skyliner Binghamton*
N40417	14123	Jun52 -Dec61	FN 417, *Skyliner Williamsport*
N40418	14124	Jun52 - Jan62	FN 418, *Skyliner Newark*
N40419	14125	Jun52 - Jan62	FN 419, *Skyliner Wilmington*
N40420	14126	Jun52 - Jan62	FN 420, *Skyliner Allentown*
N40421	14127	Jun52 - Jan62	FN 421, *Skyliner Harrisburg*, later *Skyliner Washington*
N40422	14128	Jun52 -Sep60	FN 422, *Skyliner Kansas City*
N40423	14129	Jun52 - Feb62	FN 423, *Skyliner Reading*
N40424	14130	Jun52 - Feb62	FN 424, *Skyliner Toledo*
N40425	14131	Jun52 - Mar59	FN 425, *Skyliner Zanesville*, later *Skyliner Easton*
N40426	14132	Jul52- Feb59	FN 426, *Skyliner Mansfield*, later *Skyliner Bethlehem*
N40427	14133	Jul52 - Jun60	FN 427, *Skyliner Fort Wayne*
N40428	14134	Jul52 - Jan60	FN 428, *Skyliner South Bend*
N40429	14135	Jul52 - Mar59	FN 429, *Skyliner Peoria*
N40430	14136	Jul52 -Dec61	FN 430, *Skyliner Quincy*, later *Skyliner Oklahoma City*
N40431	14166	Jul52 - Aug59	FN 431, *Skyliner Terre Haute*
N40432	14167	Jul52 - Jun60	FN 432, *Skyliner Detroit*
N40433	14168	Aug52 - Jan62	FN 433, *Skyliner Cleveland*
N40434	14169	Aug52 - Jun61	FN 434, *Skyliner Topeka*
N40435	14170	Aug52 - Feb61	FN 435, *Skyliner Wichita*

N40436	14171	Aug52 - Jun60	FN 436, *Skyliner Wilkes-Barre*, later *Skyliner Scranton*
N40438	14173	Aug52 - Jun60	FN 438, *Skyliner Endicott*
N40439	14174	Sep52 -Nov59	FN 439, *Skyliner Johnson City*
N40440	14175	Sep52 -Nov59	FN 440, *Skyliner Schenectady*
N40441	14176	Sep52 - Jun60	FN 441, *Skyliner Troy*, later *Skyliner Wilkes-Barre*

N93038	9159	Sep51 - Apr52	LF NWA
N93039	9160	Sep51 -Nov51	LF NWA
N93041	9162	Sep51 - Oct52	LT JAL
N93043	9164	Aug51 - Apr52	LT JAL
N93046	9167	Sep51 - Mar52	LF NWA
N93048	9128	Sep51 - Apr52	LF NWA
N93049	9132	Aug51 - Oct52	LT JAL
N93051	9136	Sep51 - Apr52	LF NWA
N93053	9143	Sep51 - Mar52	LF NWA
N93055	9145	Oct51 - Apr52	LF NWA
N93056	9146	Oct51 - Mar52	LF NWA
N93058	9147	Oct51 - Apr52	LF NWA
N93059	9148	Sep51 - Mar52	LF NWA
N93060	9149	Oct51 -Sep52	LF NWA
N93061	9150	Oct51 - Oct52	LF NWA/LTJAL

Although 202As were intended only for interim use pending delivery of its 404 fleet, TWA decided to exercise a purchase option and keep them. Msn 14073/N93203 Skyliner Fresno is seen in later years after the addition of a white fuselage background. (Leo J Kohn via Eric W Wagner)

Msn 9132/N93049 was one of three 202s purchased by Transocean Air Lines and used briefly on non-scheduled coast-to-coast passenger service. (A R Krieger)

TWA's 404s, introduced into service on January 15, 1952, carried a very similar red and white color scheme. At first glance Fleet Number 424 (msn 14130/N40424) Skyliner Toledo—taken at its namesake city on April 26, 1957—appears to be identical, but there is a subtle change of position for 'Trans World Airlines' in comparison to the cabin windows. Other visible changes are the anti-collision light on the top of the fuselage and modified rear fuselage radio aerial.

TWA operated its last Martin Skyliner trip (Flight 411) on Saturday, April 30, from Baltimore's Friendship International Airport to Washington-National; Columbus, Dayton, Indianapolis, and St Louis. (Howard M Svendsen)

Apart from the three purchased airplanes, Transocean also leased a dozen 202s from Northwest for domestic military airlift operations, one of which was msn 9150/N93061. Like the three owned airplanes, the leased 202s retained the basic Northwest livery. (William T Larkins)

TRANSOCEAN AIR LINES
OAKLAND, CALIFORNIA

Transocean Air Lines, which was sometimes known as TALOA (after its cable address, Transocean Air Lines OAkland), briefly used 15 202s early in the 1950s. Three were purchased from Northwest and used initially for non-scheduled passenger service between San Francisco, Los Angeles, and New York via Salt Lake City, Denver, and Chicago. The others were leased from Northwest and used on military contract flights (with 'Airlift' titles) in a 44-seat configuration. When the coast-to-coast service proved to be unprofitable, five aircraft were flown on behalf of newly resurrected Japan Air Lines (qv) under sub-contract to Northwest (qv). One crashed in military contract service and another was lost in Japan. There is an unconfirmed report that two Transocean 202s were registered TJ-ABK and TJ-ABL in 1951/1952 in Transjordan for *Hajj* flights on behalf of Air Jordan.

TRANSPORTES AÉREOS SAMUEL SELUM (TASS)
LA PAZ, BOLIVIA

Formed in 1984, TASS acquired two 404s for domestic cargo flights. One was damaged in April 1990 in an emergency landing and the other is also believed to have been written-off. Both were used for meat-hauling flights either on behalf of, or on lease to, Frigorifico Reyes.

CP-1738	14137	84 - Apr90	*El Gordo*
CP-1917	14146	Jun84 -	

Msn 14137/CP-1738 El Gordo, *one of two 404s acquired by Transportes Aéreos Samuel Selum (T.A.S.S.) for domestic Bolivian cargo flights. It is seen here at La Paz in June 1985.* (Udo Schaefer Productions via Jean-Marie Magendie)

U FLY AIRFREIGHTERS
FORT WORTH, TEXAS

This company used one 404 in an all-cargo configuration from 1973 until it was repossessed by the mortgage holder in 1975.

N468M   14139   Feb73 - Apr75

UNITED AIR LINES
CHICAGO, ILLINOIS

United ordered 35 Model 303s (msns 9222-9256) on January 20, 1946, at a cost of approximately $9 million, with an option for 35 more. The option was partially exercised the following June to include another 15 (msns 13795-13809), for a total cost of approximately $16 million, including spares. The 40-seat (at 39in pitch) 'Mainliner 303s' were to have replaced Douglas DC-3s beginning in July 1947 to offer United customers a system-wide pressurized fleet of 303s and DC-6s. In UAL's layout, they would have had a lounge separated from the main passenger cabin. The prototype 303 (NX93162 msn 9222) was flown on July 3, 1947, in United markings, but the order was canceled shortly thereafter, on September 30. United cited changed economic conditions, a need to re-evaluate its equipment requirements, and unavoidable delays as the reasons for the cancellation. A turbine-powered 304 was also to have been delivered for service evaluation, but it was never built. United's routes were later served by a large fleet of Convair 340s, which it chose over the Martin 404.

US AIRLINES, INC
ST PETERSBURG, FLORIDA

After starting intrastate freight operations in December 1945 with a DC-3, US Airlines received the first US non-scheduled air carrier operating permit for interstate carriage of cargo in October 1946. Harry R Playford, the owner of US Airlines, ordered some all-cargo 202s; however, the order was canceled before their delivery.

VERO MONMOUTH AIRLINES
VERO BEACH, FLORIDA

Vero Monmouth, an affiliate of Monmouth Airlines (qv) (later Ocean Airways), used a 404 on flights from Vero Beach to various other points in Florida. Operations ceased when its parent folded in 1981.

N149S   14141   Aug79 -Aug87

VIAS AÉREAS COLOMBIANAS SA (VIARCO)
CALI, COLOMBIA

VIARCO ordered three 202s late in 1946 to replace DC-3s on scheduled domestic services. Like many of the South American orders, it was canceled before delivery.

WILLIS AIR SERVICE, INC
TETERBORO, NEW JERSEY

This scheduled and charter air cargo carrier operated under the name The Commander Airline as its nucleus of personnel were Navy or Marine Corps veterans. Commander ordered six all-cargo 202s in mid-1946 to supplement or replace its five DC-3s; however, the order was canceled before delivery. The airline ceased operations in 1949.

OTHER COMMERCIAL OPERATORS

AEROJET-GENERAL CORP
AZUSA, CALIFORNIA

Missile, rocketry, and defense manufacturer Aerojet-General used a number of 404s for inter-plant transport.

N241AG	14166	Dec59 -Nov64	
N244AG	14106	Aug61 -Feb65	
N487A	14235	63 - 63	LF Charlotte Acft
N542AG	14175	Nov59 -Sep65	

Aerojet-General Corp purchased three 404s, including msn 14166/N241AG, for inter-plant transport of company employees. (William T Larkins)

AG INVESTORS/AG INTERNATIONAL FLYING SERVICE
MADERA, CALIFORNIA

Associated companies involved in aerial application.

N461M	14227	Dec78 -May80	
N470M	14109	Dec78 -	LF 404 Enterprises
N40408	14108	Dec78 - Jun79	
N40418	14124	Dec78 -May80	
N40445	14230	Dec78 -May80	

AIR TRAVELERS CLUB
SANTA ANA, CALIFORNIA

Leased two 404s from affiliate GSD Aircraft Leasing.

N40427	14133	Jan72 -
N40432	14167	72 -

Air Travelers Club's 404 msn 14133/N40427 at Long Beach, California, in 1972. (Steve Nation via Elliot H Greenman)

BOISE CASCADE—SEE LAKE LOS ANGELES

BROOKTRAILS—SEE LAKE LOS ANGELES

COONES FLYING SERVICE
CRANE, MISSOURI, & MADERA, CALIFORNIA

Howard I Coones received a Supplemental Type Certificate on September 19, 1977, to convert an ex-Basler 404 for granular and liquid aerial application.

N472M	14234	Aug75 - Apr79

DOTHAN AVIATION
DOTHAN, ALABAMA

Dothan Aviation acquired four ex-Piedmont 404s in 1973 that had been converted for aerial application of pesticides by Clayton Curtis (see Frontier Airways) on behalf of Charlotte Aircraft. One was a source of spares. The other three were sold in June 1977 to Marvin L Jantzen and ferried to Madera, California, for storage and subsequent sale to Ag Investors/Ag International Flying Service.

N40405	14105	Mar73 - 76	spares use only
N40418	14124	Feb73 - Jun77	
N40443	14228	Jan73 - Jun77	
N40445	14230	Jan73 - Jun77	

EG&G INC
LAS VEGAS, NEVADA

EG&G (Edgerton, Germeshausen, and Grier) operated one 404 on behalf of the US Atomic Energy Commission (later US Energy Research and Development Administration), still later US Department of Energy) as an airborne atmospheric sampler with test equipment installed in the cabin. The airplane was also operated briefly under the auspices of the US Army Research & Development Command. For some years, it was also used (along with Douglas DC-6s) to fly workers between Las Vegas-McCarran and the Nevada Test Site, with an occasional trip to Edwards Air Force Base, California, and Tonopah, Nevada. Although flown exclusively by EG&G, it was never owned by the company.

N40409	14113	Sep64 - Jun80

Msn 14113/N40409 was used by EG&G Inc to obtain test atmospheric samples on behalf of the US Atomic Energy Commission and its successors, and to fly workers from Las Vegas to the Nevada Test Site.

For many years, the airplane was in the hands of the Southern Nevada Vocational Technical Center, at Las Vegas, and was delivered to the school on June 30, 1980—which then had a 2,100ft (640m)-long airstrip—by an EG&G crew. It has since been dismantled, although the fuselage now serves as an attraction in a 'haunted house' in Fresno, California. (Steve Nation)

FLORIDA AIR TRAVEL ASSOCIATION
ORLANDO, FLORIDA

This travel club leased one 404 briefly before losing its FAA certificate on December 14, 1978.

N35JS	14162	Oct78 - Dec78

FRONTIER, INC
TUNICA, MISSISSIPPI

Owned by Howard G Hale, Frontier used two 404s converted by Clayton Curtis (see Frontier Airways) for aerial application. Another airplane, parked at Fort Lauderdale, Florida, was used as a source of spares. The two operational 404s were both withdrawn from use at Grenada, Mississippi, by 1977 and stripped for parts by Hale. Frontier was dissolved in 1980 following the death of Hale.

N469M	14148	Nov73 - Nov76	non-operational
N474M	14165	Feb74 - Feb80	
N40411	14115	Feb74 - Feb80	

FRONTIER AIRWAYS, INC
SHERIDAN, WYOMING

Frontier Airways operated a number of 404s converted for aerial application of pesticides, etc. There was no direct connection between Frontier Airways and Frontier Inc (qv), an earlier Tunica, Mississippi-based operator. However, the owner of Frontier Airways, Clayton V Curtis, did convert the earlier company's 404s for aerial application. One airplane (N40418) was used as a spares source. Two others (N40443 & N40445) were lost in accidents. The remaining two 404s were subsequently stored at Sheridan, Wyoming, where they remained in 1997.

N461M	14227	Apr82 -	
N9234C	14143	Nov73 -	
N40418	14124	Apr82 - Feb89	spares use only
N40443	14228	May82 - Jun86	
N40445	14230	Apr82 - May82	

GLENN L MARTIN CO
BALTIMORE, MARYLAND, & ORLANDO, FLORIDA

After serving as the aerodynamic prototype of the Model 404, the second 202 was retained as a company transport. Later, Martin used it and two other 202s as electronic test beds in connection with its aerospace activities.

N40400	9123	51 - 65	later based at Orlando
N93046	9167	57 - 60	LF Pioneer
N93058	9147	Jan55 - 57	LF Pioneer

GLOBAL AIR TRAVEL CLUB
OKLAHOMA CITY, OKLAHOMA

Global Air Inc operated an air travel club under this name.

N35JS	14162	Nov76 - Oct78

Global Air Inc operated msn 14162/N35JS under the name Global Air Travel Club. (Ben Ullings)

HERITAGE LAND
JACKSONVILLE, FLORIDA

This land speculation company leased a 202 around 1967, presumably to fly prospective purchasers to land development sites.

N93041	9162	67 - 67

HUBER INVESTMENT CO
DAYTON, OHIO

This company, dba Huber Homes, was another land investment operation that used a 404 to fly prospective purchasers. A second 404 was owned briefly.

N3711K	14235	Jul69 - Mar78
N9234C	14143	Sep71 - Dec71

Huber Investment Corporation obtained msn 14235/N3711K from the Kimbell Milling Co and another once owned by Ray Charles for use in connection with its Huber Homes operation. The non-standard propeller spinners are probably the same as those used on Douglas DC-6s. This aircraft was fitted with 16 seats and had an APU in the tailcone. (via Elliot H Greenman)

HUGHES TOOL CO
CULVER CITY, CALIFORNIA

One of the 404s in the TWA order (Fleet No 437) went directly to Hughes Tool Co for what was described as 'special experimental work'. In fact, it remained in storage at Culver City for more than two years, then was sold to The National Supply Co. Although that airplane was never used, Hughes did lease another 404 a few years later for electronics testing.

N40406	14106	Feb60 - Feb61	LF Calif Airmotive
N40437	14172	Sep52 - Feb55	

INTERNATIONAL CRYSTAL MANUFACTURING CO, INC
OKLAHOMA CITY, OKLAHOMA

In one of the more unusual applications of a Martin transport, International Crystal used its 202 as a flying showcase to demonstrate its wares.

N93059   9148   Sep65 - Jan67

Although not an executive airplane in the traditional sense, msn 9148/ N93059 was used by International Crystal Manufacturing Company as a flying showcase to promote sales of its products.
(Dave Lucabaugh via Walt Redmond)

INTERNATIONAL HOLIDAY CLUB
HOUSTON, TEXAS

A 202 was leased from Fun Leasing for a short period during 1968.

N93059   9148   68 -   68

KLAMATH RIVER COUNTY ESTATES—SEE LAKE LOS ANGELES

LAKE LOS ANGELES
GARDENA, CALIFORNIA

Using the name Lake Los Angeles, R R Watt Co & Caroldale Inc used two former Pacific Air Lines 404s to carry prospective purchasers to land sites in the western US. The company was also associated with the Boise Cascade Building Co, which in turn operated as Klamath River County Estates, Brooktrails, and Pacific Cascade Land Co. Lake Los Angeles, etc, were all names of individual developments.

N40432   14167   68 -   LF Pallas D & E
N40436   14171   Jul67 -Sep70

The R R Watt Company, an affiliate of Boise Cascade, used two ex–Pacific Air Lines 404s to fly prospective purchasers to land development sites. Msn 14167/N40432 is seen in the basic Pacific paint design and 'Lake Los Angeles' titles. (Lake Los Angeles was the name of one of its developments.)

Msn 14171/N40436 at Hayward, California, on September 1, 1968, with the name 'Brooktrails', another Boise Cascade development. (John P Stewart)

Msn 14171/N40436 in 1968 with the titles of Pacific Cascade Land Co, another Boise Cascade affiliate, with a development in Klamath County, Oregon. Another view of N40436, taken at Oakland, California, in 1970, shows a new color scheme and the Boise Cascade logo on the fin.
(MAP/John P Stewart)

LAKE SPORT AND TRAVEL CLUB

This travel club briefly used a 404 in 1972.

N404LS   14134   Sep72 -Dec72

LANDMARK BAPTIST TEMPLE
CINCINNATI, OHIO

This organization briefly operated one 404, reportedly for distribution of religious literature. The airplane was then sold to Penn Landmark Corp with which it may have been affiliated.

N40415   14119   Oct72 -Dec73

LEHIGH ACRES DEVELOPMENT
FORT MYERS, FLORIDA

Lehigh leased one 404 around 1969 and another in 1970 to fly prospective purchasers to its land development near Fort Myers, Florida. The second was written-off after only a few weeks.

| N40412 | 14116 | May70 -May70 |
| N474M | 14165 | 69 - 69 |

Msn 14165/N474M was leased in 1969 by Lehigh Acres Development, Inc to transport prospective purchasers to its land development near Fort Myers, Florida. (Dave Lucabaugh via John P Stewart)

MAGIC CARPET TRAVEL CLUB (MAGIC CARPET SERVICES INC, DBA)
TULSA, OKLAHOMA

| N40436 | 14171 | Oct76 -Sep77 |

Tulsa-based Magic Carpet Travel Club used N40436 (msn 14171), finished in bright green trim. (John P Stewart)

MALIBU TRAVEL CLUB
MILWAUKEE, WISCONSIN

| N40428 | 14134 | Oct70 -Sep72 |

Following a decade of executive service with Outboard Marine Corporation, N40428 (msn 14134) was acquired in 1970 by the Malibu Travel Club. (via John Wegg)

MARTIN MARIETTA CORP—SEE GLENN L MARTIN CO

MERIDIAN
Meridian was an air travel club that operated an unidentified 404 until its operating certificate was canceled on July 15, 1975.

MILE HI TRAVEL CLUB
DENVER, COLORADO

Although Mile Hi titles were applied to a 404 leased from Jack Richards Aircraft, it is not confirmed that the aircraft entered service with this travel club.

| N456A | 14147 | Nov68 - 69 |

OCEAN PINES
Ocean Pines, another Florida real estate development company, leased one 404 from East Coast Leasing.

| N542AG | 14175 | 69 - |

Ocean Pines was another Florida land development company that leased a 404 in 1969. Msn 14175/N542AG is seen in the basic livery of its former owner Aerojet-General. (MAP)

PACIFIC CASCADE—SEE LAKE LOS ANGELES

SKYLARK TRAVEL CLUB, INC
ATLANTA, GEORGIA

Another travel club, Skylark used one 202A.

| N93204 | 14074 | May68 -Dec69 |

SPERRY CO (SPERRY RAND CORP)
LONG ISLAND, NEW YORK

The Sperry Co leased two 202s from Martin Air Leasing in the mid-1960s, either as inter-plant transports or as test beds. One (N93060) was assigned to the Sperry Gyroscope Division.

| N93049 | 9132 | 66 - | LF Martin Air Lsg |
| N93060 | 9149 | Jun65 - | LF Martin Air Lsg |

SPORTSMAN AIR TRAVEL CLUB
DALLAS, TEXAS

This travel club leased one ex-Piedmont 404 from R M Richards.

N468M   14139   73 -   73

STARDUSTERS AIR TRAVEL CLUB II
YAKIMA, WASHINGTON

The Stardusters leased a 404 from Yakima Valley Leasing.

N40432   14167   Sep75 -

TWIN CITY TRAVEL CLUB
MINNEAPOLIS, MINNESOTA

Robert Wade, dba the Twin City Travel Club, acquired a sole 404.

N149S   14141   Aug75 -May76

(THE) VOYAGER TRAVEL CLUB
OKLAHOMA CITY, OKLAHOMA

The Voyager Travel Club leased a 404 in 1970, then acquired a replacement in 1971/72.

N460M   14162   70 -   70
N466M   14163   Sep72 -Nov72

The Voyager Travel Club operated msn 14163/N466M in 1972. (MAP)

WINGS AWAY
NASHVILLE, TENNESSEE

This air travel club used one 404.

N255S   14246   Mar72 - Jun75

WORLD CITIZENS INTERNATIONAL INC
WASHINGTON, PENNSYLVANIA

This air travel club leased one 404 from Air Fare Leasing, an apparent affiliate. The 404 was replaced by an ex-TWA 749 Constellation until World Citizens ceased business in 1975.

N40423   14129   Jan72 -Sep73

World Citizens International Inc retained not only the basic Piedmont livery on msn 14129/N40423, but the name Pamlico Pacemaker *as well.* (Jay L Sherlock)

MILITARY OPERATORS

UNITED STATES AIR FORCE

The former Department of Energy 404, which had been transferred to the US Army a few months earlier, was transferred to the USAF, flown briefly with passenger seats reinstalled, and then donated to the Southern Nevada Vocational Technical Center for use as a ground instructional airframe. It retained its civil registration.

N40409   14113   Jun78 -

UNITED STATES ARMY
The former Department of Energy 404 was transferred to the US Army's Research & Development Command for continued operation by EG&G.

N40409   14113   Jan78 - Jun78

UNITED STATES COAST GUARD
ARLINGTON, VIRGINIA

Two 404s were delivered to the USCG with 28-seat interiors under the military designation RM-1Z. Both were operated as public aircraft with military serial numbers and based at Washington's National Airport. When base locations were added to the USCG markings, the two airplanes displayed 'Arlington'. The first (1282) was also marked 'Washington' in lieu of Arlington at one time. The airplanes were redesignated VC-3As in September 1962 when the military services adopted a common model designation system. Both were transferred to the US Navy in 1969, but 1282 was loaned back to the USCG for a few weeks.

1282   14290   Nov52 -May69
1283   14291   Oct52 -May69

The US Coast Guard was Martin's only military 404 customer. Msn 14291 is seen in its original all-metal finish with the original military model designation RM-1 and original military serial number 1283 marked on the fin.

(D Rankin via J M G Gradidge)

MILITARY OPERATORS

The Coast Guard's msn 14290 (military s/n 1282) seen in a mid-1950s color scheme at Washington-National. (MAP)

The two Coast Guard 404s, by now re-designated VC-3As, pictured at Baltimore on April 27, 1969, in their last livery before transfer to the US Navy. Msn 14290 (military s/n 1282) is in the foreground.
(Dave Lucabaugh via John P Stewart)

Now designated RM-1Z (for VIP use) on the fin, msn 14290 appears to be finished in a red Day-Glo trim. (MAP)

UNITED STATES NAVY

The two Coast Guard airplanes were transferred to Naval Air Reserve Training Unit VR-52 at Andrews Air Force Base (AFB) in 1969 as C-3As and assigned new Navy military serial numbers. A year later they were placed in storage at Davis-Monthan AFB, Arizona, where they remained until denoted to The School of the Ozarks in July 1972.

158202	14290	May69 - Jul70
158203	14291	May69 - Jul70

By the early 1960s, RM-1Z msn 14291 (s/n 1283), was finished in a lighter Day-Glo scheme. (R W Harrison/Candid Aero-Files)

Following retirement from Coast Guard service, the two VC-3As were transferred in 1969 to Naval Air Reserve Training Unit VR-52. Although assigned the new military serial number 158202 and US Navy markings, msn 14290 is seen still retaining the basic Coast Guard livery. As VIP transport is no longer their mission, the military model designation has become simply C-3A. (Roger F Besecker via AAHS)

In yet another color scheme variation, 1282 carries its base name 'Arlington' on the fin instead of a type designation. (via John Wegg)

EXECUTIVE OPERATORS

Executive operators, in this context, refers to operators that used Martin 404 airplanes for high-level company or personal transport. Airplanes that were used by companies for other purposes, such as logistics, or research and development, may be found under **OTHER FLEET OPERATORS**. It is sometimes difficult to distinguish owners that purchased airplanes for their own transport from those that owned them for other reasons, such as a lease to another operator, trade-ins, etc. Therefore, it is possible that there were others not on this list that would also qualify as 'executive operators'. Conversely, there may be some on this list that would qualify more properly for inclusion in the **OTHER FLEET OPERATORS** section. The registrations listed are those used predominantly while the airplanes were with the operators shown. Others, such as new registrations applied pending sale of the airplanes, are not shown.

Operator	Reg	MSN
Armco Steel Corp	N40437	14172
Bass, Perry R	N22T	14231
Charles, Ray	N923RC	14143
Davis, Danny (Nashville Brass)	N404DD	14132
Denver-Chicago Trucking Co	N333G	14131
E F MacDonald Co	N636	14135
Essex Productions (Frank Sinatra)	N710E	14169
Federated Department Stores	N67B	14174
Fort Worth Pipe & Supply	N129AG	14242
Franke, Henry L	N2299S	14241
Gannett Co	N40437	14172
Gulf Underwriters Management Corp	N2299S	14241
Houston Lumber Co	N333G	14131
Hubbard Broadcasting Co	N404Z	14132
Impulsora de la Cuence de Papaloapán SA	XB-SOM	14169
Industrias Unidas SA	XB-RUK	14145
Kewanee Oil Co	N404K	14132
Kimbell Milling Co	N3711K	14235
Lone Star Steel Corp	N229LS	14242
McAllister Inc, James W	N636X	14135
Magic Chef Inc	N40412	14116
Montcrief, W A	N22T	14231
Montex Drilling Co	N636X	14135
	N40412	14116
Moreno, Mario (Cantiflas)	XB-RUK	14145
National Supply Corp	N40437	14172
Outboard Marine Corp	N40428	14134
Reyes, Major Justina	XB-SOM	14169
Secretaria de Salud y Asistencia Social	XC-DOC	14172
Stranahan, Frank R	N404K	14132
Tiffany Industries	N200JS	14114
	N636X	14135
Whirlpool Corp	N1900W	14137
Worth Manufacturing Co	N2299S	14142
Zollner Corp	N404Z	14132

Armco Steel Corp operated msn 14172/N40437 as an executive airplane. (G P H Styan via Eric W Wagner)

Ray Charles Enterprises used msn 14143/N923RC for concert tours from 1962 until 1968 when it was replaced by a Vickers Viscount. (William T Larkins)

Denver-Chicago Trucking had N333G (msn 14131), seen here at Los Angeles on New Year's Day, 1965. (Robert E Hufford)

Msn 14174/N67B was used as an executive airplane by Federated Department Stores in the early 1960s. (Roger F Besecker via Eric W Wagner)

Msn 14241 was first used as an executive airplane by Fort Worth Pipe and Supply, then acquired in 1967 by the Lone Star Steel Corp and re-registered N229LS. (John P Stewart via Peter R Keating)

Gulf Underwriters Management Corp operated msn 14241/N2299S in the early 1970s with 'Aviation Office of America' titles.
(via Elliot H Greenman)

Although it was better known for executive conversions of Convair 240s, Remmert Werner converted msn 14132/N404K in 1959 for Kewanee Oil Company.(Peter M Bowers)

Msn 14134/N40428 served the Evinrude Division of Outboard Marine Corporation as an executive airplane throughout the 1960s. (Dave Ostrowski via Elliot H Greenman)

Msn 14145/XB-RUK was acquired in 1963—the year this photo was taken—by famed Mexican actor Mario Moreno (Cantiflas), then sold the following year to Industrias Unidas. The airplane had apparently visited quite a number of countries as evidenced by the flags painted on the nose. The word 'MEXICO' appears under the right wing and the legend '777' on the rudder. (Gary Kuhn)

TWA's '41st Martin'. For all practical purposes, N40437 was a new airplane in 1955 when acquired by The National Supply Company from Hughes Tool Company. Reportedly, Hughes told Martin that he did not have room for the airplane in Burbank and it was to be stored. (E T Maloney via Eric W Wagner)

Still in the basic Outboard Marine color scheme, msn 14134 is seen with its new registration N404LS and Lake Sport & Travel Club logos. (Karl Krämer)

Msn 14135/N636X of the Montex Drilling Co at Santa Barbara, California, 1972. (Steve Nation)

Following service with The National Supply Company, Armco Steel and the Gannet Co, msn 14172 was sold to the Mexican government and operated by its office of welfare and social assistance as XC-DOC. (Gary Kuhn)

Zollner Corporation (Zollner Pistons) acquired msn 14132 in 1963 and re-registered it N404Z. Caught at San Francisco in January 1967, just visible behind its nose is one of the beached Dollar Short Solents. (John P Stewart)

EXTANT MARTINLINERS

This list includes all Martinliner airplanes (msns shown in bold type indicate those considered airworthy), or remains of aircraft, confirmed extant in recent years (with date of most recent sighting in parentheses). Unless otherwise noted, the airplanes are more or less complete, although they may be only a hulk, stripped of all useful parts. The precise fates of several other Martinliners have not yet been confirmed but as no recent sightings have been reported, they are not listed here and details may be found in the following production list.

MSN	REGN	OWNER	LOCATION/STATUS
202			
9142	N172A		remains on a farm near Wilmington, DE, c1978
9167	HK-1484	(Aeroproveedora)	hulk, Bogotá-Eldorado (Sept97)
202A			
14074	N93204	Aviation Hall of Fame & Museum	Teterboro, NJ (displayed)
404			
14106	N40406	William P Thompson	Pensacola, FL (nose only)
14107	N40407	Roberta A Rogers	Bay St Louis-Stennis Intl, MS (stored*)
14113	N40409	'haunted house'	Fresno, CA (fuselage only)
14117	N40413	Roberta A Rogers	Gulfport-Biloxi, MS (stored)
14119	N40415	US government	Bay St Louis-Stennis Intl, MS (stored*)
14125	HH-RHH	Royal Haitian Hotel	Port-au-Prince (stored)
14127	N40421	(Air Inter Sales Co)	Nassau, Bahamas (hulk
14129	YV-145C	Rentavion	Caracas/Porlamar, Venezuela (active)
14130	N40424	Roberta A Rogers	Bay St Louis-Stennis Intl, MS (stored*)
14131	N40425		San Juan, PR (abandoned)
14132	N404DD	George T Baker Aviation School	Miami, FL (ground instruction)
14135	N636X	Skylease (Jeff Whitsell)	Camarillo, CA (active)
14141	N450A	Mid Atlantic Air Museum	Reading, PA (active)
14142	N145S	Save A Connie	St Louis, MO (active)
14143	N9234C	Frontier Awys	Sheridan, WY (stored)
14153	N462M	Marvin L Jantzen	Sheridan, WY (stored)
14157	N404JS	Jesse P Soltes	Kingston, Jamaica (stored)
14158	N974M		Billings, MT (hulk on fire dump)
14161	N147S	(Holiday Investment)	Saipan-Isley Field, Marianas (hulk)
14162	N35JS	(C & S Specialities)	Nassau, Bahamas (impounded)
14164	N467M		San Francisco, CA (fuselage in club)
14171	YV-150C	Rentavion	Caracas (being made airworthy)
14227	N461M	Frontier Awys	Sheridan, WY (stored)
14231	N969M	US government	Bay St Louis-Stennis Intl, MS (stored*)
14233	N259S	Classic Airways (Tom Aarvik)	San Bernardino, CA (stored)
14234	N472M	Save A Connie	Bisbee, AZ (stored for parts)
14235	N3711K	Sam Stewart	Rialto, CA (stored)
14238	N40446		Roanoke, VA (fuselage only) (1990)
14246	N255S	I N Burchinal	Paris, TX (displayed)
14247	YV-149C	Rentavion	Caracas (stored)

An unidentified 404, registered YV-878C, was reported with Diamente Air at Caracas-Simon Bolivar, Dec95.

* These three aircraft were damaged when they were blown into each other in a storm.

The 'TolAir' 404, msn 14131, at San Juan, PR. (Michael Magnusson)

The Aviation Hall of Fame & Museum at Teterboro, NJ, displays 202A msn 14074, the only known intact survivor of the 202 series. (Brian D Charmatz)

The more or less intact msn 14234/N472M is stored at Douglass-Bisbee, Arizona. (Bob Shane)

Ex-Marco Island Airways/PBA msn 14231/N969M is one of several 404s at Bay St Louis-Stennis International, Mississippi. Strips of wood hold its broken rudder in place. (Steve Hill)

Ex-Eastern msn 14235/N3711K is stored at Rialto, California. (Bob Shane)

The trio of 404s stored at Sheridan, Wyoming: msn 14143/N9234C, msn 14153/N462M, and msn 14227/N461M. (Author)

Ex-Proair N255S/Msn 14246 is currently displayed at the Flying Tiger Museum, Paris, Texas. (Andrew Abshier)

The fuselage of Donna Lee *(N467M/msn 14164), now inside the 'Caribbean Zone' club in San Francisco, retains some of its interior.* (Nick Veronico)

MARTINLINERS REGISTRATION CROSS REFERENCE

REGN	MSN	MODEL	REGN	MSN	MODEL	REGN	MSN	MODEL
CHILE—CC			N71R	9167	202	N459A	14150	404
CC-CCK	9125	202	N129AG	14241	404	N460A	14151	404
CC-CCL	9126	202	N141S	14156	404	N460M	14162	404
CC-CCM	9127	202	N142S	14157	404	N461A	14152	404
CC-CCN	9129	202	N143S	14237	404	N461M	14227	404
CC-CLR	9125	202	N144S	14150	404	N462A	14153	404
CC-CLS	9126	202	N145S	14142	404	N462M	14153	404
CC-CLT	9127	202	N145SA	14142	404	N463A	14154	404
CC-CLU	9129	202	N146S	14223	404	N463M	14155	404
CC-CLMA	9125	202	N147S	14161	404	N464A	14155	404
CC-CLMB	9126	202	N148S	14160	404	N464M	14151	404
CC-CLMC	9127	202	N149S	14141	404	N465A	14156	404
CC-CLMD	9129	202	N170A	9163	202	N465M	14152	404
			N171A	9166	202	N466A	14157	404
BOLIVIA—CP			N172A	9142	202	N466M	14163	404
CP-1317	14163	404	N173A	9136	202	N466M	14164	404
CP-1318	14134	404	N174A	9159	202	N467A	14158	404
CP-1440	14114	404	N175A	9145	202	N467M	14163	404
CP-1441	14075	202A	N176A	9128	202	N467M	14164	404
CP-1570	14167	404	N177A	9147	202	N468A	14159	404
CP-1704	14172	404	N200JS	14114	404	N468M	14139	404
CP-1738	14137	404	N229LS	14241	404	N469A	14160	404
CP-1917	14146	404	N241AG	14166	404	N469M	14148	404
			N244AG	14106	404	N470A	14160	404
ECUADOR—HC			N251S	14243	404	N470M	14109	404
			N252S	14154	404	N471A	14162	404
N253S					14158	404	N471M	14112	404
			N254S	14159	404	N472A	14163	404
			N255S	14246	404	N472M	14234	404
			N256S	14236	404	N473A	14164	404
HAITI—HH			N257S	14110	404	N473M	14224	404
HH-RHH	14125	404	N258S	14232	404	N474A	14165	404
			N259S	14233	404	N474M	14165	404
			N302FA	14128	404	N475A	14223	404
DOMINICAN REPUBLIC—HI			(N303FA)	14173	404	N476A	14224	404
HI-285	14157	404	N333G	14131	404	N477A	14225	404
HI-334	14241	404	N404DD	14132	404	N478A	14226	404
HI-501	14129	404	N404JS	14157	404	N479A	14227	404
			N404K	14132	404	N480A	14228	404
COLOMBIA—HK			N404LS	14134	404	N481A	14229	404
HK-1484	9167	202	N404Z	14132	404	N482A	14230	404
HK-1485	14237	404	N440A	14109	404	N483A	14231	404
			N441A	14110	404	N484A	14232	404
			N442A	14111	404	N485A	14233	404
			N442D	14143	404	N486A	14234	404
			N442E	14102	404	N487A	14235	404
			N443A	14112	404	N488A	14236	404
			N444A	14121	404	N489A	14237	404
			N445A	14122	404	N490A	14238	404
			N446A	14137	404	N491A	14239	404
PANAMÁ—HP			N447A	14138	404	N492A	14240	404
HP-302	14170	404	N448A	14139	404	N493A	14241	404
HP-398	9133	202	N449A	14140	404	N494A	14242	404
HP-427	9136	202	N450A	14141	404	N495A	14243	404
HP-431	9163	202	N451A	14142	404	N496A	14244	404
			N452A	14143	404	N497A	14245	404
			N453A	14144	404	N498A	14246	404
UNITED STATES OF AMERICA—N			N454A	14145	404	N499A	14247	404
N22AA	9143	202	N455A	14146	404	N542AG	14175	404
N22T	14231	404	N456A	14147	404	N581S	14247	404
N35JS	14162	404	N457A	14148	404	N582S	14239	404
N67B	14174	404	N458A	14149	404	N583S	14111	404
N69RB	14114	404						

ECUADOR—HC

The registration HC-LVL has been reported for a Martinliner, although no other information can be traced.

C-300 to C-302 were reserved for the three 202s ordered, then canceled, by Líneas Aéreas Nacionales SA (LANSA). No msn allocation is known.

REGN	MSN	MODEL
UNITED STATES OF AMERICA—N (CONTINUED)		
N584S	14149	404
N585S	14138	404
N586S	14245	404
N587S	14231	404
N636	14135	404
N636X	14135	404
N671L	14174	404
N710E	14169	404
N923RC	14143	404
N967M	14149	404
N968M	14159	404
N969M	14231	404
N973M	14156	404
N974M	14158	404
N982M	14247	404
N1900W	14137	404
N1902M	14137	404
N2299S	14241	404
N3651B	14231	404
N3711K	14235	404
N9234C	14143	404
N9743Z	9130	202
N13415	14290	404
N13416	14291	404
N40400	9123	202
N40401	14101	404
	14106	404
N40402	14102	404
N40403	14103	404
	14174	404
N40404	14104	404
N40405	14105	404
N40406	14106	404
	14170	404
N40407	14107	404
N40408	14108	404
N40409	14113	404
N40410	14114	404
N40411	14115	404
N40412	14116	404
N40413	14117	404
N40414	14118	404
N40415	14119	404
N40416	14120	404
N40417	14123	404
N40418	14124	404
N40419	14125	404
N40420	14126	404
N40421	14127	404
N40422	14128	404
N40423	14129	404
N40424	14130	404
N40425	14131	404
N40426	14132	404
N40427	14133	404
N40428	14134	404
N40429	14135	404
N40430	14136	404
N40431	14166	404
N40432	14167	404
N40433	14168	404
N40434	14169	404
N40435	14170	404
N40436	14171	404
N40437	14172	404
N40438	14173	404
N40439	14174	404

REGN	MSN	MODEL
N40440	14175	404
	14166	404
N40441	14176	404
N40442	14225	404
N40443	14228	404
N40444	14229	404
N40445	14230	404
N40446	14238	404
N40447	14239	404
N40448	14242	404
N40450	14146	404
N67097	14145	404
N74087	14225	404
N74088	14228	404
NX93001	9122	202
NX93002	9123	202
NC93003	9128	202
NC93004	9132	202
NC93037	9158	202
NC93038	9159	202
NC93039	9160	202
NC93040	9161	202
NC93041	9162	202
NC93042	9163	202
NC93043	9164	202
NC93044	9165	202
NC93045	9166	202
NC93046	9167	202
NC93047	9133	202
NC93048	9128	202
NC93049	9132	202
NC93050	9134	202
NC93051	9136	202
NC93052	9142	202
NC93053	9143	202
NC93054	9144	202
NC93055	9145	202
NC93056	9146	202
NC93057	9135	202
NC93058	9147	202
NC93059	9148	202
NC93060	9149	202
NC93061	9150	202
NX93162	9222	303
N93201	14071	202A
N93202	14072	202A
N93203	14073	202A
N93204	14074	202A
N93205	14075	202A
N93206	14076	202A
N93207	14077	202A
N93208	14078	202A
N93209	14079	202A
N93210	14080	202A
N93211	14081	202A
N93212	14082	202A

REGN	MSN	MODEL
TRANSJORDAN—TJ		

Reportedly, the registrations TJ-ABK & TJ-ABL were assigned in 1951/1952 to two 202s of Transocean Air Lines for Hajj flights on behalf of Air Jordan, although no confirmation has been traced.

MEXICO—XA, XB, XC

XA-NEK	14075	202A
XA-SEX	9143	202
XA-SOX	14147	404
XB-RUK	14145	404
XB-SOM	14169	404
XC-DOC	14172	404

VENEZUELA—YV

YV-C-AMB	9130	202
YV-C-AMC	9131	202
YV-145C	14129	404
YV-149C	14247	404
YV-150C	14171	404

The registration YV-878C was reported on a 404 of Diamente Air at Caracas-Simon Bolivar in December 1995.

MILITARY

US COAST GUARD

1282	14290	404
1283	14291	404

US NAVY

158202	14290	404
158203	14291	404

EARLY PRODUCTION PLANS

The best of plans can go awry, and those for 202 and 303 production were certainly no exception. In order to place actual production and deliveries in proper perspective, it is first necessary to review 202/303 production as it was originally intended. Martin assigned manufacturer's serial numbers (msns) according to the sequence in which the orders were placed; therefore, a higher number did not necessarily indicate a newer airplane. The sequence in which the airplanes were scheduled to go into final assembly was indicated instead by what Martin referred to as the 'ship number' (marked as M 1 etc on the nose of each airframe). Although clouded considerably by the rework required for certification, and by the many cancellations and reassignments, the first 57 Model 202s were intended to be produced as follows:

Ship Number	MSN	Customer
1-3	9122-9124	test airplanes, Martin Nos 1-3
4-6	9125-9127	Líneas Aérea Nacional Chile (LAN), Nos 1-3
7-8	9158-9159	Northwest Airlines (NW) Nos 1-2
9	9128	Pennsylvania-Central Airlines (PCA) No 1
10-11	9160-9161	NW Nos 3-4
12	9129	LAN No 4
13	9168	Eastern Air Lines No 1, scrapped
14	9162	NW No 5
15	9130	Foreign (FOR) No 1, delivered as Línea Aéropostal Venezolana (LAV) No 1
16	9163	NW No 6
17	9132	PCA No 2, delivered as NW No 13
18-21	9164-9167	NW Nos 7-10
22	9131	FOR No 2, delivered as LAV No 2
23	9133	FOR No 3, later LAV No 3, delivered as NW No 11
24-25	9134/9136	PCA Nos 3-4, delivered as NW Nos 14-15
26	9193	Chicago & Southern Airlines (C&S) No 1, scrapped
27-31	9142-9146	PCA Nos 5-9, delivered as NW Nos 16-20
32	9135	FOR No 4, delivered as NW No 21
33	9194	C&S No 2, scrapped
34	9147	PCA No 10, delivered as NW No 22
35	9195	C&S No 3, scrapped
36	9148	PCA No 11, delivered as NW No 23
37	9196	C&S No 4, scrapped
38	9149	PCA No 12, delivered as NW No 24
39-40	9197-9198	C&S Nos 5-6, scrapped
41	9150	PCA No 13, delivered as NW No 25
42	9199	C&S No 7, scrapped
43-44	9151-9152	PCA Nos 14-15, stored
45	9200	C&S No 8, scrapped
46	9137	FOR No 2, stored
47	9201	C&S No 9, scrapped
48	9153	PCA No 16, stored
49	9202	C&S No 10, scrapped
50	9154	PCA No 17, stored
51	9138	FOR No 6, stored
52	9155	PCA No 18, stored
53	9139	FOR No 7, stored
54	9156	PCA No 19, stored
55	9140	FOR No 8, stored
56	9157	PCA No 20, stored
57	9141	FOR No 9, stored

According to other documents, the airplanes listed above as 'Foreign' were intended for a French airline—undoubtedly Air France.

The cancellations by all but LAN and Northwest left Martin with customers for only 14 airplanes. The company managed to sell LAV two of those originally assigned to Air France, and it was anticipated that the first three would be retained by Martin for test purposes. That still left 38 unsold airplanes in various stages of completion.

In the manufacture of airline airplanes, production planning and parts procurement for a specific airplane typically begin at least a year before the airplane is scheduled for completion. As 202 production was well underway long before the cancellations, Martin was faced with a very difficult decision—whether to invest the additional resources needed to complete the 38 unsold airplanes in the hope that customers would eventually be found, or abandon them and accept as losses the manufacturing costs already incurred.

In its zeal to sell 202s to as many airlines as possible, Martin offered 202s with several different interior and door configurations. The 27 202s originally assigned to Air France and PCA were similar to the airplanes ordered by Northwest. Martin was, therefore, able to sell 15 to its only remaining US customer. The dozen left seemed to have some market potential—perhaps Martin held the vain hope that Northwest would eventually purchase those as well—so they were placed in storage partially completed. Eventually they were completed with new msns as 202As for Transcontinental & Western Air (TWA—soon to be officially renamed Trans World Airlines.) On the other hand, the 11 slated for Eastern Air Lines and Chicago & Southern differed considerably from the others, and, with little prospect for eventual sale, the components for those airplanes were scrapped.

Although the correlation of ship numbers beyond 57 is unknown, the following msns are known to have been assigned:

MSN	Customer
9168-9192	Eastern 202s
9203-9220	Braniff Airways 202s
9221	Delta Air Lines 202
9222-9256	United Air Lines 303s
13727-13751	Northwest 303s
13767-13775	Delta 202s
13776-13787	Braniff 303s
13788-13794	Pan American-Grace Airways 303s
13795-13809	United 303s
13833-13882	TWA 303s
13907-13911	Aeroposta Argentina 202s

One of the 202s from the Eastern order, reportedly msn 9171, was partially assembled later. It was intended to serve as the Merchantman all-cargo prototype, but, like so many other 202s, never completed.

Each airplane has been listed in sequential order of its manufacturer's serial number (msn). As noted in *Early Production Plans*, a higher number does not necessarily indicate a newer airplane.

The letter 'A' was sometimes added as a suffix to the serial number of a Martin 202. Contrary to popular belief, this suffix did not indicate that a 202 was converted to a 202A; it was used by Martin to denote a 202 with nacelles tilted upward $1^1/_2°$. This feature, which was standard on the 202As, was to increase propeller-ground clearance and lessen the possibility of propellers striking the ground in a hard landing. Serial numbers 9123, 9135, 9148, and 9162 are reported to have been converted, and it appears that all other surviving 202s were converted around 1948 as well.

Fortunately, serial number assignment was relatively straightforward during 404 production. As with the 202s, a higher serial number did not necessarily indicate a newer airplane.

Before 1949, the US nationality marks 'NC' and 'NX' were used for aircraft with standard and experimental airworthiness certificates, respectively. For aircraft registered for the first time after December 31, 1948, only 'N' was used regardless of the type of airworthiness certificate issued. In lieu of 'NX', the word 'experimental' was placed on the exterior adjacent to each entrance to denote an airplane with an experimental airworthiness certificate. Aircraft already in service, such as the 202s, were permitted to retain the 'NC' or 'NX' marks until the surfaces were refinished, if used only within the US, or until December 31, 1950, if operated outside the country. It is, therefore, impossible to determine when a specific airplane was changed from 'NC—' to 'N—'. For convenience, the original registration numbers of all 202s that were delivered with standard airworthiness certificates are shown only as 'NC—' even though they may have flown initially as 'NX—' and later became 'N—'. The 202As and 404s were produced after 1948, so they were all 'N—' from the time of delivery.

All references to registrations in this list are those that have been assigned officially to the airplanes in question. Generally, they would be the registrations displayed on the airplanes. It must be recognized, however, that the official registration does not have to appear on an airplane if it is not flown. There can, therefore, be discrepancies between the official registrations and those that appear in photos taken on the ground. Registrations reserved, but not actually used, are shown in parentheses.

Individual airplane names, such as fleet names, are shown in italics. It should not be taken for granted that an individual airplane name was displayed during the whole period with an operator.

Most operators use the registration number or manufacturer's serial number for record-keeping purposes; however, some, particularly those with large fleets, assign their own fleet number (FN) to each airplane for such purposes. All known fleet numbers are shown in this list. Generally, a fleet number is displayed in a prominent exterior location for the benefit of ground personnel. It should not be taken for granted, however, that a fleet number was displayed on the airplane the entire time it was in the possession of the operator or, for that matter, that it was ever displayed.

The dates of sale may differ in some instances from previously published information. Whenever available, the dates shown in official records on the bills of sale have been used. Those represent the dates on which title passed to the new owners and are not necessarily the dates on which the new owners actually took possession of the airplanes. 'Owner', of course, refers to the registered owner. Generally, the registered owner did not have legal ownership because of a mortgage or other encumbrance. To avoid confusion among the US and European forms of date presentation, the latter style of day-month-year has been adopted and the month has been spelled out in three-letter abbreviated form.

The term 'sold' is used when it appears that ownership actually did pass from one owner to another. In other cases when it appears that the airplane was merely re-registered to another part of the same company or another member of the same family, the general term 'transferred' (trf) is used. US states are shown in their standard two-letter abbreviated form.

Crashed (cr) is used in reference to any accident from which the airplane was not rebuilt, regardless of the extent of damage, and bears no relation to the degree of trauma that might have been involved. Obviously, this would mean damage short of complete destruction when the airplane was new and relatively valuable. As the airplane depreciated in value, it could mean a relatively minor accident, eg, a gear-up landing.

Just what constitutes being 'scrapped' or 'broken-up' (BU) is somewhat subjective as the airframe may be cut up in some instances or may languish for years as an abandoned hulk. As used in this list, BU means that the airframe has been dismantled, cut up, or cannibalized to the point of destruction.

The following abbreviations are used:

BU	broken up
c	about (circa)
config	configuration
cvtd	converted
cr	crashed
dba	doing business as
DD	delivered (delivery date)
dereg	de-registered
dmgd	damaged
FF	first flight
FN	fleet number
IS	in service (date) (not always confirmed as a revenue flight)
LRF	last revenue flight
LT	leased to
mfd	manufactured
msn	manufacturer's serial number
NTU	not taken up
R (r)	registered
regn	registration number
RR	re-registered
RT	returned to
RTS	returned to service
ST	sold to
trf	transferred to
TT	total (flying) time (hours)
WFU	withdrawn from use
WO	written-off

MODEL 202

9122   NX93001   prototype mfd 20Nov46
FF 22Nov46; dereg Dec47, BU c1948 Baltimore, MD.

9122 *NX93001—the first 202 seen in 1947 before the addition of 8-degree dihedral in the outer wing panels.* (Logan Coombs via Peter M Bowers)

9123   NX93002   prototype mfd 20Jan47
FF 27Jan47, used for certification tests; cvtd to Model 202A prototype 10Jan50. **N40400** cvtd 1950 to partial Model 404 config for use as flight test aerodynamic prototype and FF 21Oct50; used 1961 as electronics testbed by Glenn L Martin Co/Martin Marietta Corp; dmgd in ground incident; ST Piedmont Airlines for parts; BU c1965 (TT 8200).

9123 *N40400 (previously NX93002)—in use by Martin in 1954 as a company transport. The aircraft was used for experimental night photography work in 1964 and 1965.* (A R Krieger via John Wegg)

9124   non-flying 3rd prototype
mfd 1946 for structural tests; later BU.

9125   CC-CLR   mfd 1947
DD 13Nov47 to LAN-Chile, FN 0299; **CC-CLMA** RR 1954, FN 261; **CC-CCK** RR Jan63; subsequently BU.

9125 *CC-CLR—Linea Aérea Nacional de Chile before delivery.* (Martin P31965 via Jack L King)

9126   CC-CLS   mfd 1947
DD 05Nov47 to LAN-Chile; **CC-CLMB** RR 1954, FN 262; **CC-CCL** RR Jan63; subsequently BU.

9126 *CC-CLS of Linea Aérea Nacional de Chile, probably before delivery.* (Martin via Peter M Bowers)

9127   CC-CLT   mfd 1947
DD 04Aug48 to LAN-Chile, FN 0058; **CC-CLMC** RR 1954, FN 263; **CC-CCM** RR Jan63; subsequently BU.

9127 *CC-CLMC (previously CC-CLT)—LAN Chile Fleet No 263.* (Peter R Keating via Eric W Wagner)

9128   NC93003   mfd 1947 (originally assigned to PCA)
Used as sales demonstration airplane. DD 23Dec47 to Northwest Airlines, **NC93048** RR 1948 (NW quotes delivery 27Jan48), FN 548; WFU 17Mar51 and stored; LT Transocean Air Lines 19Sep51. ST Pioneer Air Lines 29Apr52 *Pacemaker David Crockett*; lost right-hand engine cowl in flight 07Jul53 over Breckenridge, TX, en route Dallas–Albuquerque, landed safely at Abilene; WFU 1953 and stored Dallas-Love Field, TX; trf to Pioneer Aeronautical Services 06Nov53. ST Allegheny Airlines 31Dec56, **N176A** RR 12Apr57, FN 176, *The Detroiter*, IS 01May57; gear collapsed on landing 05Dec60 at Avoca, PA—no injuries; cvtd 31Mar64, to cargo config. ST Fairchild Hiller Corp 14Oct66. ST Associated Products of America 14Oct66, stored Wildwood, NJ; BU 1977.

9128 *N93048 (previously NC93003)—Pioneer Air Lines.* (Leo J Kohn)

9129   CC-CLU   mfd 1947
DD 04Aug48 to LAN-Chile; **CC-CLMD** RR 1954, FN 264; **CC-CCN** RR Jan63; BU c1965.

9129 *CC-CLU in production for Linea Aérea Nacional de Chile on April 30, 1947. Both msn 9127 and 9129 were delivered on August 4, 1948, and departed from Washington the same day on their delivery flight.* (Martin via A R Krieger)

9130   **YV-C-AMB**   mfd 1947 (originally assigned to Air France)
DD 19Dec47 to LAV *Rafael Urdaneta*. **N9743Z** ST California Airmotive Corp c1963 and stored Lancaster, CA; BU 1965.

9130 *N9743Z (previously YV-C-AMB)—final days at Lancaster, California, April 26, 1964.* (Clay Jansson via Walt Redmond)

9131   **YV-C-AMC**   mfd 1947 (originally assigned to Air France)
DD 19Dec47 to LAV *Andres Bello*; dmgd 26Aug52, Cuidad Bolívar, Venezuela, in belly landing—no injuries; BU following accident 18Oct58.

9131 *YV-C-AMC—Linea Aeropostal Venezolana (unnamed), Piaro, November 20, 1953.* (Peter R Keating)

9132   **NC93004**   mfd 09Dec47 (originally assigned to Air France.)
DD 23Dec47 as **NC93049** to Northwest Airlines (NW quotes delivery 27Jan48); FN 549; WFU 17Mar51 and stored. ST Transocean Air Lines 15Aug51; DD 10Sep51; flown on behalf of Japan Air Lines Oct51-Oct52 *Kinsei*. ST Southwest Airways (later Pacific Air Lines) 31Oct52 (Southwest quotes 03Nov52). ST TWA 30Jun60 and stored San Francisco, CA. ST Martin Air Leasing Inc 21Nov61; LT Admiral Airways c1961; LT The New Riverside Hotel 1962; LT Sperry Co 1966; stored Burbank, CA. ST International Aerodyne 31Dec69 and left in storage Burbank. ST National Aircraft Leasing Ltd 06Apr70. ST SKH Inc 06Apr70. Repossessed 12Jan71 by National Aircraft Leasing. ST Arturo Mendez 27Jan71. ST

Eloy E Perez and Raymond Degui 30Apr71, stored San Juan, PR. ST Reynaldo Segui Ortiz dba Rey Segui Co 08Oct74, remained in storage San Juan; derelict by 1976 and presumed BU.

9132 *N93049 (previously NC93004)—leased to Sperry Co for use as a test bed, New York-JFK, October 1966.* (Harry Sievers via Peter R Keating)

9133   **NC93047**   mfd 11Dec47 (originally assigned to Air France, then LAV)
DD 23Dec47 to Northwest Airlines, FN 547; used Apr48 by Glenn L Martin Co as demonstrator; WFU 17Mar51 and stored; LT California Central Airlines 29Jun51. ST California Central Airlines 29Sep51, FN 047 *City of San Diego*; WFU cFeb54 and stored. ST Southwest Airways (later Pacific Air Lines) 03Mar55 (Southwest quotes 14Feb55). ST TWA 30Jun60 TWA and stored San Francisco, CA. ST Martin Air Leasing Inc 17Nov61. ST Jim Sorthun dba Admiral Air Service 12Nov62. **HP-398** ST Rutas Aéreas Panamenas SA (RAPSA) 15Sep64; WFU cFeb72 Panama City, Panamá, BU after 1973.

9133 *N93047—Southwest Airways, San Francisco, February 8, 1958.* (Robert Hufford)

9134   **NC93050**   mfd 1948 (originally assigned to PCA)
DD 06May48 to Northwest Airlines, FN 550; cr 07Mar50 Minneapolis, MN—lost control after hitting flag pole at Fort Snelling National Cemetery during instrument approach to Wold-Chamberlain Field en route Washington, DC–Winnipeg, all 13 aboard fatal, 2 others on ground fatal and 3 others injured.

9134 *NC93050—Northwest Airlines, crashed March 7, 1950, at Minneapolis.* (via Jim Borden)

9135   **NC93057**   mfd 26May48 (originally assigned to Air France)

DD 15Jun48 to Northwest Airlines, FN 557; WFU 17Mar51 and stored. ST California Central Airlines 06Sep51, FN 057 *City of Los Angeles*. ST Glenn L Martin Co 30Sep53, used for electronic equipment tests, later static tests; WFU 08Jul60 (TT 13737); BU Oct61.

9142 *N93052—California Central Airlines* City of San Francisco, *Oakland, December 12, 1954. ('Fly now…pay later' advertising appears on aft fuselage.* (Larry Smalley via Walt Redmond)

9135 *N93057—with Martin in 1954, scrapped October 11, 1961.* (A R Krieger)

9136   NC93051   mfd 14May48 (originally assigned to PCA)
DD 18May48 to Northwest Airlines, FN 551; dmgd 04Sep50 Billings, MT, following forced landing because of smoke in cockpit—no injuries; WFU 17Mar51 and stored; LT Transocean Air Lines Sep51. ST Pioneer Air Lines 09Apr52 *Pacemaster Ben Milam*; WFU Mar53 and stored; trf to Pioneer Aeronautical Services 06Nov53. **N173A** ST Allegheny Airlines 13May55, FN 173 *The Pennsylvanian*, IS 01Jun55; ST Fairchild Hiller Corp 23Feb66. **HP-427** ST Rutas Aéreas Panamenas SA (RAPSA) 10Mar66; WFU cFeb72 Panama City, Panamá, and presumed later BU.

9136 *N93051—Northwest Airlines, Minneapolis-St Paul International Airport, 1950.* (Leo J Kohn)

9137 through **9141**—all originally assigned to Air France but not completed as 202s.

9142   NC93052   mfd 03May48 (originally assigned to Air France)
DD 19May48 to Northwest Airlines, FN 552; WFU 17Mar51 and stored. ST California Central Airlines 06Sep51, FN 052 *City of San Francisco*; WFU cFeb54 and stored. **N172A** ST Allegheny Airlines 03Mar55, FN 172 *The Ohio Valley*, DD 06Mar55, IS 01Jul55; WO 14Nov55 New Castle, DE, on training flight—gear collapsed on landing because of mid-air engine fire which damaged wing spar, 1 injured (TT 11915); airplane trucked to Dover, DE, and used for spares; remains in scrapyard near Wilmington, DE, 1960; later moved to a farm, extant c1978.

9143   NC93053   mfd 04May48 (originally assigned to PCA)
DD 22May48 to Northwest Airlines, FN 553 *Minneapolis*; WFU 17Mar51 and stored; LT Transocean Air Lines Sep51 (op with 'Airlift' titles). ST Pioneer Air Lines 27Mar52 *Pacemaster William B. Travis*; WFU Mar53 and stored; trf to Pioneer Aeronautical Services 06Nov53. ST Southwest Airways (later Pacific Air Lines) 14Jan56. ST Edde Aircraft Inc 09Mar64; trf to Edde Airlines 09Mar64. ST Caltex Air Parts 09Feb66; **XA-SEX** LT Servicio Aéreo Baja (Baja Air Lines) Feb66; **N93053** RT Caltex Air Parts 15Jan68 and stored Burbank, CA. **N22AA** ST Ewell K Nold Jr 11Apr69. ST I N Burchinal Jr 27Jul72. ST Jungle Aviation & Radio Service 1975. RT I N Burchinal Jr 1976 and displayed at the Flying Tiger Air Museum, Paris, TX. ST Richards Spraying 21Jan77, believed BU after 1978.

9143 *N93053—Pacific Air Lines, San Francisco, May 3, 1963.* (Robert E Hufford)

9144   NC93054   mfd 10May48 (originally assigned to PCA)
DD 29May48 to Northwest Airlines, FN 554, IS 06Jun48; nose gear failed to lower 02Aug50 on approach to Aberdeen, SD, and returned to Minneapolis for main gear only landing, minor damage, no injuries; gear collapsed on landing 09Oct50 Detroit, MI—no injuries; cr 16Jan51, 3½mi north of Edwall, WA, near Reardan, en route Twin Cities–Spokane–Wenatchee–Yakima–Seattle after sudden loss of control during cruise, cause could not be determined, all 3 crew and 7 passengers aboard fatal (TT 5874).

9144 *NC93054—Northwest Airlines, crashed January 16, 1951, near Reardan, Washington.* (A R Krieger)

9145   NC93055   mfd 18May48 (originally assigned to PCA)
DD 09Jun48 to Northwest Airlines, FN 555; WFU 17Mar51 and stored; LT Transocean Air Lines 30Oct51. ST Pioneer Air Lines 09Apr52 *Pacemaster Kit Carson*; WFU Mar53 and stored; trf to Pioneer Aeronautical Services 06Nov53. **N175A** ST Allegheny Airlines 20Jan56, FN 175 *The Pittsburgher*, IS 01May56; nose landing gear collapsed 26Feb60 at Erie, PA, after veering off runway into snowbank on takeoff—no injuries; cvtd 30Jun64 to all-cargo config as an 'Allegheny Cargo-Liner'. ST Fairchild Hiller Corp 01Aug66. ST Associated Products of America 09Aug66 and stored Wildwood, NJ; BU late 1977.

9145 *N175A (previously N93055)—Allegheny Airlines, Greater Wilmington, March 29, 1963.* (G P H Styan via Eric W Wagner)

9146   NC93056   mfd 21May48 (originally assigned to PCA)
DD 29May48 to Northwest Airlines, FN 556; WFU 17Mar51 and stored; LT Transocean Air Lines Oct51. ST Pioneer Air Lines 27Mar52 *Pacemaster James Bowie*; WFU Mar53 and stored; trf to Pioneer Air Services 06Nov53. ST Southwest Airways (later Pacific Air Lines) 25Jan56. ST TWA 30Jun60 and stored San Francisco, CA. ST Martin Air Leasing Inc 17Nov61. ST Walston Aviation 20Jun62; trf to Walston Aircraft Sales & Service 03Jul62. ST George W Perry 30Mar63. ST Joe G Marrs dba Marrs Aviation 29Dec69; stored Sarasota, FL, and stripped for spares, hulk extant until c1983.

9146 *N93056—leased by Northwest to Transocean Air Lines for military contract flights with 'Airlift' titles, Oakland, California.* (A R Krieger)

9147   NC93058   mfd 01Jun48 (originally assigned to PCA)
DD 17Jun48 to Northwest Airlines, FN 558; WFU 17Mar51 and stored; LT Transocean Air Lines Oct51. ST Pioneer Air Lines 09Apr52 *Pacemaster Mirabeau B. Lamar*; WFU Mar53 and stored; trf to Pioneer Aeronautical Services 06Nov53; LT Glenn L Martin Co Jan55 as an electronics testbed; LT Allegheny Airlines 31Jul57. **N177A** ST Allegheny Airlines 01Dec57, FN 177; BU following taxi accident 02Nov63 at Newark, NJ, with TWA Boeing 707-131B N752TW (msn 18391).

9147 *N93058—leased back to Martin (photo: October 2, 1956). Radar is fitted to the rear fuselage and the emblem on the nose is a pilot astride a rocket or missile.* (Sommerich via Peter M Bowers)

9148   NC93059   mfd 1948 (originally assigned to PCA)
DD 24Jun48 to Northwest Airlines, FN 559; WFU 17Mar51 and stored; LT Transocean Air Lines Sep51. ST Pioneer Air Lines 27Mar52 *Pacemaster James Fannin*; WFU Mar53 and stored; trf to Pioneer Aeronautical Services 06Nov53. ST Southwest Airways (later Pacific Air Lines) 05Jan56. ST California Time Airlines 31Dec63. ST Jack Richards Aircraft Sales Inc 07Sep65. ST International Crystal Mfg Co 07Sep65. ST Jack Adams Aircraft Sales Inc 20Jan67. ST Jack Richards Aircraft Co 20Jan67. ST Tex-Hou Corp 15Dec67. ST Fun Leasing Inc 26Apr68; LT International Holiday Club 1968; WFU and stored Galveston, TX. ST Tex-Hou Corp 01Mar69 (remained in storage). ST Ewell K Nold Jr 09Sep71; BU 1972 near Houston, TX.

9148 *N93059—Southwest Airways.* (A R Krieger)

9149   NC93060   mfd 11Jun48 (originally assigned to PCA)
DD 30Jun48 to Northwest Airlines, FN 560; WFU 17Mar51 and stored; LT Transocean Air Lines Oct51; flown on behalf of Japan Air Lines Oct51-Sep52 *Dosei*. ST Transocean 04Sep52. ST Southwest Airways (later Pacific Air Lines) 01Oct52. ST TWA 30Jun60 and stored San Francisco, CA. ST Martin Air Leasing 17Nov61; LT Sperry Gyroscope Co Jun65. ST International Aerodyne Inc 31Dec69. ST Major Air Transport Inc 23Apr70. ST M Enterprises 24Apr70; impounded Sep70 at Athens, Greece, for alleged smuggling; believed BU after 1976.

9149 *N93060—International Aerodyne, Long Beach, California.* (Steve Nation)

9150   NC93061   mfd 18Jun48 (originally assigned to

PCA)

DD 30Jun48 to Northwest Airlines, FN 561; WFU 17Mar51 and stored; LT Transocean Air Lines Oct51; flown on behalf of Japan Air Lines Oct51-Sep52 *Kasei*. ST Transocean 04Sep52. ST Southwest Airways 24Sep52; landed gear-up 15Mar54 at Oxnard, CA—no injuries; WO in hangar fire 30Dec55, San Francisco, CA; center section and wing stored at San Francisco until c1961.

9150 *N93061—Southwest Airways, photographed on January 16, 1956, after the hangar fire at San Francisco, December 30, 1955.*
(William T Larkins)

9151 through **9157**—all originally assigned to Pennsylvania-Central Airlines (PCA) but not completed as 202s.

9158   NX93037   mfd 05Apr47 (used by Martin for certification tests, radio call-sign KHVIY)

NC93037 DD 02Aug47 to Northwest Airlines, FN 537 *The Province of Alberta*; cr 13Oct50, Almelund, MN—unwanted propeller reverse during training flight, all 6 aboard fatal (TT 5289).

9158 *NX93037—shown pre-delivery in 1947 in the World War II-era livery of Northwest Airlines; crashed October 13, 1950, at Almelund, Minnesota.* (Logan Coombs via Peter M Bowers)

9159   NC93038   mfd 12Aug47

DD 30Aug47 to Northwest Airlines, FN 538; WFU 17Mar51 and stored; LT Transocean Air Lines Sep51. ST Pioneer Air Lines 09Apr52 *Pacemaster Stephen F. Austin*; WFU Mar53 and stored; trf to Pioneer Aeronautical Services 06Nov53. **N174A** ST Allegheny Airlines 14Jan56, FN 174 *The Clevelander*, IS 25Mar56; cr 01Dec59 near Williamsport, PA—flown into Bald Eagle Mountain during instrument approach to Montoursville Airport, en route Philadelphia–Bradford–Erie–Cleveland; 3 crew and 23 passengers fatal (one survivor).

9159 *N174A (previously N93038)—Allegheny Airlines 'Martin Executive' The Clevelander photographed at Newark, New Jersey, May 9, 1957; crashed December 1, 1959, into Bald Eagle Mountain near Williamsport, Pennsylvania.*
(Charles Trask via A R Krieger)

9160   NC93039   mfd 1947

DD 22Sep47 to Northwest Airlines, FN 539; WFU 17Mar51 and stored; LT Transocean Air Lines Sep51; cr 05Nov51 at Tucumcari, NM—port wing struck ground during landing approach in poor weather, en route Oakland–Indiantown Gap, PA–Fort Devens, MA; 1 military passenger fatal, 9 injured (TT 6790); salvaged parts purchased by Southwest Airways for spares.

9160 *N93039—Northwest Airlines, 1949.* (Logan Coombs via Peter M Bowers)

9161   NC93040   mfd 27Aug47

DD 29Sep47 to Northwest Airlines, FN 540, IS 12Oct47; cr 07Nov50, Butte, MT—flown into mountain during instrument approach operating NW115 Chicago–Seattle via Minneapolis, Aberdeen, Bismarck, Great Falls, and Billings, all 4 crew and 17 passengers aboard fatal (TT 6166).

9161 *NC93040—Northwest Airlines, crashed November 7, 1950, at Butte, Montana.* (Jane's All the World's Aircraft via John Wegg)

9162   NC93041   mfd 04Sep47

DD 09Oct47 to Northwest Airlines, FN 541; WFU 17Mar51 and stored. ST Transocean Air Lines 05Sep51; flown on behalf of Japan Air Lines Oct51-Oct52 *Suisei*. ST Southwest Airways (later Pacific Air Lines) 30Oct52, DD 31Oct52. ST TWA 30Jun60 and stored San Francisco, CA. ST Delta Aircraft & Engine Co 08Sep60; trf to Delta Leasing Corp 21Oct60; trf back to Delta Aircraft & Engine Co 22Feb63. ST Carolina Fleets Inc 22Feb63. ST Charlotte Aircraft Corp 20May65. ST Brennan Aviation Co 20Jul66; leased 1967 to an operator dba Heritage Land. ST Westernair of Albuquerque Inc 13May71. ST Distributaire Inc 13May71.

ST Sky Aircraft Sales 29Oct71, ST James Outlaw Jr 30Oct71, dba Sunshine Choral Aires and dba Adventures in Flying. ST W E Hamilton 20Oct73. ST Global Aeronautical Museum Inc 20Sep74. ST I N Burchinal Jr 01Aug75 and displayed at the Flying Tiger Air Museum, Paris, TX. ST Milt Stollak 12Jul78 (reportedly airworthy at Bimini, Bahamas, Dec77). ST Emory J Burns 06May79. Fate unconfirmed.

9162 *N93041—Heritage Land, Jacksonville, Florida, May 24, 1967.* (Clay Jansson via Walt Redmond)

9163 **NC93042** mfd 1947
DD 19Oct47 to Northwest Airlines, FN 542; WFU 17Mar51 and stored. ST California Central Airlines 15Aug51, FN 042 *City of Oakland*, IS 31Aug51; WFU cFeb54 and stored. **N170A** ST Allegheny Airlines 03Mar55, FN 170 *The Atlantic Shore*, IS 01Jun55. ST Fairchild Hiller Corp 27Apr66. **HP-431** ST Rutas Aéreas Panamenas SA (RAPSA) 21Jul66; WFU c1969 Panama City, Panamá; believed BU c1972.

9163 *N170A (previously N93042)—Allegheny Airlines, Baltimore, October 9, 1965.* (Dave Lucabaugh via Walt Redmond)

9164 **NC93043** mfd 1947
DD 25Oct47 to Northwest Airlines, FN 543; WFU 17Mar51 and stored. ST Transocean Air Lines 15Aug51; flown on behalf of Japan Air Lines Co Jan52 *Mokusei*; cr 09Apr52 on O-Shima Island, Japan—flown into Mt Mihara en route Tokyo-Fukuoka, all 33 passengers and 4 crew aboard fatal.

9164 *NC93043—Northwest Airlines, 1948. Later flown by Transocean Air Lines under contract to NW on behalf of Japan Air Lines and crashed on Mount Mihara, O-Shima Island.* (Logan Coombs via Walt Redmond)

9165 **NC93044** mfd 1947
DD 08Nov47 to Northwest Airlines, FN 544; cr 29Aug48 at Winona, MN—structural failure of left wing en route Chicago–Minneapolis, all 3 crew and 34 aboard fatal (TT 1321).

9165 *NC93044—Northwest Airlines experimental color scheme; crashed on August 29, 1948, at Winona, Minnesota.* (A R Krieger)

9166 **NC93045** mfd 01Oct47
DD 12Nov47 to Northwest Airlines, FN 545; WFU 17Mar51 and stored. ST California Central Airlines 06Sep51, FN 045 *City of Burbank*; WFU cFeb54 and stored. **N171A** ST Allegheny Airlines 03Mar55, FN 171 *The New Yorker*, DD 05Mar55, IS 01Jul55; cvtd 30Nov64 to all-cargo config as an 'Allegheny Cargo-Liner'. ST Fairchild Hiller Corp 11Nov66. ST Associated Products of America 14Nov66; stored Wildwood, NJ; BU May77.

9166 *NC93045—Northwest Airlines experimental color scheme, applied at the factory.* (Logan Coombs via Walt Redmond)

9167 **NC93046** mfd 07Oct47
DD 13Nov47 to Northwest Airlines, FN 546 *North Star*, later *Topliner North Star*; WFU 17Mar51 and stored; LT Transocean Air Lines Sep51. ST Pioneer Air Lines 27Mar52 *Pacemaster Sam Houston*; WFU Mar53 and stored; trf to Pioneer Aeronautical Service 06Nov53; LT Glenn L Martin Co 1957-60 for use as an electronics testbed; RT Pioneer Hydrotex (new name effective 12Jun59). ST Hubert M Covert 04Nov60. ST Lloyd Airlines 22Nov60. ST Hubert M Covert 31Mar61. ST International Aviation Corp 30Oct61. ST Aero Enterprises 17Sep63. ST Laurel Walsh Inc 11Nov63. ST Aero Enterprises 02Dec63. Repossessed by Pullman Bank & Trust 21May64. ST Flying W Airways 02Nov64. ST Sanlo Inc Nov64. **N71R** ST Central American Airways Flying Service 28Jul65. **HK-1484** ST Aeroproveedora Ltda 'Proa' Sep73 and operated as a freighter; accident 24Jun75 at Eldorado Airport, Bogotá—no injuries; WFU 1977 and stored Bogotá, hulk extant Sep97.

9167 *NC93046—Northwest Airlines* Topliner North Star, *1948. This experimental color scheme, applied at the factory, was very close to the new scheme eventually adopted by Northwest.* (Logan Coombs via Walt Redmond)

9168 through **9170**—all assigned to Eastern Air Lines but not built, completed components scrapped.

9171*

Originally assigned to Eastern Air Lines, then as prototype Marketer/Merchantman; stored partially completed; used 1955 for CAA's *Operation Ditch* evacuation tests; used 1956 for simulated ditching evacuation in San Francisco Bay, CA; presumed BU.
(* msn as reported, but not confirmed)

9171—*the uncompleted 'Merchantman' all-cargo 202 at San Francisco after being modified for static ditching evacuation tests. Drums have been added to the nose and wing center section for bouyancy.* (William T Larkins)

9172 through **9192**—all assigned to Eastern Air Lines but not built, completed components scrapped.

9193 through **9202**—all assigned to Chicago & Southern but not built, completed components scrapped.

9203 through **9220**—all assigned to Braniff Airways but not built.

9221 assigned to Delta Air Lines but not built.

THE MODEL 303

9222   **NX93162**   prototype mfd 01Jul47
FF 03Jul47 in United Air Lines livery; BU 1947 (TT 87).

9222 *NX93162—the prototype 303 in final assembly in 1947 in D Building. The 303 in jigs behind is believed to have been msn 9223.*
(Martin via Smithsonian Institution)

9223   **(NC93163)**   2nd prototype
Intended for United Air Lines but scrapped 1947 before completion (assigned registration likely, but not confirmed).

9224 through **9256**—all assigned to United Air Lines but not built.

MODEL 202A

14071   **N93201**   mfd 08Jun50
DD 14Jul50 to TWA (on lease), FN 211 *Skyliner San Francisco*, IS 11Sep50; purchased 01May52 by TWA; WFU 02Feb58, stored Kansas City, MO (TT 15557). ST Allegheny Airlines 15Apr58, DD 17Apr58, FN 178, IS 17May58. ST Fairchild Hiller Corp 01Aug66. ST Associated Products of America 09Aug66, stored Wildwood, NJ; BU May77.

14071 *N93201—Trans World Airlines Fleet No 211.* (Martin via Author)

14072 N93202   mfd 30Jun50

DD 20Jul50 to TWA (on lease), FN 212 *Skyliner Oakland*, IS 01Sep50; dmgd 11Sep51 by flood Kansas City, MO, and RT Martin for repairs 14Sep-16Nov51, RTS 30Nov51; purchased 01May52 by TWA; WFU 31Jan58 and stored Kansas City, MO (TT 14406). ST California Airmotive Corp 17Jul59; LT Pacific Air Lines 11Aug59; WO 21Aug59, Burbank, CA, when tail torn off by Curtiss C-46 N111E (msn 30225) operated by Sourdough Air Transport which ground looped during an emergency landing (the C-46 survived); BU by California Airmotive.

14072 N93202—Trans World Airlines Skyliner Oakland *after addition of the white fuselage background.* (via Eric W Wagner)

14073 N93203   mfd 30Jun50

DD 22Jul50 to TWA (on lease), FN 213 *Skyliner Fresno*, IS 02Sep50; purchased 10Apr52 by TWA; WFS 01Feb58 and used only for training at Kansas City, MO, 21Mar-31Oct58; WFU 31Oct58 (TT 15194); LT Allegheny Airlines 10Nov58. ST Allegheny Airlines 31Dec58, FN 179, IS 02Jan59. ST Fairchild Hiller Corp 01Aug66. ST Associated Products of America 09Aug66, stored Wildwood, NJ; BU May77.

14073 N93203—Allegheny Airlines, Cape May, New Jersey, 1960. (via Walt Redmond)

14074 N93204   mfd 10Jul50

DD 03Aug50 to TWA (on lease), FN 214 *Skyliner Burbank*, IS 11Sep50; purchased 01May52 by TWA; nose gear collapsed after hitting fence on approach 08Sep54, Philadelphia, PA—no injuries, RTS 16Dec54; WFU 01Feb58 Kansas City, MO (TT 14659). ST California Airmotive Corp 17Jul59, DD 03Aug59; LT Lone Star Airlines 1960, stored Las Vegas, NV, 1960. ST TWA 1961 (remained in storage Las Vegas). ST Allegheny Airlines 21Jul61, FN 184 (still in store Nov61). ST Fairchild Hiller Corp 17Jun66. ST Associated Products of America 31Aug66 and stored Linden, NJ. ST Skylark Travel Club Inc 31May68; LT Herman's Hermits and The Animals for rock concert tour. ST Associated Products of America 05Dec69 and stored Wildwood, NJ; acquired by Aviation Hall of Fame & Museum of New Jersey, and displayed at Teterboro, NJ.

14074 N93204—Trans World Airlines Skyliner Burbank. (Peter M Bowers)

14075 N93205   mfd 17Jul50, FF 25Jul50

DD 29Jul50 to TWA (on lease), FN 215 *Skyliner Los Angeles*, IS 01Sep50; purchased 10Apr52 by TWA; landing gear inadvertently raised during landing roll 17Oct53, Philadelphia, PA—no injuries; WFU 21Mar58, Kansas City, MO (TT 15397); LT Pacific Air Lines 09Apr58-27Jun59. ST California Airmotive Corp 17Jul59, DD 27Jun59 (TWA date). **XA-NEK** ST Líneas Aéreas Unidas SA (LAUSA) 28Jan60, repossessed by California Airmotive 27Dec60 as **N93205** and stored Las Vegas, NV. ST Allegheny Airlines 14Aug61, FN 185 (still stored Nov61). ST Fairchild Hiller Corp 01Aug66. ST Associated Products of America 09Aug66. ST Modern Air Transport 24Aug66. ST Southeast Airlines 28Oct69; WFU 1973 and stored Miami, FL. ST J Patrick Soltes 26Mar75; trf to Martin Air Transport 31Jul75. ST Sky Commerce Inc 25Sep79. **CP-1441** ST Nacional Can Ltda Oct79 for resale or lease to Comercializadora Aérea Mixta Boliviana Ltd (CAMBA); ST (or LT) Compañia Aérea Nacional (CAN) 1981; believed to have crashed in 1984.

14075 CP-1441 (previously N93205)—for Comercialisadora Aerea Mixta Boliviana (CAMBA), Miami, October 1979. (D Thirwall via Michael Magnusson)

14076 N93206   mfd 1950

DD 11Aug50 to TWA (on lease), FN 216 *Skyliner Phoenix*, IS 01Sep50; purchased 10Apr52 by TWA; dmgd 20Nov56 Pittsburgh, PA—nose gear strut failed on retraction; WFU 11Mar58 and stored Kansas City, MO (TT 15300); LT Pacific Air Lines 14Jan-02May59; LT Allegheny Airlines 13Jun59, IS 22Jun59. ST Allegheny Airlines 01Oct59, FN 183. ST Fairchild Hiller Corp 01Aug66. ST Modern Air Transport 09Aug66; LT Air Atlantic c1968. ST Southeast Airlines 28Oct69; WFU and stored Miami, FL. ST Charlotte Aircraft Corp 21Jan72; BU Miami 1972.

14076 N93206—leased to Pacific Air Lines, San Francisco, April 4, 1959. (Larry Smalley via Walt Redmond)

14077   N93207   mfd 27Jul50

DD 17Aug50 to TWA (on lease), FN 217 *Skyliner Las Vegas*, IS 01Sep50; ran off runway 20Jan51 landing at Louisville, KY—repaired; purchased 01May52 by TWA; WFU 01Feb58 and stored Kansas City, MO (TT 15206). ST California Airmotive Corp 17Jul59, DD 28Jul59; LT Lone Star Airlines 1960 then stored Las Vegas, NV. ST Allegheny Airlines 01Sep61, FN 186. ST Fairchild Hiller Corp 01Aug66. ST Associated Products of America 11Aug66 and stored Wildwood, NJ. ST Wildwood Boardwalk Amusement Park 1975 and used as park attraction 'Amusement Airlines'; BU 1980.

14077 *N93207—Trans World Airlines.* (A R Krieger)

14078   N93208   mfd 03Aug50

DD 18Aug50 to TWA (on lease), FN 218 *Skyliner Albuquerque*, IS 02Sep50; purchased 01May52 by TWA; WFU 01Feb58 and stored Kansas City, MO (TT 15233); LT Pacific Air Lines 24Dec58-02May59; LT Allegheny Airlines 06Jun59, IS 21Jun59. ST Allegheny Airlines 01Oct59, FN 182. ST Fairchild Hiller Corp 01Aug66. ST Modern Air Transport 09Aug66. ST Southeast Airlines 30Jan70 for spares and stored Miami, FL. ST Charlotte Aircraft Corp 21Jan72; BU early 1972 Miami, FL.

14078 *N93208—final days at Miami, September 1970.* (Gordon Reid)

14079   N93209   mfd 24Aug50

DD 06Sep50 to TWA (on lease), FN 219 *Skyliner Santa Fe*, IS 10Sep50; purchased 10Apr52 by TWA; WFU 02Feb58 and stored Kansas City, MO (TT 15104). ST California Airmotive Corp 17Jul59, DD 20Jul59; LT Lone Star Airlines 1960 then stored Las Vegas, NV. ST TWA Jun61. ST Allegheny Airlines 30Jun61, FN 187. ST Fairchild Hiller Corp 01Aug66. ST Associated Products of America 09Aug66. ST Modern Air Transport 24Aug66. ST Mid America Airlines 18Nov67; repossessed 30Aug69 by National Bank of Commerce of Tulsa. ST Stan Burnstein dba Continental Aviation Co 25May70. ST Carolina Aircraft Corp 29May70; BU 1971 Fort Lauderdale, FL.

14079 *N93209—Trans World Airlines* Skyliner Santa Fe *about to flare at Chicago-Midway on April 14, 1956.* (A R Krieger)

14080   N93210   mfd 31Aug50

DD 16Sep50 to TWA (on lease), FN 220 *Skyliner Amarillo*, IS 24Sep50; purchased 10Apr52 by TWA; WFU 01Feb58 and stored Kansas City, MO (TT 15040); LT Allegheny Airlines 21Nov58. ST Allegheny Airlines 31Dec58, FN 180, IS 28Jan59. ST Fairchild Hiller Corp 01Aug66. ST Associated Products of America 09Aug66 and stored Wildwood, NJ; BU May77.

14080 *N93210—Allegheny Airlines, Baltimore, August 10, 1965.* (Dave Lucabaugh via Walt Redmond)

14081   N93211   mfd 1950

DD 28Sep50 to TWA (on lease), FN 221 *Skyliner Lancaster*, IS 30Sep50; gear collapsed on landing 19Feb51, Dayton, OH—no injuries, repaired by Martin and RTS 24Apr51; purchased 10Apr52 by TWA; cr 12Jan55 Covington, KY—mid-air collison with DC-3 N999B (msn 4255), all 13 aboard 202 and both aboard DC-3 fatal (TT 7958).

14081 *N93211—Trans World Airlines* Skyliner Lancaster, *crashed January 12, 1955, at Covington, Kentucky, following a mid-air collision with DC-3 N999B.* (A R Krieger)

14082   N93212   mfd 30Sep50

DD 29Sep50 to TWA (on lease), FN 222 *Skyliner Hannibal*, IS 01Oct50; purchased 10Apr52 by TWA; later *Skyliner Denver*, WFU 01Feb58 and stored Kansas City, MO (TT 15007). ST Allegheny Airlines 31Dec58, FN 181, DD 30Apr59 (TWA quotes 12Feb59). ST Fairchild Hiller Corp 09Jun66. ST Associated Products of America 11Aug66. ST Modern Air Transport 24Aug66. ST Southeast Airlines 30Jan70; WFU Sep71, Miami, FL; used by Clayton Curtis for high-speed taxi tests to evaluate suitability of type for aerial application work. ST Charlotte Aircraft Corp 21Jan72; BU early 1972 Miami, FL.

14082 *N93212—Southeast Airlines, Miami, October 1970. This airplane was used by Clayton V Curtis in 1969 to test the suitability of the Martinliner for aerial application work.* (Gordon Reid)

MODEL 404

A non-flying airframe was manufactured c1951 for structural tests, probably not assigned a msn, later scrapped.

14101   **N40401**   mfd 05Jul51
FF 27Jul51. DD 19Feb52 to TWA, FN 401 *Skyliner Baltimore*, IS 20Feb52; gear-up landing 28Feb60, NAS Olathe, KS, after wheel loss after takeoff from Midway en route Peoria—no injuries; WFU and stored Kansas City-Fairfax. ST Piedmont Airlines 31Jul61 (TT 19326), FN 401 *Tidewater Pacemaker*, DD 02Feb62, IS 02Mar62; cr 22Aug62, Wilmington, NC, on training flight—lost control on landing because of unselected propeller reversal—no injuries to 3 crew.

14101 *N40401—Trans World Airlines at Chicago-Midway.* (A R Krieger)

14102   **N40402**   mfd 16Jul51
DD 31Jan52 to TWA, FN 402 *Skyliner Indianapolis*, IS 02Feb52, later renamed *Skyliner Chicago*. **N442E** ST East Coast Flying Service 28Jun61 (TT 19328), DD 29Jun61 to Washington-National; operated for rock group Dave Clark Five in 1965 with 'The DC5' titles. **N40402** ST Piedmont Airlines 01Feb65, FN 402 *Savannah River Pacemaker*, DD 02Feb65, IS 25Mar65; WFU 06Mar71. ST Alpha Aviation 17Nov72. ST Jack Adams Aircraft Sales 21Nov72. ST Mark Aero Inc 21Nov72; WFU 1972 St Louis, MO; BU Jul76.

14102 *N442E (previously N40402)—East Coast Flying Service, 1965. 'The DC5' on the nose indicates it was leased to The Dave Clark Five for a rock concert tour.* (MAP)

14103   **N40403**   mfd 1951
DD 09Nov51 to TWA, FN 403 *Skyliner Pittsburgh*, IS 10Nov51; cr 01Apr56, Pittsburgh, PA—lost control following takeoff because of high drag of unfeathered propeller, operating TW400 Pittsburgh–Harrisburg–Reading–Allentown–Newark, 22 fatal, 7 injured (TT 9177).

14103 *N40403—Trans World Airlines (unnamed), crashed April 1, 1956, at Pittsburgh.* (TWA via Author)

14104   **N40404**   mfd 1951
DD 29Nov51 to TWA, FN 404 *Skyliner Philadelphia*, IS 30Nov51; gear-up landing 08Dec51, St Joseph, MO, during training—no injuries; repaired by Lockheed Air Service, Burbank, 08-29Jan52, RTS 01Feb52; cr 15Nov56, Las Vegas, NV—failed to make successful single-engine go-around, no injuries (TT 10452).

14104 *N40404—Trans World Airlines Skyliner Philadelphia, crashed November 15, 1956 at Las Vegas.* (A R Krieger)

14105   **N40405**   mfd 12Nov51
DD 04Dec51 to TWA, FN 405 *Skyliner New York*, IS 06Dec51; WFU and stored Kansas City-Fairfax. ST Piedmont Airlines 02Feb62 (TT 19232), FN 405 *Ohio Valley Pacemaker*, DD 06Feb62, IS 29Aug62; WFU 31Dec69. ST US Aircraft Sales 12Jan70. ST Charlotte Aircraft Corp 20Mar70; cvtd to aerial applicator 07May70 by Clayton V Curtis; WFU Dec72, Sebring, FL. ST Dothan Aviation Inc 02Mar73 for spares; BU 1976, Sebring, FL.

14105 *N40405—Piedmont Airlines* Ohio Valley Pacemaker, *Wilmington, North Carolina, March 1, 1969.* (Elliot H Greenman)

14106   **N40406**   mfd 23Nov51
DD 10Dec51 to TWA, FN 406 *Skyliner Washington DC*; IS 13Dec52. ST California Airmotive Corp 15Feb60 (TT 17359); LT Hughes Tool Co 18Feb60-Feb61 for radar testing. **N244AG** ST Aerojet-General Corp 28Aug61. **N40401** ST Piedmont Airlines 04Feb65, FN 401 *Great Smokies Pacemaker*, IS 16Apr65; WFU May69. ST US Aircraft Sales 17Dec69, DD 05Dec69. ST Charlotte Aircraft Corp 20Mar70, stored Sebring, FL. ST CEC Corp 09Dec71. ST H J Caldwell and Badr Halwany 07Mar72; trf to Atlantic Southeast Airlines 28Mar72; BU 1979, Sebring, FL; nose preserved by William P Thompson, Pensacola, FL.

14106 *N40406—Aerojet-General.* (A R Kreiger)

14107   **N40407**   mfd 30Nov51
DD 13Dec51 to TWA, FN 407 *Skyliner Indianapolis*, IS 14Dec52; lost left-hand engine cowl 19May57—landed safely Kansas City, MO; WFU and stored Kansas City-Fairfax; ST Piedmont Airlines 31Jul61, DD 19Oct61 (TT 19292). FN 407 *Blue Grass Pacemaker*, IS 01Jan62; WFU 05Dec70. ST Africair Inc 28Mar72. ST Southeast Airlines 01Apr72. ST Provincetown-Boston Airline 06Jan76; WFU Nov84 and stored Naples, FL; stored Gulfport-Biloxi, MS, 1987. ST Roberta A Rogers dba Erickson & Remmert 26Sep88, moved to Bay St Louis-Stennis Intl, MS, Mar89; proposed sale to Aero Sierra de Durango not completed and remained stored. Extant (Jun97).

14107 *N40407—Piedmont Airlines* Blue Grass Pacemaker, *Wilmington, North Carolina, August 16, 1969.* (Elliot H Greenman)

14108   **N40408**   mfd 07Dec51
DD 21Dec51 to TWA, FN 408 *Skyliner Columbus*, IS 25Dec51; left main gear collapsed 20Dec58 on landing at Columbus, OH—repaired. ST Pacific Air Lines 26Sep60 (TT 19089), DD 28Sep60, IS 08Oct60. ST Piedmont Airlines 09Apr66, FN 408 *Rappahannock Pacemaker*, DD 03May66; WFU 15May68. ST Alpha Aviation Inc 17Jan73. ST Equilease Corp 28Nov73; LT Bennett Paper Corp 28Nov73. ST Engine Air Ltd 10Jan77. ST Marvin L Janzen 18Jan77. ST Valley Martin Inc 28Dec78; LT Ag Investors 28Dec78; cvtd to aerial applicator 20Feb79 by Howard Coones; cr 29Jun79 near Pampa, TX—collided with ground when windshield became obscured by spray from another sprayer—1 injured.

14108 *N40408—Pacific Air Lines, San Francisco, March 30, 1965.* (Author)

14109   **N440A**   mfd 20Aug51
DD 09Oct51 to Eastern Air Lines, FN 440 (the first 404 delivered, although EAL quotes 21Oct51—probably the arrival date in New York). **N470M** ST Mohawk Airlines 24Sep62, *Air Chief Montagnais*. ST Ozark Air Lines 02Jun65, IS 05Jul65. ST Fairchild Hiller Corp 07Jul67 and stored Las Vegas, NV. ST Jack Richards Aircraft Sales Co, Inc 29Jul70; LT Golden Eagle Aviation 1970, seized 05Oct70 by FAA for violation of FARs. ST John E Beaven 16Oct70. ST Supply Forwarding Co (later renamed Salefish Inc) 04Jan72; released from seizure 05Jan72. ST R M Richards 21Sep72. ST W E Hamilton 06Oct73. ST Arizona Land Air Co Inc 30Jan74. ST Onyx Aviation Inc 12Jan77. ST Marvin L Janzen 25Jan77; cvtd to aerial applicator 1978 by Howard Coones. ST 404 Enterprises Inc 27Dec78; LT Ag International Flying Service 30Dec78; WFU c1980 and abandoned at Oakland, CA. ST G L Ellison 24Jul96; hulk BU Oct96, dereg 25Oct96.

14109 *N470M (previously N440A)—Ozark Air Lines, Chicago-O'Hare, April 6, 1967.* (Robert E Hufford)

14110   **N441A**   mfd 31Oct51
DD 17Nov51 to Eastern Air Lines, FN 441. ST Charlotte Aircraft Corp 20Dec62 and believed stored Louisville, KY. **N257S** ST Southern Airways 03Jun64, FN 116, IS 28Oct64. ST Transexecutive Airlines Inc 26Jan76; LT Shawnee Airlines 31Jan76. ST Dolphin Aviation Inc 20Apr76 for continued lease to Shawnee Airlines (carried Air South titles by Dec77); lease trf to Florida Airlines 01Mar78, *Sea Island*, although already operated by Florida Als Apr77; trf to Dolphin International Inc 29Jun78 for continued lease to Florida Airlines; WFU and stored Sarasota, FL; used for parts; RT Dolphin International 08Jan80. ST Ocean Airways Inc 08Jan80. ST David

S Stempler 23Jan81; donated to Sarasota-Manatee Airport Authority 28Jun83 for fire and rescue training; hulk extant Oct86, believed subsequently BU.

14110 *N257S (previously N441A)—Florida Airlines in livery of affiliate Shawnee Airlines, 1977.* (MAP)

14111   **N442A**   mfd 12Nov51

DD 27Nov51 to Eastern Air Lines, FN 442. ST East Coast Flying Service 20Jul60. ST Charlotte Aircraft Corp 10May65. **N583S** ST Southern Airways 17May65, FN 121, IS 21Jul65; WFU 1975 Atlanta, GA; BU 11Jun76.

14111 *N442A—Eastern Air Lines.* (A R Krieger)

14112   **N443A**   mfd 19Nov51

DD 01Dec51 to Eastern Air Lines, FN 443. **N471M** ST Mohawk Airlines 18Sep62, *Air Chief Manhanset.* ST Ozark Air Lines 01Oct65, IS 19Dec65. ST Fairchild Hiller Corp 29Jul67 and stored Las Vegas, NV. ST Interstate Airmotive 14Nov67. ST Alpha Aviation 18Oct72. ST Taku Lands Inc 11Dec73; trf to H S Stinson Jr 12Dec73; LT Mark Aero Jan74 for planned operation as Missouri Commuter Airlines. ST Petroleum Air Transport Inc 12Jul76; trf to DHL Corp dba DHL Airlines 23Mar79; WFU Jul79, Honolulu, HI; BU 1983.

14112 *N443A—one of the few 404s painted in Eastern's later livery.* (via Clinton H Groves)

14113   **N40409**   mfd 14Dec51

DD 27Dec51 to TWA, FN 409 *Skyliner Dayton*, IS 28Dec51; LT Pacific Air Lines 24Apr60 (TT 17626), DD 09May60. ST Pacific Air Lines 30Jun60. ST United States Leasing Corp 30Sep64; LT Edgerton,

Germeshausen and Grier Inc (EG&G) 30Sep64; modified to incorporate infra-red scanner and air sampling equipment. ST US Atomic Energy Commission 24Jan67, continued operation by EG&G; trf to US Energy Research and Development Administration 19Jan75, continued operation by EG&G; trf to US Department of Energy 01Oct77, continued operation by EG&G; trf to US Army Missile R & D Command 12Jan78, continued operation by EG&G; trf to US Air Force, DET 1, AFEREG 02Jun78; continued operation by EG&G. Donated to Southern Nevada Vocational Technical Center, Las Vegas, NV, by EG&G and delivered 30Jun80 to adjacent dirt strip by air for use as training aid; BU Aug96, fuselage trucked to Fresno, CA, for use in a 'haunted house' attraction.

14113 *N40409—operated by EG&G on behalf of the US Atomic Energy Commission, Las Vegas, 1976.* (MAP)

14114   **N40410**   mfd 19Dec51

DD 31Dec51 to TWA, FN 410 *Skyliner Cincinnati*, IS 03Jan52; WFU and stored Kansas City-Fairfax. ST Piedmont Airlines 31Jul61 (TT 19592), FN 410 *Shenandoah Pacemaker*, DD 08Feb62, IS 14Mar62; WFU 27Nov68. ST US Aircraft Sales Corp 02Dec68. ST Francis Y Sogi 02Dec68. ST Skagitt Corp 24Jan69. ST S S McIntyre, Jr 15Oct71. ST Mark Aero Inc 24Oct72. **N69RB** ST Red Baron Charter Co 30Mar73. ST Joe Simkins (Tiffany Industries) 17Feb75. **N200JS** RR Jun75 to Joe Simkins; WFU and stored c1978, St Louis, MO. ST Sky Commerce Inc 25Jan79. **CP-1440** ST Comercializadora Aérea Mixta Boliviana Ltd (CAMBA) Jan79, DD 26Jan79 at Miami, left Miami 09Feb79; cr 12Dec79 Apolo airstrip, Bolivia, just after takeoff, 10 fatal, 1 injured.

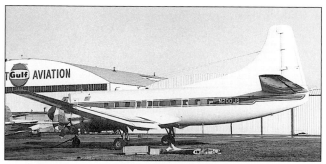

14114 *N200JS (previously N40410/N69RB)—Joe Simkins dba Tiffany Industries, St Louis, March 1976.* (John P Stewart via Peter R Keating)

14115   **N40411**   mfd 20Dec51

DD 04Jan52 to TWA, FN 411 *Skyliner St Louis*, IS 15Jan52; WFU and stored Kansas City-Fairfax. ST Piedmont Airlines 31Jan61 (TT 19491), FN 411 *Tennessee Valley Pacemaker*, DD 07Feb62, IS 22Mar62; WFU 18Jan70. ST US Aircraft Sales Corp 28Jan70. ST Charlotte Aircraft Corp 20Mar70 and stored Sebring, FL. ST American Jet Industries Inc 28Oct71, remained stored Sebring, FL. ST CMH Leasing Corp 24Oct72; LT Flamingo Airlines 1972. ST Clayton V Curtis 17Nov73. ST Frontier Inc 15Feb74; cvtd to aerial applicator 02Apr74 by Clayton V Curtis; stored 1977, Grenada, MS. ST F & B Aircraft 12Feb80; BU at Grenada by Apr85.

14115 *N40411—Trans World Airlines (unnamed), New York-LaGuardia, January 11, 1952.* (Leo J. Kohn)

14116   **N40412**   mfd 1951
DD 23Jan52 to TWA, FN 412 *Skyliner Wheeling*, IS 27Jan52. ST California Airmotive Sales Corp 11Mar60 (TT 17501). ST W A Moncrief 11Mar60, trf to Montex Drilling Co 11Mar60, DD from TWA 12Mar60. ST Magic Chef Inc 29Mar65. ST Vanderbilt University 19Aug69 for the McGugin Center. ST Carolina Aircraft Corp 03Apr70; trf to Florida Aircraft Leasing Corp 06Apr70; LT Lehigh Acres Development Inc May70; cr 30May70, Atlanta, GA—forced landing on I-285 after being refueled with turbine fuel at DeKalb-Peachtree Airport en route Fort Myers, FL; 1 of 30 passengers plus 5 in an automobile on ground fatal, 27 injured.

14116 *N40412—Magic Chef Inc.* (via Denis Goodwin)

14117   **N40413**   mfd 01May52
DD 19May52 to TWA, FN 413 *Skyliner Louisville*, IS 22May52; WFU and stored Kansas City-Fairfax. ST Piedmont Airlines 31Jul61 (TT 18978), FN 413 *Sand Hills Pacemaker*, DD 12Jan62, IS 09Feb62; WFU 08Nov70. ST Southeast Airlines 07Jun72. ST Provincetown-Boston Airline 06Jan76; WFU Nov84; stored Gulfport-Biloxi, MS, 1987. ST Roberta A Rogers dba Erickson & Remmert 26Sep88; proposed sale to Aero Sierra de Durango not completed and remained stored. Extant (Jun97).

14117 *N40413—Southeast Airlines, Miami, October 1975.* (John Wegg)

14118   **N40414**   mfd 1952
DD 19May52 to TWA, FN 414 *Skyliner Boston*, IS 01Jun52, later *Skyliner Dayton*; WFU and stored Kansas City-Fairfax; ST Piedmont Airlines 31Jul61, DD 16Oct61 (TT 19187), FN 414 *Commonwealth Pacemaker*, IS 01Jan62; WFU 12Dec70. ST Alpha Aviation 17Jan73; WFU St Louis, MO, 1976 and stripped for spares, hulk to airport fire service, extant 1984.

14118 *N40414—final days at St Louis.* (Gordon Reid)

14119   **N40415**   mfd 08May52
DD 26May52 to TWA, FN 415 *Skyliner Albany*, IS 02Jun52; left landing gear collapsed on landing 08May53, Wheeling, WV—no injuries; WFU and stored Kansas City-Fairfax. ST Piedmont Airlines 31Jul61, DD 04Jan62 (TT 18863), FN 415 *Yadkin Valley Pacemaker*, IS 29Jan62; hard landing 06Aug62, Rocky Mount, NC—no injuries; WFU 22Jan71. ST Landmark Baptist Temple 19Oct72. ST Penn Landmark Corp 08Dec73, stored Pinehurst, NC. ST Provincetown-Boston Airline 01Dec76; WFU Oct77 and stored Naples, FL; stored Gulfport-Biloxi, MS, 1987. ST Roberta A Rogers dba Erickson & Remmert 26Sep88 and moved to Bay St Louis-Stennis Intl, MS, Mar89; proposed sale to Aero Sierra de Durango not completed; seized by US Customs Service 15Mar90. ST Mario Duenas 01Nov95 but documentation of sale never completed. Extant.

14119 *N40415—Provincetown-Boston Airline with Naples Airlines titles, Naples, March 1978.* (Karl Krämer)

14120   **N40416**   mfd 1952
DD 27May52 to TWA, FN 416 *Skyliner Binghamton*, IS 02Jun52; nose gear failed on landing 25Mar54, Chicago-Midway, IL—no injuries; RTS 27May54; cr 19Feb55, nr Albuquerque, NM: flown into Sandia Mountain operating TW260 Albuquerque–Santa Fe, 13 passengers and 3 crew aboard fatal (TT 5614).

14120 *N40416—Trans World Airlines (unnamed), crashed February 19, 1955, into Sandia Mountain near Albuquerque.* (Ed Peck via Clinton H Groves/Airliners America/ATP)

14121   N444A   mfd 28Nov51
DD 07Dec51 to Eastern Air Lines, FN 444. ST Falair Inc 13Jun61; LT ASA International Airlines 20Jun61, FN 444. ST Pacific Air Lines 24May62, DD 25May62, IS 16Jul62. ST Pallas Design & Engineering Corp 01Aug68 and stored Las Vegas, NV. ST W Patrick Moriarty 12Jun72; BU Las Vegas, Sep-Oct79.

14121 *N444A—Eastern Air Lines, Washington-National, May 2, 1957.*

14122   N445A   mfd 1951
DD 16Dec51 to Eastern Air Lines, FN 445; cr 17Feb56, Owensboro, KY—stalled on approach to Davies County Airport operating EA156 Evansville–Owensboro–Louisville–Chicago, right wing separated in very hard landing, fuselage rolled inverted, one injury (TT 12373).

14123   N40417   mfd 15May52
DD 02Jun52 to TWA, FN 417 *Skyliner Williamsport*, IS 03Jun52; WFU and stored Kansas City-Fairfax. ST Piedmont Airlines 31Jul61 (TT 18207), FN 417 *Piedmont Pacemaker*, DD 27Dec61, IS 18Jan62; WFU 04Sep68. ST US Aircraft Sales Corp 09Oct68. ST Francis Y Sogi 09Oct68. ST Charlotte Aircraft Corp 20Mar70 and stored Sebring, FL. ST CEC Corp 13Apr71. ST Carolina Fleets Inc 24May71 and stored Miami, FL; trf to American Lease Plans Inc Jul72. ST Atlantic Southeast Airlines 19Aug74, remained stored Miami, FL. ST Air Agency Inc 08Oct76. ST Provincetown-Boston Airline 21Feb78 for parts and dismantled at Miami 27Feb78, fuselage trucked to Naples, FL, 14Mar78; hulk BU 1987 although registered to Air Agency Inc Sep89.

14123 *N40417—ex-Piedmont's* Piedmont Pacemaker *chained to a flatbed at Miami in March 1978 for its final journey to Naples, Florida.* (Karl Krämer)

14124   N40418   mfd 19May52
DD 02Jun52 to TWA, FN 418 *Skyliner Newark*, IS 03Jun52; WFU and stored Kansas City-Fairfax. ST Piedmont Airlines 31Jul61, DD 24Jan62 (TT 19192), FN 418 *Hampton Roads Pacemaker*, IS 15Feb62; WFU 15May68. ST US Aircraft Sales Corp 26Dec68; trf to Francis Y Sogi 06Jan69. ST Charlotte Aircraft Corp 23Jun69 and stored Sebring, FL; cvtd to aerial applicator 25Jan70 by Clayton V Curtis. ST Dothan Aviation Inc 15Feb73. ST Marvin L Janzen 17Jun77 and stored Madera, CA. ST Ag International Flying Service 28Dec78. Repossessed by Marvin L Janzen 02May80. ST Frontier Airways Inc 12Apr82 for spares use; hulk BU at Madera Feb89 and remains trucked to Fresno for recycling; dereg 03Jun91.

14124 *N40418—Piedmont Airlines* Hampton Roads Pacemaker, *Atlanta, April 30, 1966.* (Robert E Hufford)

14125   N40419   mfd 22May52
DD 05Jun52 to TWA, FN 419 *Skyliner Wilmington*, used by Martin 05-10Jun52 for gross weight tests, IS 13Jun52; WFU and stored Kansas City-Fairfax. ST Piedmont Airlines 31Jul61, DD 05Dec61 (TT 18052), FN 425 *Kanawha River Pacemaker*, IS 17May62; WFU 23Aug71. ST Caribbean International Hotel Corp 26Feb72. ST Transport Facilities Inc 21Jun72 (operated for Royal Haitian Hotel). ST International Transport Leasing 24Mar77; trf to Royal Haitian Hotel 15Jul77, used by Duvalier as HH-RHH (although still reg N40419) c1983, including for flights between Punta Paitilla, Panamá, and Haiti; WFU and stored Port-au-Prince c1987. ST Mid South Airways 21Jan87, dereg 26Feb87. Extant (Nov96).

14125 *HH-RHH (previously N40419)—Royal Haitian Hotel, Panama City, April 1983.* (Jaime Escobar Corradine)

14126   N40420   mfd 26May52

DD 06Jun52 to TWA, FN 420 *Skyliner Allentown*, IS 07Jun52; lost control after aborted takeoff because gust lock was engaged 18Nov55, Allentown, PA—no injuries; WFU and stored Kansas City-Fairfax. ST Piedmont Airlines 31Jul61, DD 09Dec61 (TT 18850), FN 420 *Tarheel Pacemaker*, IS 04Jan62; WFU 10Feb69. ST US Aircraft Sales Corp 09Apr69. ST Charlotte Aircraft Corp 09Apr69 and stored Sebring, FL. ST Provincetown-Boston Airline 04May77 and used for parts; BU 1987, Naples, FL.

14126 *N40420—previously Piedmont Airlines* Tarheel Pacemaker, *Sebring, Florida, September 1970.* (Gordon Reid)

14127   N40421   mfd 28May52

DD 13Jun52 to TWA, FN 421 *Skyliner Harrisburg*, IS 14Jun52, later *Skyliner Washington*; WFU and stored Kansas City-Fairfax. ST Piedmont Airlines 31Jul61 (TT 19041), FN 421 *Appalachian Pacemaker*, DD 29Jan62, IS 22Feb62; WFU 15Nov69. ST US Aircraft Sales Corp 17Nov69. ST Charlotte Aircraft Corp 20Mar70 and stored Sebring, FL; LT Flamingo Airlines 1971; WFU cNov71 and stored Nassau, Bahamas. ST CEC Corp 09Dec71. ST Harold J Caldwell and Badr Halwany 06Mar72; trf to Atlantic Southeast Airlines 28Mar72, remained stored Nassau. ST Air Inter Sales Co 04Aug72, reportedly impounded at Nassau Sep76 for smuggling; hulk extant Sep92.

14127 *N40421—Trans World Airlines* Skyliner Harrisburg. (via John Wegg)

14128   N40422   mfd 04Jun52

DD 18Jun52 to TWA, FN 422 *Skyliner Kansas City*, IS 19Jun52. ST Pacific Air Lines 26Sep60 (TT 18324), DD 28Sep60, IS 11Oct60. ST Pallas Design & Engineering Corp 01Aug68 and stored Litchfield Park (Goodyear), AZ. ST M Silverman 05Mar70; trf to Hawthorne Christian Schools dba Fiesta Air 06Mar70. **N302FA** RR Aug72 to Hawthorne Christian Schools; WFU Nov72, Long Beach, CA; proposed sale Dec73 to Mark Aero for Missouri Commuter Airlines not completed. ST Universal Applicators 21Apr75; LT California Internationale 1975. ST Kodiak Western Alaska Airlines 19Mar76 for spares to support N40438 (msn 14173); BU Long Beach, CA, Jul77.

14128 *N40422—Hawthorne Christian Schools, Long Beach, California, April 1970.* (Steve Nation)

14129   N40423   mfd 04Jun52

DD 19Jun52 to TWA, FN 423 *Skyliner Reading*, IS 31Jul61; WFU and stored Kansas City-Fairfax. ST Piedmont Airlines 31Jul61 (TT 18143), FN 423 *Pamlico Pacemaker*, DD 16Feb62, IS 02Aug62; WFU 06Nov70. ST Air Fare Leasing Corp 03Jan72; LT World Citizens Intl Inc 1972. ST Penn Landmark Corp 17Sep73; WFU c1976 and stored Pinehurst, NC. ST Provincetown-Boston Airline 27Jun77. ST F.I.R.S.T. Cargo Inc 20Feb87, dereg Mar87. **HI-501** ST Santiago Freight Cargo CXA Mar87; WFU 1987 and stored Santo Domingo, DR. **YV-145C** ST Rentavion CA 26May89, stored until made airworthy 1996. Current.

14129 *N40423—Provincetown-Boston Airline with Naples Airlines titles, Naples, March 1978.* (Karl Krämer)

14130   N40424   mfd 06Jun52

DD 20Jun52 to TWA, FN 424 *Skyliner Toledo*, IS 20Jun52; WFU and stored Kansas City-Fairfax. ST Piedmont Airlines 31Jul61, DD 13Feb62 (TT 18292), FN 424 *Pee Dee Pacemaker*, IS 13Jul62; WFU 17Jul68. ST US Aircraft Sales Corp 09Oct68; trf to Francis Y Sogi 09Oct68. ST Charlotte Aircraft Corp 12Mar69 and stored Sebring, FL. ST Southeast Airlines 02Dec71. ST Provincetown-Boston Airline 28Nov75; used for campaign of presidential candidate John Anderson Aug80; WFU Naples, FL; stored Gulfport-Biloxi, MS, 1987. ST Roberta A Rogers dba Erickson & Remmert 26Sep88 and moved to Bay St Louis-Stennis Intl, MS, Mar89; proposed sale to Aero Sierra de Durango not completed and remained stored. Extant (Jun97).

14130 *N40424—Southeast Airlines, Miami, October 1975.* (John Wegg)

14131 **N40425** mfd 17Jun52

DD 27Jun52 to TWA, FN 425 *Skyliner Zanesville*, IS 28Jun52, later renamed *Skyliner Easton*. **N333G** ST California Airmotive Sales Corp 24Mar59 (TT 15019), DD 25Mar59. ST Houston Lumber Co (Max Houston) 25Jul59, *Lumber City I*, also *Lumber Lady*. ST Denver-Chicago Trucking Co 08Sep61. **N40425** ST Piedmont Airlines 01Apr66, FN 425 *Manassa Pacemaker*, IS 18May66. ST US Aircraft Sales Corp 26Dec68; trf to Francis Y Sogi 06Jan69. ST Charlotte Aircraft Corp 23Jun69.. ST Holman & Moody Inc 18Jul69. ST Albert Q Crisler 10Dec70. ST Africair Inc 27Mar72. ST Southeast Airlines 01Apr72; engine fire 16Jun75, Key West, FL—no injuries. ST Provincetown-Boston Airline 28Nov75. ST Roberta A Rogers dba Erickson & Remmert 29May86. ST Borinquen Air Leasing Inc 17Nov86; LT Aero Virgin Islands 1987 and operated occasionally for Taino Airways; WFU and stored San Juan, PR; reported as 'destroyed' 17Sep89 by *Hurricane Hugo*; moved to airport restaurant/bar in 1992 as an attraction and repainted in Tol-Air colors (a local cargo operator) but abandoned by Feb94. Extant (1997).

14131 *N40425—'TolAir' titles (although never operated by this company), San Juan, Puerto Rico.* (Hernán Matos)

14132 **N40426** mfd 20Jun52

DD 03Jul52 to TWA, FN 426 *Skyliner Mansfield*, IS 04Jul52, later renamed *Skyliner Bethlehem*. ST Remmert Werner (Beldex Corp) 11Feb59 (TT 14895), DD 16Feb59. **N404K** RR 02Apr59 to Remmert Werner. ST Kewanee Oil Co 04Aug59. ST National Flight Services Inc 02Feb62. ST Chicago Industries Association Inc 02Feb62, renamed The National Strancar Corp later. ST Frank R Stranahan 05Feb63. **N404Z** ST Page Airways Inc 01Jun63. ST Zollner Corp 07Jun63. ST Hubbard Broadcasting Co 29Aug69. ST First National Aircraft Inc 08Jan72. ST Danny Davis (Nashville Brass) 08Jan72, *Lady Barbara*. **N404DD** RR 04Dec73 to Danny Davis. ST Monarch Aircraft Inc (Samuel T Stewart) 28Mar79; LT The Doobie Brothers; repainted as N404D in error Nov79, subsequently corrected. ST Gradin Properties Inc 24Sep81. ST Dade County Public School System, George T Baker Aviation School 23Jul84 and used for ground training at Miami, FL. Extant (1997).

14132 *N404DD (previously N40426/N404K/N404Z, mismarked N404D)—Monarch Aircraft, Inc, Chino, California, November 1979.* (John Wegg)

14133 **N40427** mfd 24Jun52

DD 11Jul52 to TWA, FN 427 *Skyliner Fort Wayne*, IS 12Jul52; LT Pacific Air Lines 25Apr60 (TT 16637), DD 13May60. ST Pacific Air Lines 30Jun60. ST Pallas Design & Engineering Corp 01Aug68. ST M Silverman 15Jul71. ST Samuel T Steward and George M Hansen 01Sep71; trf to GSD Aircraft Leasing 01Feb72; LT Air Travelers Club Jan72; LT Doobro Corp (The Doobie Brothers) 06Jun74, *Doobieliner*; WO 01Sep74 in ground cabin fire, Norfolk, VA.

14133 *N40427—Doobieliner, leased to The Doobie Brothers rock band; destroyed by ground cabin fire September 1, 1974, at Norfolk, Virginia.* (Steve Nation via Elliot H Greenman)

14134 **N40428** mfd 27Jun52

DD 15Jul52 to TWA, FN 428 *Skyliner South Bend*, IS 16Jul52; landing gear collapsed on landing 22Sep53, Fort Wayne, IN—no injuries; landed very hard short of the runway, struck approach lights and skidded down runway 07Jun56, Pittsburgh, PA, operating TW509—no injuries, RTS 01Oct56. ST Outboard Marine Corp, Evinrude Division 15Jan60 (TT 15551). ST Malibu Travel Club 22Oct70. **N404LS** ST Lake Sport & Travel Inc 13Sep72. ST Northridge Bank 11Dec72 and stored Oshkosh, WI. ST Roman J Lisowski Jr dba Lisowski Realty Co 27Sep74. ST Midland National Bank 14Sep76, still stored Oshkosh. ST LTA Export Inc 27May77; trf to Landy Taylor Aircraft Sales 14Jun77. ST Bellomy Lawson Inc 14Jun77. **CP-1318** ST Comercializadora Aérea Mixta Boliviana Ltd (CAMBA) 14Jul77, departed from Miami 16Jul77 on dely; cr 15Jul81, Pista el Perú, Beni, Bolivia—undershot on landing and right wing torn off—no injuries (TT 22990).

14134 *CP-1318 (previously N40426/N404LS)—in orange trim with Comercialisadora Aérea Mixta Boliviana (CAMBA), La Paz, December 1, 1977.* (ALPS via Michael Magnusson)

14135 **N40429** mfd 01Jul52

DD 16Jul52 to TWA, FN 429 *Skyliner Peoria*, IS 17Jul52. ST California Airmotive Sales Corp 10Mar59 (TT 15072), 12Mar59. **N636** ST E F MacDonald Co 02Apr59. **N636X** ST James W Mc Allister Inc 12Jul65. ST Montex Drilling Co 19Jul67. ST World Service Life Insurance Co 18Jan73. ST Airworld Inc 18Jan73. ST United Trading Corp 06Apr73. ST Whitesell Construction Inc 06Apr73. ST Joe Simkins (Tiffany Industries) 14Nov75. ST Institute of Marine Sciences Inc 13Aug82. ST Dick Maxwell 24Feb83. ST American Institute of Marine Sciences 06May86. ST Phase II Inc 15Oct86. ST Sun & Wind Inc 24Aug87, stored Pueblo, CO. ST Skylease Inc (Jeff Whitesell, Airliners of America) 04Jun94, ferried

Pueblo–Billings–Spokane–Seattle (Boeing Field) 02Jul94; restored and reflown 08Mar97; repainted 1997 in Pacific Air Lines colors and based at Camarillo, CA. Current.

14135 *N636X—Dick Maxwell, Chino, California, November 1983 (now with Airliners America at Camarillo, California).* (John Wegg)

14136   N40430   mfd 03Jul52
DD 21Jul52 to TWA, FN 430 *Skyliner Quincy*, IS 21Jul52, later *Skyliner Oklahoma City*; WFU and stored Kansas City-Fairfax. ST Piedmont Airlines 31Jul61, DD 26Dec61 (TT 18857), FN 430 *Chesapeake Pacemaker*, IS 12Jan62. ST US Aircraft Sales Corp 26Dec68; trf to Francis Y Sogi 06Jan69. ST Charlotte Aircraft Corp 23Jan69; stored 24Feb69, Sebring, FL. ST CEC Corp 24May71. ST Harold J Caldwell and Badr Halwany 06Mar72; trf to Atlantic Southeast Airlines 28Mar72. ST Knight Airlines Inc 15Aug79, remained stored Sebring. ST Sebring Airport Authority in sheriff's sale 18Oct82; BU Sebring.

14136 *N40430—Piedmont Airlines* Chesapeake Pacemaker, *Greater Cincinnati, Ohio, March 17, 1962.* (G P H Styan via Eric W Wagner)

14137   N446A   mfd 1951
DD 22Dec51 to Eastern Air Lines, FN 446; gear collapsed 17Apr53, Greensboro, SC—no injuries. ST Charlotte Aircraft Corp 15Nov62. ST East Coast Flying Service 15Nov62. **N1900W** ST Whirlpool Corp 17Jan63. **N1902M** donated to Michigan State University 31Dec68. ST Erie Air Service Inc 24Apr70. ST Robert G Carlton dba United Flight Services 21Apr71 and stored Watsonville, CA. ST Northern United Inc 27Nov76, remained stored Watsonville; later stored Concord, CA. **CP-1738** ST Transportes Aéreos Samuel Selum (TASS) c1984, *El Gordo*; operated on behalf of or LT Frigorifico Reyes; WO 07Apr90 (17Apr90 also quoted), overran at Yacuma, Bolivia, following emergency landing.

14137 *CP-1738 (previously N446A/N1900W/N1902M)—Transportes Aéreos Samuel Selum (TASS).* (Denis Goodwin via J M G Gradidge)

14138   N447A   mfd 1951
DD 29Dec51 to Eastern Air Lines (EAL quotes 27Dec51), FN 447. ST Charlotte Aircraft Corp 15Nov62. ST East Coast Flying Service 15Nov62. **N585S** ST Southern Airways 27Aug65, FN 123, IS 16Sep65. ST Marco Island Airways 20Sep73 for spares; BU Opa-locka, FL, Sep75.

14138 *N585S (previously N447A)—Southern Airways, Atlanta, May 4, 1969.* (John P Stewart)

14139   N448A   mfd 20Dec51
DD 06Jan52 to Eastern Air Lines, FN 448. **N468M** ST Mohawk Airlines 05Oct61, *Air Chief Montauk*, DD 09Oct61, IS 17Oct61. ST Ozark Air Lines 13Apr65, IS 05May65. ST Fairchild Hiller Corp 30Mar67 and stored Las Vegas, NV; LT Piedmont Airlines 20May67-22Jul68, FN 468 *Brazos River Pacemaker*, DD 02Jun67, IS 01Jul67. ST Jack Richards Aircraft Co Inc 16Sep68. ST Ronald C Witt 22Nov68; trf to Cut Price Gas & Oil Inc 07Jun72. ST R M Richards 18Oct72; LT Sportsman Air Travel Club 1973. ST U Fly Airfreighters Inc 06Feb73. Repossessed by First National Bank of Bethany, OK 28Apr75. ST Onyx Aviation Inc 29Apr75. ST Dolphin Aviation Inc 03May76; WFU Fort Lauderdale, FL, after planned rebuild by Shawnee Airlines was abandoned; BU 07Oct78.

14139 *N468M (previously N448A)—leased to Sportsman Air Travel Club still as* Brazos River Pacemaker, *San Jose, California, January 1974.* (John Whitehead via John P Stewart)

14140   **N449A**   mfd 02Jan52

DD 17Jan52 to Eastern Air Lines, FN 449. ST Charlotte Aircraft Corp 05Dec62; LT Mohawk Airlines 06Jun63; cr 02Jul63, Rochester, NY—lost control in severe thunderstorm just after takeoff from Runway 28 operating MO112 White Plains–Newark, 2 crew and 5 passengers fatal, 1 crew and 29 pax injured (TT 29818).

14140 *N449A—Eastern Air Lines, Louisville, Kentucky, September 1962.* (via Peter R Keating)

14141   **N450A**   mfd 07Jan52

DD 23Jan52 to Eastern Air Lines, FN 450. **N149S** ST Southern Airways 20Dec62, FN 109, IS 21Jan63; WFU 1972 and stored Atlanta, GA. ST Robert Wade dba Twin City Travel Club 08Aug75. ST James H Osborn 13May76. ST Jim Malone Aircraft Sales Co 17Feb78. ST Crown Regency 720 Inc 08Mar78; trf to Royal Regency Inc 19Apr78 and stored Tulsa, OK; later stored Dallas, TX. ST Vero Monmouth Airlines Inc 08Aug79 and operated by Ocean Airways as required. ST Rover Sales Inc (Vortex International) 18Aug87 and stored Miami, FL. ST Mid Atlantic Air Museum, Reading, PA, 05Aug91 (delivered 01Aug91); **N450A** RR 14Jul92 and repainted in Eastern Air Lines colors. Current.

14141 *N149S (previously N450A)—Southern Airways, Fleet No 109.* (via Elliot H Greenman)

14142   **N451A**   mfd 21Jan52

DD 31Jan52 to Eastern Air Lines, FN 451. ST The Hayes Corp 05Sep61. ST Southern Airways 05Sep61, FN 105, IS 06Nov61. **N145SA** RR 02Oct61 by FAA in error. **N145S** Regn corrected 19Oct61; hard landing 17Jun63, Baton Rouge, LA, and overran—no injuries. ST Dolphin Aviation Inc 25May78; trf to Dolphin International Inc 29Jun78; LT Florida Airlines Jun78, *Hilton Head Island*, later *City of Ft. Myers*. ST Ocean Airways Inc 08Jan80; WFU Oct80 and stored Orlando, FL. ST David S Stempler 23Jan81 (for operation by Florida Airlines Inc); operated 01Feb–01Dec81 for Air Florida Commuter (Florida Airlines reorganized 07Aug81 as Southern International Airways); stored Dec81, Lakeland, FL. ST Wheeler Systems Inc 15Feb85; trf to Systems-International Airways Inc 30Apr88. ST Federal Leasing Company Inc 19May89. RT Systems-International Airways 15Aug89; repossessed by Sun Bank, Miami, and stored Fort Lauderdale, FL. ST Florida Aviation Inc 14Nov89. ST Save A Connie Inc 17Sep90, DD 11Dec90 to Kansas City (TT 60168); minor damage 21Jun91 when Cessna 172 was blown into 404 during storm at Kansas City; repainted in red/white colors Aug92 *Skyliner Kansas City*. Current.

14142 *N145S (previously N451A)—Air Omni (tentative name for a proposed merger of Florida Airlines and Marco Island Airways), 1980.* (MAP)

14143   **N452A**   mfd 25Jan52

DD 12Feb52 to Eastern Air Lines, FN 452. ST Falair Inc 13Jun61; LT ASA International Airlines Jun61, FN 452. **N442D** ST East Coast Flying Service Inc 09Jan62. ST Graubert Aviation Inc 24Jul62; LT Ray Charles Enterprises 25Jul62. **N923RC** ST Ray Charles Enterprises 16Aug65. **N9234C** ST East Coast Leasing Inc (S Ross Lipscomb) 21Feb68. ST DC Leasing Corp 17Mar69. Repossessed by S Ross Lipscomb 28Feb70. ST Washington Aircraft Leasing Corp 17Apr70. Repossessed by S Ross Lipscomb 31Aug71. ST Huber Investment Co dba Huber Homes 15Sep71. ST Carolina Aircraft Corp 10Dec71; LT Flamingo Airlines 1972. trf Florida Aircraft Leasing Corp 01Sep72. ST CMH Leasing Corp 01Sep72; cvtd to aerial applicator 22Jun73 by Clayton V Curtis. ST Clayton V Curtis 17Nov73. ST Frontier Inc 15Feb74. ST Clayton V Curtis 14Jun74; trf to Frontier Airways Inc 26May75; stored Sheridan, WY. Extant (Aug97).

14143 *N442D (previously N452A)—Graubert Aviation, Inc, leased to Ray Charles Enterprises, Los Angeles, August 13, 1963.* (Robert E Hufford)

14144   **N453A**   mfd 1952

DD 19Feb52 to Eastern Air Lines, FN 453; cr 10Mar57, Louisville, KY—left wing separated in very hard landing at Standiford Field operating EA181 Chicago–Miami, fuselage rolled inverted—1 injured (TT 15365).

14144 *N453A—Eastern Air Lines, written off March 10, 1957, at Louisville, Kentucky.* (Howard M Svendsen)

14145   N454A   mfd 06Feb52
DD 27Feb52 to Eastern Air Lines, FN 454. ST Falair Inc 13Jun61; LT ASA International Airlines 20Jun61, FN 454. ST East Coast Flying Service 22Jan63. **XB-RUK** ST Mario Moreno (Cantiflas) 28Jun63. ST Industrias Unidas SA 28Jan64. **N67097** ST Westernair of Albuquerque Inc 24Mar75 and stored Miami, FL. ST Southeast Airlines 11Dec75 for parts; dismantled 08Jul76, fuselage hulk BU Jul79.

14145 *XB-RUK (previously N454A)—Industrias Unidas SA, with non-standard propeller spinners, probably the same as used on DC-6s.* (MAP)

14146   N455A   mfd 08Feb52
DD 26Feb52 to Eastern Air Lines, FN 455. ST Falair Inc 13Jun61; LT ASA International Airlines 20Jun61, FN 455. ST Pacific Air Lines 24May62, DD 25May62, IS 04Sep62. **N40450** ST Piedmont Airlines 15Jul66, FN 450 *York River Pacemaker*, DD 20Jul66, IS 26Jul66; WFU 16Jun68. ST US Aircraft Sales Corp 17Dec69. ST Charlotte Aircraft Corp 20Mar70 and stored Sebring, FL. ST CEC Corp 13Apr71. ST Carolina Fleets Inc 24May71; trf to American Lease Plan Inc Jul72; LT Atlantic Southeast Airlines 1972. ST Atlantic Southeast Airlines 19Aug74; LT Kwin-Air 1975. ST Jet Power dba Trans Global Airlines 09Nov76. ST Knight Airlines Inc 15Nov76; seized 23Sep77, Porto Velho, Rondônia, Brazil, with alleged contraband; RT Knight Airlines 1980 and stored Opa-locka, FL. ST Sekman Aviation Corp May84. **CP-1917** ST Transportes Aéreos Samuel Selum (TASS) Jun84; operated on behalf of or LT Frigorifico Reyes; believed crashed after 1987.

14146 *CP-1917 (previously N455A/N40450)—Transportes Aéreos Samuel Selum (TASS).* (Paul Howard)

14147   N456A   mfd 1952
DD 29Feb52 to Eastern Air Lines, FN 456. ST Falair Inc 13Jun61; LT ASA International Airlines 20Jun61, FN 456. ST East Coast Flying Service 22Jan63. ST Charlotte Aircraft Corp 01Feb65; LT Ozark Air Lines 16Mar65, IS 24Jul65. ST Ozark Air Lines 27Oct65. ST Fairchild Hiller Corp 04Aug67 and stored Las Vegas, NV. (**XA-SOX**) planned LT Baja Air Lines 1968 not consummated, remained stored Las Vegas. ST Jack Richards Aircraft Co 16Sep68; LT Mile Hi Travel Club Nov68; WFU 1969, Tulsa, OK. ST Tulsa Air Leasing Inc 03Feb70. RT Jack Richards Aircraft Co 09Jun70; dismantled 1970, Tulsa, OK, fuselage hulk BU 1974.

14147 *XA-SOX (previously N456A)—re-registered for planned lease to Baja Air Lines, Las Vegas, July 1968.* (Jay L Sherlock)

14148   N457A   mfd 20Feb52
DD 07Mar52 to Eastern Air Lines (EAL quotes 01Mar52), FN 457. ST Mohawk Airlines 28Feb62, *Air Chief Susquehanna*, IS 01Apr62. **N469M** RR 16Apr62 to Mohawk. ST Ozark Air Lines 29Dec64, IS 07Jan65. ST Fairchild Hiller Corp 02Apr68 and stored Las Vegas, NV. ST Jack Richards Aircraft Co 29Jul70. ST H J Steakley 16Oct70. ST C M H Leasing Corp 11May72; gear up landing 25Aug72, Fort Lauderdale, FL—no injuries; WFU Fort Lauderdale. ST Clayton V Curtis 17Nov73. ST Frontier Inc 15Feb74. ST Cavico Alamo Aircraft Sales Inc 24Nov76. ST Shawnee Airlines 24Nov76, still stored Fort Lauderdale; BU 1976.

14148 *N469M (previously N457A)—Ozark Air Lines, Moline, Illinois, May 29, 1965.* (A R Krieger)

14149   N458A   mfd 22Feb52
DD 14Mar52 to Eastern Air Lines, FN 458. ST Charlotte Aircraft Corp 15Nov62. ST East Coast Flying Service 15Nov62. **N584S** ST Southern Airways 17Aug65, FN 122, IS 09Sep65; WFU 1972 Atlanta, GA. **N967M** ST Marco Island Airways 20Sep73. ST Citicorp Leasing Inc 12Dec73 for lease-back to Marco Island Airways. ST Marco Island Airways 11May79; operated 1980-1982 for Air Florida Commuter. Acquired by Provincetown-Boston Airline 05Oct84 through merger; WFU Nov84, stored Naples, FL. ST Roberta A Rogers dba Erickson & Remmert 26Sep88, still stored Naples. ST City of Naples Airport Authority Feb93; hulk BU c1995, dereg 05Mar96.

14149 *N484S (previously N458A)—Southern Airways Fleet No 122, Atlanta, June 9, 1967.* (Robert E Hufford)

14150 N459A   mfd 27Feb52
DD 12Mar52 to Eastern Air Lines, FN 459. ST The Hayes Corp 16Oct61. **N144S** ST Southern Airways 16Oct61, FN 150, IS 17Nov61; LRF 30Apr78 Atlanta–Gadsden (AL)–Atlanta (final scheduled passenger piston service by a 'major' US carrier). ST Dolphin Aviation Inc 25May78; trf to Dolphin International Inc 29Jun78; LT Florida Airlines Jun78, *Sanibel Island*, later *City of Sarasota/Bradenton*. ST Ocean Airways Inc 08Jan80; WFU Oct80 and stored Orlando, FL. ST David S Stempler (for use by Florida Airlines Inc) 23Jan81; operated 01Feb-01Dec81 for Air Florida Commuter (Florida Airlines reorganized 07Aug81 as Southern International Airways); WFU Dec81, Lakeland, FL. ST Wheeler Systems Inc 15Feb85; trf to Systems-International Airways Inc 30Apr88; cvtd to cargo config; WFU and stored Bartow, FL. ST Federal Leasing Co Inc 19May89. RT Systems-International Airways 28Aug88. Repossessed by Allstate Financial Corp 31Jan92. ST Business Funding of Florida Inc 26Jun92, remained stored Bartow. ST Save A Connie Inc 26Jan95 for spares and BU late 95.

14150 *N144S (previously N459A)—Systems-International Airways, stored at Bartow, Florida, March 7, 1987.* (Karl Krämer)

14151 N460A   mfd 04Mar52
DD 21Mar52 to Eastern Air Lines, FN 460. **N464M** ST Mohawk Airlines 31Aug61, *Air Chief Huron*, IS 28Sep61. ST Ozark Air Lines 19Dec65, IS 08Mar66. ST Fairchild Hiller Corp 12Jun67 and stored Las Vegas, NV. ST Jack Richards Aircraft Sales 29Jul70; LT Golden Eagle Aviation 1970; cr 02Oct70, 40mi west of Denver, CO—flown into Mt Trelease at 10,750ft elevation with Wichita State University football team aboard, en route Denver–Logan, UT—32 fatal, 8 injured.

14151 *N464M (previously N460A)—Mohawk Airlines Air Chief Huron, New York–LaGuardia 1967. The word 'Mohawk' appears on both upper wing surfaces.* (Peter W Black via Peter J Marson)

14152 N461A   mfd 05Mar52
DD 26Mar52 to Eastern Air Lines, FN 461. **N465M** ST Mohawk Airlines 12Sep61, *Air Chief Sauk and Fox*, IS 19Sep61. ST Ozark Air Lines 13Sep65, IS 17Feb66. ST Fairchild Hiller Corp 17Aug67 and stored Las Vegas, NV. ST Interstate Airmotive Corp 26May70. ST Alpha Aviation Inc 18Oct72. ST Taku Lands Inc 11Dec73; trf to Harold S Stinson Jr 12Dec73; LT Mark Aero 1974 for planned operation as Missouri Commuter Airlines. ST Petroleum Air Transport Inc 12Jul76; trf to DHL Corp dba DHL Airlines 23Mar79; WFU Jul79, Honolulu, HI; BU 1983.

14152 *N465M (previously N461A)—Mark Aero, Minneapolis, July 28, 1975.* (George Poling)

14153 N462A   mfd 10Mar52
DD 22Mar52 to Eastern Air Lines, FN 462. **N462M** ST Mohawk Airlines 18Aug61, *Air Chief Abnaki*, IS 04Sep61. ST Ozark Air Lines 11Mar65, IS 22Mar65. ST Fairchild Hiller Corp 29Dec66 and stored Las Vegas, NV; LT Piedmont Airlines 09Jun67, FN 462 *Long Island Pacemaker*, DD 20Jun67, IS 17Jul67; RT Fairchild Hiller 07Aug68. ST Jack Richards Aircraft Co 31Mar69; WFU 1970 and stored Long Beach, CA; trf World Aviation Inc c02Apr71. ST Alvin L Fuller 18Oct71. ST Continental Aviation Inc 21Nov72. ST R M Richards 29Dec72; trf to Onyx Aviation Inc 14Nov73. ST Resources Development Corp 29Jan75. ST Marvin L Janzen cApr77; WFU Oct77, Galveston, TX, following single-engine landing. ST James Martin & Assoc (voided by court action), ST High Timber Development Co Inc 21Jun83. Repossessed by Marvin L Janzen 19Nov86; cvtd by Clayton V Curtis to aerial applicator 15Jun87 but believed never used; stored Sheridan, WY. Extant (Aug97).

14153 *N462M (previously N462A)—Marvin L Janzen, Long Beach, California, June 1983.* (John Wegg)

14154 N463A   mfd 1952
DD 29Mar52 to Eastern Air Lines, FN 463. **N252S** ST Southern Airways 20Dec62, FN 111, IS 15Feb63; WFU 1970 Atlanta, GA; BU 1972.

14154 *N463A—Eastern Air Lines, Philadelphia, c1961.* (R Armstrong via George W Pennick)

14155   N464A   mfd 18Mar52
DD 07Apr52 to Eastern Air Lines, FN 464. ST Mohawk Airlines 31Aug61, IS 09Sep61. **N463M** RR 07Feb62 to Mohawk. ST Ozark Air Lines 24Aug64, IS 03Nov64. ST Fairchild Hiller Corp 07Jul67 and stored Las Vegas, NV. ST Jack Richards Aircraft Co 29Jul70. ST Tom Steele 09Feb71, derelict at Las Vegas. ST M Silverman 22Jun71; trf to Prairie Avenue Gospel Center dba Fiesta Air 1971 for parts. ST Ben Widfeldt Aug74. ST Nevada Recycling Corp 15Apr77; BU Las Vegas, 1977.

14155 *N463M (previously N464A)—Ozark Air Lines, St Louis, February 11, 1967.* (Dave Ostrowski)

14156   N465A   mfd 21Mar52
DD 04Apr52 to Eastern Air Lines, FN 465. ST The Hayes Corp 26Jul61. **N141S** ST Southern Airways 26Jul61, FN 101, DD 28Jul61, IS 29Oct61. **N973M** ST Marco Island Airways 29Sep76; operated 1980-82 for Air Florida Commuter; WFU Marco Island, FL; dereg 11Oct83 and used for spares; acquired by Provincetown-Boston Airline through merger Oct84; BU Dec85.

14156 *N141S (previously N465A)—Southern Airways, Atlanta, June 9, 1967.* (Robert E Hufford)

14157   N466A   mfd 26Mar52
DD 15Apr52 to Eastern Air Lines, FN 466; mid-air collision 01Oct60, Orlando, FL, en route Jacksonville–Orlando–Miami with Beech Bonanza—one fatal aboard Bonanza, 404 landed safely with damage to right wing tip, no injuries in 404. ST The Hayes Corp 31Jul61. **N142S** ST Southern Airways 31Jul61, FN 102, DD 24Jul61, IS 29Oct61; gear-up landing 17Feb67, Atlanta, GA—no injuries; WFU c1972 and stored Atlanta. ST Air Lease Inc 25Sep73. Repossessed by National Community Bank 07Oct75. ST East Coast Aircraft Sales Inc 23Oct75. **HI-285** ST Aerolíneas Dominicanas SA (ADSA/Dominair) 08Mar76 and left Miami 12Mar77; LT Aerovías Quisqueyana Jan-May78; WFU Santiago, DR; later stored in Panamá, then stored at Port-au-Prince, Haiti (c1987), then Kingston-Norman Manley, Jamaica. ST Santiago Air SA; ST R Kirchheimer not completed. ST Jesse P Soltes 25Jun86, **N142S** R 15Sep89, remained stored; **N404JS** RR 29Apr90. Extant (Jan97).

14157 *HI-285 (previously N466A/N142S)—Aerolíneas Dominicanas SA (ADSA—aka Dominair).* (MAP)

14158   N467A   mfd 01Apr52
DD 14Apr52 to Eastern Air Lines, FN 467. **N253S** ST Southern Airways 20Dec62, FN 112, IS 01Mar63. **N974M** ST Marco Island Airways 07Oct77; operated 1980-82 for Air Florida Commuter; acquired by Provincetown-Boston Airline 05Oct84 through merger; WFU Nov84. ST Graceville Air Service Inc 01May86. ST Warren C Eastman 10May86. ST Wade Properties Inc 25Jun86. Repossessed by Clinton State Bank 01Oct88 and stored Billings, MT; dereg Feb92; to Billings fire dump. Extant (Jul95).

14158 *N974M (previously N467A/N253S)—Marco Island Airways, Marco Island, Florida, March 1978.* (Karl Krämer)

14159   N468A   mfd 03Apr52
DD 17Apr52 to Eastern Air Lines, FN 468. **N254S** ST Southern Airways 20Dec62, FN 113, IS 23Mar63; WFU Atlanta, GA, 1970. **N968M** ST Marco Island Airways 31Oct73. ST Citicorp Leasing Inc 12Dec73 for lease-back to Marco Island Airways. ST Marco Island Airways 11May79; operated 1980-82 for Air Florida Commuter; WFU 1982 and stored Marco Island, FL; acquired by Provincetown-Boston Airline 05Oct84 through merger. ST Roberta A Rogers dba Erickson & Remmert 26Sep88, ST Steve Braun 04Apr94 for $50; hulk BU Marco Island 94; dereg 17Jun94.

14159 *N254S (previously N468A)—Southern Airways, decaying at Atlanta, September 1970. The rudder is mismatched with paint from an earlier livery.* (Gordon Reid)

14160   N469A   mfd 07Apr52
DD 23Apr52 to Eastern Air Lines, FN 469. ST The Hayes Corp 17Sep62.
N148S ST Southern Airways 17Sep62, FN 108, IS 10Oct62; WFU
Atlanta, GA, 1970; BU 1971.

14160 *N469A—Eastern Air Lines, Richmond, Virginia, October 14, 1961.
Eastern has added a Chamberlain nose radome.* (Modlin via A R Krieger)

14161   N470A   mfd 10Apr52
DD 29Apr52 to Eastern Air Lines, FN 470; lost directional control on
takeoff 03Nov60, Wilmington, DE—no injuries. ST The Hayes Corp
23Aug62. **N147S** ST Southern Airways 23Aug62, FN 107, DD 28Aug62,
IS 21Sep62. ST Dolphin Aviation Inc 02Mar78; LT Florida Airlines
Mar78, *Longboat Key*, later *City of Miami*; trf to Dolphin International Inc
29Jun78 for continued lease to Florida Airlines. ST Ocean Airways Inc
08Jan80; WFU Oct80 and stored Orlando, FL. ST David S Stempler (for
use by Florida Airlines Inc) 23Jan81; operated 01Feb-01Dec81 for Air
Florida Commuter (Florida Airlines reorganized 07Aug81 as Southern
International Airways); WFU Dec81, Lakeland, FL. ST Roy H Elliot Jr
dba Air Marianas 10Sept82, *Flagship Saipan*; trf to Holliday Investment
Corp 04Mar83; presumed to be the 404 derelict at Isley Field, Saipan, 1990.

14161 *N147S (previously N469A)—Southern Airways, Greenville-
Spartanburg Jetport, South Carolina, October 5, 1970.* (Elliot H Greenman)

14162   N471A   mfd 14Apr52
DD 30Apr52 to Eastern Air Lines, FN 471. **N460M** ST Mohawk Airlines
02Aug61, *Air Chief Delaware*, IS 14Aug61. ST Ozark Air Lines 10Aug65,
IS 24Aug65. ST Fairchild Hiller Corp 14Sep67 and stored Las Vegas, NV.
ST Jack Richards Aircraft Co 31Mar69; LT The Voyager Travel Club 1970;
trf to World Aviation Inc 23Feb71. ST Del Rio Springs Inc 08Mar72. ST
Hughie Demore & Walter H Cave 19Apr73. ST Jet Air Flying Corp
31Oct79. **N35JS** ST International Air Leasing Inc 01Aug75. ST Global
Air Inc dba Global Air Travel Club 09Nov76. ST Janet Arcona 20Oct78;
LT Florida Air Travel Association 1978. ST Andres Rodriguez 21Apr79.
ST International Casino World Tours Inc 03Aug79. ST C & S Specialties
Inc 29Sep80; reportedly stolen from New Orleans c1983 and subsequently
impounded Nassau, Bahamas, for alleged drug running; dereg 02May91 but
extant Mar94.

14162 *N471A—Eastern Air Lines, St Louis, Missouri, February 2, 1954.*
(Howard M Svendsen)

14163   N472A   mfd 17Apr52
DD 06May52 to Eastern Air Lines, FN 472. **N467M** ST Mohawk Airlines
24Sep61, *Air Chief Potawatomi*, DD 19Sep61, IS 25Sep61. **N466M** RR
08Dec62 to Mohawk, regn switched with msn 14164. ST Ozark Air Lines
20May65, IS 11Jun65. ST Fairchild Hiller Corp03Jun67 and stored Las
Vegas, NV. ST Jack Richards Aircraft Co 20Nov68; trf to World Aviation
Inc 23Feb71. ST Voyager 1000 Inc, dba The Voyager Travel Club 27Sep72.
ST Business Aircraft Leasing Inc 06Nov72. ST B M Richards 25Apr73. ST
Onyx Aviation Inc 25Jul73. ST Voyagers Aircraft Inc 04Jun74. ST Onyx
Aviation 05Feb76. ST Rene Montenegro 17Sep76. **CP-1317** ST
Comercializadora Aérea Mixta Boliviana Ltda (CAMBA) 24Nov76, DD
23Dec76; damaged in accident before Mar77 and WFU; believed BU.

14163 *N466M (previously N472A/N467M)—Mohawk Airlines* Air Chief
Potawatomi *at New York-Idlewild, September 22, 1963.* (Author)

14164   N473A   mfd 22Apr52
DD 08May52 to Eastern Air Lines, FN 473. **N466M** ST Mohawk Airlines
18Sep61, *Air Chief Ottawa*, DD 21Sep61, IS 25Sep61. **N467M** RR
08Dec62 to Mohawk, regn switched with msn 14163. ST Ozark Air Lines
26Oct64, IS 01Nov64. ST Fairchild Hiller Corp 11Mar67 and stored Las
Vegas, NV; LT Piedmont Airlines 20May67, FN 467 *Cherokee Pacemaker*,
DD 13Jun67, IS 05Jul67; RT Fairchild Hiller 18Jul68. ST Jack Richards
Aircraft Co 26Nov68. ST Business Aircraft Inc 05Feb70; trf to Basler
Flight Service Inc dba Basler Airlines 24Feb72; WFU Oshkosh, WI, 1974.
ST Samuel T Stewart 08Aug75; LT The Doobie Brothers, *Donna Lee*;
WFU Chino, CA; dismantled c1986 and fuselage used in the 'Caribbean
Zone' restaurant in San Francisco, CA, at First & Natomas Streets. Extant
(1996).

14164 *N467M (previously N473A/N466M)—leased to The Doobie Brothers
rock band, Chino, California, December 1976.* (John Wegg)

14165   N474A   mfd 29Apr52

DD 09May52 to Eastern Air Lines, FN 474; propeller blade tip failed because of hard landing 08Apr54, Houston, TX, and penetrated fuselage—no injuries; propeller blades damaged in hard landing 24Aug56, Chicago-Midway, IL—no injuries. **N474M** ST Mohawk Airlines 06Dec62, DD 12Dec62, used for spares and not operated. ST Charlotte Aircraft Corp 18Sep65. ST East Coast Flying Service 21Sep65 and rebuilt; trf to East Coast Leasing Inc 17Aug67. ST Flying W Airways 09Jan68. ST Florida Aircraft Leasing 15Mar69; LT Lehigh Acres Development Inc; trf to Carolina Aircraft Corp 13Aug69. ST Air Seco Inc dba Colony Airlines Oct69; WFU 1970 and stored Fort Lauderdale, FL. ST Clayton V Curtis 18Dec72. ST Frontier Inc 15Feb74; WFU 1977 and stored Grenada, MS. ST F & B Aircraft 12Feb80; BU at Grenada c1985.

14165 *N474A—Eastern Air Lines, St Louis, Missouri, September 10, 1961.*
(Dave Ostrowski)

14166   N40431   mfd 09Jul52

DD 23Jul52 to TWA, FN 431 *Skyliner Terre Haute*, IS 23Jul52. ST California Airmotive Sales Corp 04Aug59 (TT 15489). ST Aerojet-General Corp 10Dec59. **N241AG** RR 22Nov60 to Aerojet-General. **N40440** ST Piedmont Airlines 20Nov64, FN 440 *Santee Pacemaker*, IS 28Dec64; WFU 04Sep68. ST US Aircraft Sales Corp 09Oct68. ST Francis Y Sogi 09Oct68. ST Charlotte Aircraft Corp 12Mar69 and stored Sebring, FL. ST CEC Corp 13Apr71. ST Harold J Caldwell and Badr Halwany 06Mar72; trf to Atlantic Southeast Airlines 28Mar72 and stored Miami, FL. ST Air Agency Inc 08Oct76. ST Provincetown-Boston Airline 21Feb78 for parts; dismantled Miami 01Mar78 and fuselage trucked to Naples, FL, 18Mar78; remains BU 1988.

14166 *N40440 (previously N40431/N241AG)—ex-Piedmont* Santee Pacemaker *languishing at Sebring, Florida, September 1970.* (Gordon Reid)

14167   N40432   mfd 11Jul52

DD 25Jul52 to TWA, FN 432 *Skyliner Detroit*, IS 25Jul52; LT Pacific Air Lines 12Nov59 (TT 16141), DD 30Jan60. ST Pacific Air Lines 30Jun60; LT R A Watt Co 15Mar–May68. ST Pallas Design & Engineering Corp 01Aug68; LT Lake Los Angeles c1968; LT Fiesta Air Apr–Aug71. ST GSD Leasing Inc 12Jun72; LT Air Travelers Club Inc 1972. ST Yakima Valley Leasing Corp 22Jul75; LT Stardusters Air Travel Club II 08Sep75. ST Onyx Aviation Inc 19Jan77. ST Marvin L Janzen 19Jan77. ST Valley Ag 07Dec77; stored Bisbee, AZ, 1979. ST Sky Commerce Inc 21Mar80. **CP-1570** ST Comercializadora Aérea Mixta Boliviana Ltda (CAMBA)

24Jul80; cr 16Jun87, Paraparau, Beni, Bolivia—gear-up landing following engine problem on test flight—3 fatal.

14167 *N40432—Pacific Air Lines, Los Angeles, December 28, 1963.*
(Robert E Hufford)

14168   N40433   mfd 16Jul52

DD 13Aug52 to TWA, FN 433 *Skyliner Cleveland*, IS 14Aug52; WFU Kansas City-Fairfax and stored; ST Piedmont Airlines 31Jul61, DD 24Oct61 (TT 18399), FN 433 *Peach Tree Pacemaker*, later *Tidewater Pacemaker*; WFU 21Dec69. ST US Aircraft Sales Corp 12Jan70. ST Charlotte Aircraft Corp 20Mar70 and stored Sebring, FL. ST CEC Corp 24May71. ST Harold J Caldwell and Badr Halwany 06Mar72; trf to Atlantic Southeast Airlines 28Mar72. ST Knight Airlines Inc 15Aug79, still stored Sebring. ST Sebring Airport Authority in sheriff's sale 18Oct82 and BU 1983.

14168 *N40433—final days at Sebring, Florida, March 1978, in company with other former Piedmont Airlines 404s.*(Karl Krämer)

14169   N40434   mfd 1952

DD 20Aug52 to TWA, FN 434 *Skyliner Topeka*, IS 20Aug52. **N710E** ST Essex Productions (Frank Sinatra) 11Jul61 (TT 18114), *Christina*. **XB-SOM** ST Major Justina Reyes. ST Impulsora de la Cuenca de Papaloapan SA 05Nov63, *El Compadre*. ST Westernair of Albuquerque Inc cAug75. ST Sky Sales & Service Inc 25Aug75; dereg cSep75 in México. ST R J Stevenson 16Oct75. **N67274** trf to Continental Aircraft Leasing Ltd 19Feb76; BU St Louis, MO, Jul76.

14169 *XB-SOM (previously N40434/N710E)—at Los Angeles International Airport, December 7, 1963, in the basic livery of its previous owner, Frank Sinatra, but renamed* El Compadre. (Robert E Hufford)

14170   N40435   mfd 24Jul52
DD 20Aug52 to TWA, FN 435 *Skyliner Wichita*, IS 21Aug52; landing gear hit dike short of the runway on landing approach 01Aug55, Binghamton, NY—no injuries, RTS 21Oct55. **HP-302** ST Pan-Air Trading 02Feb61 (TT 17087) for Compania Panameña de Aviación (COPA), *Chiriqui*. **N40406** ST Piedmont Airlines 28Sep65, FN 406 *Appomattox Pacemaker*, DD 01Oct65, IS 03Nov65; cr 20Nov66, New Bern, NC—crashed into Croatan National Forest on approach operating positioning flight from Wilmington—all 3 crew aboard fatal.

14170 *N40435—Trans World Airlines* Skyliner Wichita, *Chicago-Midway*. (A R Krieger)

14171   N40436   mfd 12Aug52
DD 29Aug52 to TWA, FN 436 *Skyliner Wilkes-Barre*, IS 29Aug52, later *Skyliner Scranton*; LT Pacific Air Lines 18Jan60 (TT 16810), DD 08Feb60. ST Pacific Air Lines 30Jun60; gear-up landing 17Apr62, Vandenburg AFB, CA—no injuries. ST R R Watt Co and Caroldale Inc 20Jul67, dba Lake Los Angeles, Klamath River Country Estates, and Brooktrails; trf to Boise Cascade Bldg Co 24Feb69. ST Universal Air Leasing 23Sep70. ST T L Industries Inc 26Feb73. ST Alpha Aviation Inc 05Jul73; trf to Mark G Morris 24Feb75; trf to Petroleum Air Transport Inc 30Jan76. ST The Golden Era Aircraft Corp 17Sep76. ST Magic Carpet Services Inc 13Oct76, dba Magic Carpet Travel Club. ST William J Weaver 24Sep77; trf to Weaver Aircraft Services Inc 24Sep77. ST Sims and Associates 08Nov78; trf to W Gilmore Sims 02Jan79; stored Fort Lauderdale, FL, Feb79. ST William E Harris 05Jun79. ST W Gilmore Sims 27May80. ST Société National de Transport (Haiti) 05Jun80, but never dereg in US. ST Kenneth Rayburn 25Aug80, still stored Fort Lauderdale. ST Hill Air Inc 07May84 at auction. **YV-150C** ST Rentavion CA 08Oct88, left Fort Lauderdale Oct89; reportedly being made airworthy.

14171 *N40436—Petroleum Air Transport, 1976, with 'KMI' titles by the forward door.* (MAP)

14172   N40437   mfd 1952
DD 04Sep52 to TWA and assigned FN 427 and name *Skyliner Scranton* but not used, completed for Howard Hughes with special interior; trf to Hughes Tool Co 10Sep52 and ferried Baltimore–Culver City, CA, 09Sep52 by

TWA crew and stored. ST The National Supply Co 04Feb55; trf to NSX Supply Co 30Apr58. ST Armco Steel Corp 03Jan61. ST Ontario Airways Inc 23Jan63. ST Gannet Co (Gannet Newspapers) 24Jan63. ST Page Airways Inc 06Nov68. ST Jimmy Williams Aircraft Sales 27Feb69. **XC-DOC** ST Secretaria de Salud y Asistencia Social 06May69. **CP-1704** ST Compañia Aérea Nacional c1981; accident 15Jan84, Nieves, Bolivia—emergency landing following engine failure on takeoff—no injuries; cr 19Aug85, La Paz, Bolivia—engine failure on takeoff and struck airport fence during emergency landing—no injuries.

14172 *CP-1704 (previously N40437/XC-DOC) complete with propeller spinners—Compañia Aérea Nacional, crashed August 19, 1985, at La Paz, Bolivia (six months after this photo was taken).* (Michael Magnusson)

14173   N40438   mfd 1952
DD 29Aug52 to TWA, FN 438 *Skyliner Endicott*, IS 30Aug52; LT Pacific Air Lines 12Jan60 (TT 16227), DD 08Feb60. ST Pacific Air Lines 30Jun60; cvtd to cargo config May67; trf to Air West Inc 09Apr68. ST Pallas Design and Engineering Corp 01Aug68. ST M Silverman 19Aug68 and stored Long Beach, CA. ST Prairie Avenue Gospel Center dba Fiesta Air 20Oct71, remained stored Long Beach. ST Universal Applicators Inc 21Apr75. ST Kodiak Western Alaska Airlines 21Apr76; LT Kachemak Seafoods Inc 10Jul-cSep76. ST Stanley Booker 24Jan78; dba Nevada Airlines; cr 16Nov79, Tuscavan, AZ—unwanted autofeather just after takeoff en route Grand Canyon–Las Vegas—10 injured.

14173 *N40438—Prairie Avenue Gospel Center dba Fiesta Air, Long Beach, California, June 1973.* (Steve Nation)

14174   N40439   mfd 22Aug52
DD 12Sep52 to TWA, FN 439 *Skyliner Johnson City*, IS 13Sep52; landing gear retracted inadvertently on landing 10Nov52, Pittsburgh, PA—no injuries, RTS 16Dec52. ST California Airmotive Sales Corp 12Nov59 (TT 15617). **N67B** ST Federated Department Stores 12Nov59. **N671L** RR 27Dec63 to Federated Dept Stores. ST Lockheed Aircraft Corp 06Feb64. ST Southern Airways 21May65, **N40403** ST Piedmont Airlines 21May65, FN 403 *Mount Mitchell Pacemaker*, IS 16Sep65; WFU 22Sep68. ST US Aircraft Sales Corp 09Oct68; trf to Francis Y Sogi 09Oct68. ST Charlotte Aircraft Corp 12Mar69 and stored Sebring, FL. ST Provincetown-Boston Airline 06Apr77 for spares and moved to Naples, FL; hulk BU 1994.

14174 *N40439—Trans World Airlines* Skyliner Johnson City, *San Francisco.* (William T Larkins)

14175　**N40440**　mfd 27Aug52
DD 19Sep52 to TWA, FN 440 *Skyliner Schenectady*, IS 19Sep52. ST California Airmotive Sales Corp 06Nov59 (TT 15607). **N542AG** ST Aerojet-General Corp 06Nov59. ST East Coast Flying Service 17Sep65; trf to East Coast Leasing Inc 17Aug67; LT Ocean Pines 1969. ST Luan Air Transport Inc 14Feb69. ST Neuland Development Inc 01Apr71. ST Onyx Aviation Inc 02Mar74; LT Balantic 1975. ST I Tran Ltd 20Aug76; grounded by FAA at Chicago-Midway because of unairworthy condition but flown to Pennhold, AB, Canada by Jul76; (fate unknown).

14175 *N542AG (previously N40440)—Onyx Aviation, Inc, Oklahoma City, March 1974.* (Jay L Sherlock)

14176　**N40441**　mfd 04Sep52
DD 25Sep52 to TWA, FN 441 *Skyliner Troy*, IS 26Sep52, later renamed *Skyliner Wilkes-Barre*; landing gear inadvertently retracted on landing 13Sep54, Fort Wayne, IN—no injuries, RTS 22Oct54; LT Pacific Air Lines 12Nov59 (TT 15593), Pacific quotes DD 19May60. ST Pacific Air Lines 30Jun60 via California Airmotive Corp. ST Mars Aviation Corp 08Sep67; BU 1967.

14176 *N40441—Pacific Air Lines, San Francisco, February 29, 1964.* (Robert E Hufford)

(14177 through 14222—not 404s)

14223　**N475A**　mfd 08Sep52
DD 26Sep52 to Eastern Air Lines, FN 475. ST Hayes Aircraft Corp 04May62. **N146S** ST Southern Airways 04May62, FN 106, IS 13Jun62; WFU 1970 and stored Atlanta, GA; BU 1971.

14223 *N475A—Eastern Air Lines, New York-LaGuardia, January 7, 1956.* (Robert E Hufford)

14224　**N476A**　mfd 11Sep52
DD 30Sep52 to Eastern Air Lines, FN 476. **N473M** ST Mohawk Airlines 26Oct62, *Air Chief Micmac*. ST Ozark Air Lines 23Aug65, IS 08Nov65. ST Fairchild Hiller Corp 17Aug67 and stored Las Vegas, NV. ST Jack Richards Aircraft Co 21Jan70. ST Interstate Airmotive Corp 17Aug70. ST Alpha Aviation Inc 18Oct72. ST Taku Lands Inc 11Dec73; trf to Harold S Stinson 12Dec73; LT Mark Aero 1974 for planned operation as Missouri Commuter Airlines. ST Petroleum Air Transport Inc 12Jul76; trf to DHL Corp dba DHL Airlines 23Mar79; WFU Nov79, Honolulu, HI; BU 1983

14224 *N473M (previously N476A)—Ozark Air Lines.* (Elliot H Greenman)

14225　**N477A**　mfd 16Sep52
DD 30Sep52 to Eastern Air Lines, FN 477. **N74087** ST Charlotte Aircraft Corp 30Aug62; LT Piedmont Airlines 19Sep62, FN 442 *Blue Ridge Pacemaker*, IS 12Sep62. **N40442** ST Piedmont Airlines 09Oct62 and RR; WFU 27Oct69. ST US Aircraft Sales Corp 17Nov69 and stored Charlotte, NC. ST Charlotte Aircraft Corp Dec70; believed BU.

14225 *N40442 (previously N477A/N74087)—Piedmont Airlines* Blue Ridge Pacemaker, *Asheville, North Carolina, October 1, 1967.* (Robert E Hufford)

14226   N478A   mfd 19Sep52
DD 09Oct52 to Eastern Air Lines, FN 478. ST Charlotte Aircraft Corp 15Nov62. ST East Coast Flying Service 15Nov62; used for Dave Clark Five rock tour with 'DC-5' titles; BU Apr68.

14226 N478A—East Coast Flying Service, Baltimore, June 25, 1965. 'DC-5' on the nose and ventral stair indicates that it was leased to the Dave Clark Five at the time for a rock concert tour. (Dave Lucabaugh via Eric W Wagner)

14227   N479A   mfd 24Sep52
DD 13Oct52 to Eastern Air Lines, FN 479. **N461M** ST Mohawk Airlines 09Aug61, *Air Chief Manhattan*, IS 26Aug61. ST Ozark Air Lines 29Dec64, DD 29Dec64, IS 22Feb65. ST Fairchild Hiller Corp 07Jul67 and stored Las Vegas, NV. ST Jack Richards Aircraft Co 26Nov68. ST Aero Leasing Corp 19Sep69; LT Koscot Interplanetary 1969; WFU 1971 and stored Detroit, MI. ST Marvin L Janzen 02Jun77; stored Madera, CA. ST Ag Investors 28Dec78. Repossessed by Marvin L Janzen 02May80. ST Frontier Airways Inc 12Apr82; stored Madera, CA, then Sheridan, WY. Extant (Aug97).

14227 N461M (previously N479A)—Marvin L Janzen, Madera, California, September 1977. (John Wegg)

14228   N480A   mfd 29Sep52
DD 13Oct52 to Eastern Air Lines (EAL quotes 12Oct52), FN 480. **N74088** ST Charlotte Aircraft Corp 30Aug62; LT Piedmont Airlines, FN 443 *Tidewater Pacemaker*, DD 07Sep62, IS 14Sep62. **N40443** ST Piedmont Airlines 09Oct62 and RR; WFU 30Sep69. ST US Aircraft Sales Corp 23Oct69. ST Charlotte Aircraft Corp 20Mar70 and stored Sebring, FL; cvtd to aerial applicator 10Apr70 by Clayton V Curtis. ST Dothan Aviation Inc 20Jan73; WFU Macon, GA, 1976. ST Marvin L Janzen 17Jun77; stored Madera, CA. ST Ag Investors 28Dec78. Repossessed by Marvin L Janzen 02May80. ST Frontier Airways Inc 26May82; cr 27Jun86, Buffalo, WY—failed to clear obstruction on takeoff from Johnson County Airport, destroyed by fire—3 fatal; dereg 02May91.

14228 N40443 (previously N480A/N74088)—Piedmont Airlines Tidewater Pacemaker, Wilmington, North Carolina, March 1, 1969. (Elliot H Greenman)

14229   N481A   mfd 01Oct52
DD 16Oct52 to Eastern Air Lines, FN 481. ST Charlotte Aircraft Corp 20Dec62. **N40444** ST Piedmont Airlines 31Dec62, FN 444 *West Virginia Centennial 1863-1963 Pacemaker*, IS 15Feb63, later *New River Pacemaker*; WFU 23Oct69. ST US Aircraft Sales Corp 17Nov69. ST Charlotte Aircraft Corp 20Mar70 and stored Charlotte, NC; later BU.

14229 N40444 (previously N481A)—Piedmont Airlines New River Pacemaker. (Gordon Reid)

14230   N482A   mfd 03Oct52
DD 22Oct52 to Eastern Air Lines, FN 482. ST Charlotte Aircraft Corp 20Dec62. **N40445** ST Piedmont Airlines 31Dec62, FN 445 *Potomac Pacemaker*, IS 28Feb63; WFU 09Feb70. ST US Aircraft Sales Corp 12Feb70. ST Charlotte Aircraft Corp 20Mar70 and stored Sebring, FL; cvtd to aerial applicator 10Sep70 by Clayton V Curtis. ST Dothan Aviation Inc 20Jan73; WFU Macon, GA, 1976. ST Marvin L Janzen 17Jun77; stored Madera, CA, 1977. ST Ag Investors 28Dec78. Repossessed by Marvin L Janzen 02May80. ST Frontier Airways Inc 12Apr82; cr 15May82, Madera, CA—wing torn off during emergency landing following engine failure after takeoff on ferry flight to Sheridan, WY—no injuries.

14230 N40445 (previously N482A)—Marvin L Janzen (still with Dothan Aviation Corp titles on rear fuselage), in company with msn 14167 and (foreground) msn 14227, at Madera, California, September 1977. (John Wegg)

14231 N483A mfd 08Oct52
DD 29Oct52 to Eastern Air Lines, FN 483. ST Charlotte Aircraft Corp 20Dec62. **N22T** ST Perry R Bass 02May63 dba Richardson & Bass Oil Co. ST W A Montcrief 09Jul65. **N3651B** RR 31Dec65 to W A Montcrief. ST Southern Airways 18Jan66, FN 125. **N587S** RR 26Apr66 to Southern; WFU Atlanta, GA, 1971. ST Citicorp Leasing Inc 23May74. **N969M** LT Marco Island Airways 23May74. ST Marco Island Airways 11May79; operated 1980-82 for Air Florida Commuter; acquired by Provincetown-Boston Airline 05Oct84 through merger; WFU Nov84 and stored Naples, FL; stored Gulfport-Biloxi, MS, 1987. ST Roberta A Rogers dba Erickson & Remmert 26Sep88 and moved to Bay St Louis-Stennis Intl Mar89; proposed sale to Aero Sierra de Durango not completed and remained stored; seized 15Mar90 by US Customs Service. ST Mario Duenas 01Nov95, but documentation of sale never complete. Extant.

14231 *N483A—Eastern Air Lines.* (MAP)

14232 N484A mfd 10Oct52
DD 31Oct52 to Eastern Air Lines (EAL quotes 01Nov52), FN 484. ST Charlotte Aircraft Corp 20Dec62 and believed stored Louisville, KY. **N258S** ST Southern Airways 03Jun64, FN 117, IS 31Aug64. ST A C Allyn 30Dec77; LT Air South. ST Dolphin Aviation Inc 12Mar79; trf to Dolphin Leasco Inc 14Aug79; lease trf to Florida Airlines, *St. Simon Island*, later *City of Atlanta*; operated 01Feb-01Dec81 for Air Florida Commuter (Florida Airlines reorganized 07Aug81 as Southern International Airways); WFU Dec81 and stored Miami, FL; trf back to Dolphin Aviation Inc 23Aug83; trf to R D Ciaravella 14Nov84. ST Eastland Educational Corp 19Dec85. ST Aggressive Investments Inc 22Aug86; BU Miami, Dec88.

14232 *N258S (previously N484A) ex-Florida Airlines (Aggressive Investments Inc) awaiting the cutter's torch at Miami, March 1987.* (Karl Krämer)

14233 N485A mfd 15Oct52
DD 04Nov52 to Eastern Air Lines, FN 485. ST Charlotte Aircraft Corp 20Dec62 and believed stored Louisville, KY. **N259S** ST Southern Airways 03Jun64, FN 118, IS 01Oct64. ST Transexecutive Airlines Inc 21Jan76; LT Shawnee Airlines Feb76. ST Dolphin Aviation Inc Apr76; lease trf to Florida Airlines May76, *City of Ft. Lauderdale*; trf to Dolphin International

Inc 29Jun78. ST Ocean Airways Inc 08Jan80; WFU Oct80. ST David S Stempler 23Jan81 (for use by Florida Airlines Inc); operated 01Feb-01Dec81 for Air Florida Commuter (Florida Airlines reorganized 07Aug81 as Southern International Airways); WFU Dec81, Lakeland, FL. ST Wheeler Systems Inc 15Feb85; trf to Systems-International Airways Inc 30Apr88; WFU and stored Bartow, FL. ST Federal Leasing Co Inc 19May89. RT Systems-International Airways 15Aug89; reposeessed by Allstate Financial Corp 08May92. ST Business Funding of Florida Inc 24Jun92; later stored Russellville, AR. ST Save A Connie Inc 26Jan95 (TT 52330) and ferried to Kansas City, MO. ST Classic Airways (Tom Aarvik) 16Jan96 delivered 20Jan96 Kansas City–San Diego, CA, then to Long Beach, CA; stored San Bernardino, CA. Current.

14233 *N259S (previously N485A) of Systems-International Airways, in storage at Bartow, Florida, March 1987.* (Karl Krämer)

14234 N486A mfd 18Oct52
DD 12Nov52 to to Eastern Air Lines, FN 486. **N472M** ST Mohawk Airlines 07Sep62, *Air Chief Powhaten*; landing gear inadvertently retracted on landing 29Feb64 Binghamton, NY—no injuries (and nose gear remained down). ST Ozark Air Lines 09Jul65, IS 13Sep65. ST Fairchild Hiller Corp 12Jan67; LT Piedmont Airlines 26May67, DD 26Jun67, FN 472 *Fox River Valley Pacemaker*; RT Fairchild Hiller 28Jul68. ST Jack Richards Aircraft Co 18Oct68. ST Basler Flight Service Inc dba Basler Airlines 18Oct68; trf to Business Aircraft Corp 18Oct68, trf back to Basler Flight Service 28Feb72. ST Howard I Coones dba Coones Flying Service 12Aug75; cvtd to aerial applicator 19Sep77. ST co-owners Donald C Fink, Michael B Krinsky and Roger J Kaughan 16Apr79; repossessed by Michael B Krinsky 30Jun86. ST Ralph S Johnson dba Master Equipment Co 16Dec86; WFU Bisbee, AZ. ST Alan B Johnson 07Dec93. ST Save A Connie Inc 03Mar94 as a parts source. Extant.

14234 *N472M (previously N486A) of Basler Flight Service (dba Basler Airlines), Oshkosh, Wisconsin, August 1975.* (Karl Krämer)

14235 N487A mfd 22Oct52
DD 13Nov52 to Eastern Air Lines, FN 487; landed long and ran off snow-covered runway over steep slope on landing 15Jan56, Huntington (Tri-State Airport), WV, operating EA175 Chicago–Louisville–Charlotte—no injuries. ST Charlotte Aircraft Corp 20Dec62; LT Aerojet-General Corp 1963. **N3711K** ST Kimbell Milling Co 31Jan64, *Lady Velma*. ST Huber Investment Corp dba Huber Homes 17Jul69. ST Landy Taylor Aircraft

Sales 28Mar78. ST Monarch Aircraft Inc 20Oct78; LT The Doobie Brothers, *Doobie Liner*. ST Sam Stuart 02May79; cvtd to aerial applicator 20Mar87 (with dual airworthiness certificate for standard category operation); WFU Chino, CA, by 1991; later stored at Rialto, CA, *El Dago*. Extant.

14235 *N3711K (previously N487A) leased to The Doobie Brothers as a* Doobie Liner, *Chino, California, June 1979.* (John Wegg)

14236 N488A mfd 24Oct52
DD 18Nov52 to Eastern Air Lines, FN 488. ST Charlotte Aircraft Corp 20Dec62 and believed stored Louisville, KY. **N256S** ST Southern Airways 03Jun64, FN 115, IS 16Jun64; WFU Atlanta, GA, and BU Feb72.

14236 *N256S (previously N488A) of Southern Airways, Atlanta, June 9, 1967.* (Robert E Hufford)

14237 N489A mfd 29Oct52
DD 19Nov52 to Eastern Air Lines, FN 489; gear-up landing 15Sep59, Plattsburgh AFB, NY. ST Hayes Aircraft 06Nov61. **N143S** ST Southern Airways 06Nov61, FN 103, IS 13Dec61. **HK-1485** ST Aeroproveedora Ltda 'Proa' 05Apr74; cr 07Aug74, Mariquita, Colombia, on training flight—stalled and crashed on approach—2 fatal, 4 injured.

14237 *HK-1485 (previously N489A/N143S) of Aero Proveedora Ltda (Proa Colombia) at Mariquita, Colombia, after its last landing on August 7, 1974.* (Peter J Marson collection via F Kirby)

14238 N490A mfd 06Nov52
DD 22Nov52 to Eastern Air Lines, FN 490. ST Charlotte Aircraft Corp 20Dec62. **N40446** LT Piedmont Airlines 09Apr64, FN 446 *Buckeye Pacemaker*, IS 13Apr64. ST Piedmont Airlines 30Sep64; BU following gear

collapse 07Jul66, Roanoke, VA; fuselage reported by railroad yards 1990.

14238 *N490A—Eastern Air Lines. Scrapped July 9, 1966, Roanoke, Virginia, following landing gear collapse with Piedmont (as N40446).* (Howard M Svendsen)

14239 N491A mfd 07Nov52
DD 22Nov52 to Eastern Air Lines, FN 491. ST Charlotte Aircraft Corp 20Dec62 and believed stored Louisville, KY. **N40447** LT Piedmont Airlines 13Aug-13Nov64, FN 447. **N582S** ST Southern Airways 24Nov64, FN 120; WFU Atlanta, GA, and BU 1976.

14239 *N491A—Eastern Air Lines, Chicago-Midway, 1954.* (Leo J Kohn)

14240 N492A mfd Nov52
DD 26Nov52 to Eastern Air Lines, FN 492; cr 14Nov57, Massena, NY—both engines separated during very hard landing at Richards Field operating EA18 New York–Albany–Plattsburg–Malone–Massena—no injuries (TT 15677); remains ST to Association Aviation Underwriters and fuselage stored at Massena until at least 1959.

14240 *N492A—Eastern Air Lines; crashed November 14, 1957, at Massena, New York.* (A R Krieger)

14241 N493A mfd 14Nov52
DD 06Dec52 to Eastern Air Lines (EAL quotes 05Dec52), FN 493. ST Charlotte Aircraft Corp 15Nov62. ST East Coast Flying Service 15Jan63. **N129AG** ST Fort Worth Pipe & Supply 29Jul63, *Queen Bee*. **N229LS** ST Lone Star Steel Corp 27Mar67. **N2299S** RR 16Jan69 to Lone Star Steel. ST Gulf Underwriters Management Corp 29Sep70 and operated with 'Aviation Office of America' titles. ST Worth Manufacturing Co 14Mar73. ST Henry L Franke 19Dec74. ST Onyx Aviation Inc 15Jun78. ST

Executive Trans Air Inc 19Jun78. **HI-334** ST Aerolíneas Dominicanas SA (ADSA/Dominair) 20Mar79, left Miami 04May79 (as N2299S); WFU Santiago, DR, and cannibalized for spares; BU 1983.

14241 *N129AG (previously N493A) Fort Worth Pipe & Supply* Queen Bee, *Baltimore, January 23, 1964.* (via Peter R Keating)

14242 N494A mfd 19Nov52
DD 18Dec52 to Eastern Air Lines, FN 494. ST Charlotte Aircraft Corp 20Dec62. **N40448** ST Piedmont Airlines 14Aug64, FN 448 *Albemarle Pacemaker*, IS 16Sep64; landed short 21Jan65, Weyers Cave, VA, causing left gear to collapse—no injuries; WFU 31Jul68. ST US Aircraft Sales Corp 09Oct68. ST Francis Y Sogi 09Oct68. ST Charlotte Aircraft Corp 12Mar69 and stored Sebring, FL; LT Flamingo Airlines 16Aug71; WFU 1972 and stored Fort Lauderdale, FL, then Miami; used as spares source by Southeast Airlines; BU Sep76.

14242 *N40448 (previously N494A) leased to Flamingo Airlines.* (via Clinton H Groves/Airliners America/ATP)

14243 N495A mfd 1952
DD 24Dec52 to Eastern Air Lines, FN 495. **N251S** ST Southern Airways 20Dec62, FN 110, IS 04Feb63; cr 01Jan68, Oxford, MS—fire following hard landing and gear collapse on flight from Tuscaloosa, AL, no injuries to 3 crew.

14243 *N495A—Eastern Air Lines.* (R W Harrison/Candid Aero Files)

14244 N496A mfd 1952
DD 03Jan53 to Eastern Air Lines, FN 496; dmgd Morgantown, WV, 16Oct55, in minor accident; cr 17Mar58, Melbourne, FL—burned after hitting gravel pile on landing approach, no injuries.

14245 N497A mfd 11Dec52
DD 15Jan53 to Eastern Air Lines, FN 497. ST Charlotte Aircraft Corp 20Dec62 and believed stored Louisville, KY. ST East Coast Flying Service 03Jun64. **N586S** ST Southern Airways 20Sep65, FN 124, IS 28Sep65; WFU Atlanta, GA, 1970; BU 1971.

14245 *N586S (previously N497A)—Southern Airways withdrawn from service at Atlanta, September 1970.* (Gordon Reid)

14246 N498A mfd 08Jan53
DD 23Jan53 to Eastern Air Lines, FN 498. ST Charlotte Aircraft Corp 20Dec62 and believed stored Louisville, KY; LT Southern Airways 21Aug63. **N255S** ST Southern Airways 03Mar64, FN 114. ST Wings Away Inc 31Mar72. ST American Omni Corp 30Jun75. ST Transecutive Aviation Inc 03Sep76; LT Shawnee Airlines Feb77; lease trf to Florida Airlines Inc Sep77. ST Dolphin Aviation Inc 27Feb79; trf to Dolphin Leasco Inc 14Aug79; lease trf to Shawnee Airlines; lease trf to Florida Airlines, *City of Macon*; operated 01Feb-01Dec81 for Air Florida Commuter (Florida Airlines reorganized 07Aug81 as Southern International Airways); trf to Pilot Leasing Inc 01Jan82; WFU Sarasota, FL, 1982; trf back to Dolphin Aviation 06Jan83. ST Coastal Airways Inc 06Jan83. ST International Transfer Corp dba Proair 01Mar84. ST Graceville Air Service Inc 30Dec85. Repossessed by Clinton State Bank 01Oct88 and stored Paris, TX. ST I N Burchinal (Flying Tiger Air Museum) 04Sep92. Extant (Jun97).

14246 *N255S (previously N498A) of Florida Air Lines (later Florida Airlines) in the livery of affiliate Shawnee Airlines, Sarasota, Florida, March 1978.* (Karl Krämer)

14247 N499A mfd 02Feb53
DD 19Feb53 to Eastern Air Lines, FN 499; gear-up landing 06Jun59, Syracuse, NY—no injuries. ST Charlotte Aircraft Corp 20Dec62 and believed stored Louisville, KY. **N581S** ST Southern Airways 05Oct64, FN 119, IS 05Oct64; WFU Atlanta, GA, 1972. **N982M** ST Marco Island

Airways 29Dec77; operated 1980-81 for Air Florida Commuter; WFU Marco Island, FL, 1981; acquired by Provincetown-Boston Airline 05Oct84 through merger. ST Graceville Air Service Inc 01May86. ST Gerald Martin and James P Furlong 01May86. **YV-149C** ST Rentavion CA 22Sep88, DD 17Oct88; WFU c1992, Caracas-Maiquetia. Extant (Feb97).

14247 *N982M (previously N499A/N581S) of Marco Island Airways, Miami, March 1978.* (Karl Krämer)

(**14248** through **14289**—not 404s)

14290   1282   mfd 1952
DD 25Nov52 as RM-1Z to US Coast Guard and based at NAF Washington, DC (National Airport) assigned to USCG Arlington, later USCG Washington; redesignated as VC-3A 18Sep62. **158202** trf to US Navy 27May69 as C-3A and assigned to Naval Air Reserve Training Unit VR-52, Andrews AFB, MD, coded '6A-202'; RT USCG 12Nov-31Dec69; trf to Military Aircraft Storage and Disposition Center, Davis-Monthan AFB, AZ, 30Jul70 and stored with park code '8C001'. **N13415** donated to The School of the Ozarks 13Jul72. ST Royal Regency Inc 29Aug78. ST Lisle Aircraft Inc 24Oct78; cr 10Nov78, in Caribbean off Punta Fija, Venezuela.

14290 *1282—US Coast Guard Arlington.* (MAP)

14291   1283   mfd 1952

DD 31Oct52 as RM-1Z to US Coast Guard and stationed NAF Washington, DC (National Airport) assigned to USCG Arlington; redesignated as VC-3A 18Sep62. **158203** trf to US Navy 27May69 as C-3A and assigned to Naval Air Reserve Training Unit VR-52, Andrews AFB, MD, coded '6A-203'; trf to Military Aircraft Storage and Disposition Center, Davis-Monthan AFB, AZ, 30Jul70 and stored with park code '8C002'. **N13416** donated to The School of the Ozarks 13Jul72. ST Royal Regency Inc 29Aug78; BU Point Lookout, MO, Jun79.

14291 *N13416 (previously 1283) derelict at Lookout Point, Missouri, September 15, 1979.* (A R Krieger)

THE EVOLUTION OF A MARTINLINER: MSN 14233

As originally delivered with Eastern Air Lines trim applied over a bare metal fuselage and class name 'Silver Falcon' by the ventral stairway; New York-Idlewild, December 28, 1955. (Robert E Hufford)

At Atlanta in July 1980 during brief service with Ocean Airways. (Jay L Sherlock)

In service with its second-generation owner Southern Airways. The nose shape has been altered by the installation of a radome. (Leo J Kohn)

Stored at Lakeland, Florida, after flying connecting services on behalf of Air Florida in its livery. (via John Wegg)

Decidedly in need of care and attention in the livery of Florida Airlines affiliate Shawnee Airlines at Fort Lauderdale, April 1979. (Karl Krämer)

Storage at Bartow, Florida, in March 1987, pristine in the markings of Systems-International Airways. (Karl Krämer)

Restored to operational status as City of Ft. Lauderdale *with the more conservative paint scheme of Florida Airlines.* (MAP)

Final owner? After its acquisition by Save A Connie, N259S was sold to Classic Airways and flown to California in January 1996. Currently, it is stored at San Bernardino (formerly Norton AFB). (Winfried Giese)

INDEX TO MAIN TEXT

(Additional information on operators and owners may be found in the relevant appendices.)